THREE PLAYS

THREE PLAYS

Dockers • *The Interrogation of Ambrose Fogarty*
Pictures of Tomorrow

MARTIN LYNCH

edited by
Damian Smyth

LAGAN PRESS
BELFAST
1996

Published by
Lagan Press
PO Box 110 BT12 4AB, Belfast

The publishers wish to acknowledge the financial assistance
of the Arts Council of Northern Ireland in the production of this book.

© Martin Lynch, 1981, 1982, 1994
Introduction © Damian Smyth, 1996

The moral right of the author has been asserted.

A catalogue record of this book is available from the British Library.

ISBN: 1 873687 60 5
Author: Lynch, Martin
Title: Three Plays
1996

Front Cover: Alan Bennion and James Green
in the Lyric Theatre's production of *Pictures of Tomorrow*
(Courtesy of the Lyric Players Theatre, Belfast)
Set in New Baskerville
Printed by Noel Murphy Printing, Belfast

for
Jimmy, Vina, Moira, Gráinne, Briege, Ann, Malachy, Deirdre, Eamonn, Grainne, Patrick, Veronica, Martin, Seamus, Anne, Seamus, Caragh, Finnuala, Tiernan, Chris, Seamus, Paul, Siobhan, Colm, Bronagh, Ailish, Maeve, Mary, Alec, Roisin, Seamus, Oonagh, Kevin, Conor, Sean, Eamonn, Betty, Eamonn Og, Brian, Janet, Ceara, Brian, Barry, Sinead, Theresa, Charlie, Catrina, Ronan, Tierna, Veronica, Marty, Martin Og, Ciaran, Emer, Loreen, Frankie, Gavin, Orlagh, Riain, Nuala and Sinead.

CONTENTS

Introduction	9
Dockers	17
The Interrogation of Ambrose Fogarty	87
Pictures of Tomorrow	165

Introduction

Martin Lynch is one of that generation of northern Irish playwrights which came to imaginative maturity and popular prominence in the late 1970s and early 1980s. Of those dramatists—Graham Reid, Anne Devlin, Christina Reid and Frank McGuinness—his career has been most fraught with the peculiar tensions of working-class politics, the empowerment creatively of debilitated communities, the commitment to a place and an idiom still seeking full dramatic expression, and the often uncomfortable demands of a medium perceived as the preserve of an intellectual élite, both on the stage and in the stalls. Of those dramatists, too, his work has been the most precocious, the most angry, the most didactic and the most annoying—few Irish playwrights exact from audiences the measures of discomfort and disagreement Lynch does with his work.

This is a gauge of his attunement to the locations of raw nerves, particularly those laid bare by sectarianism and political violence; but, in a fuller sense, it is a tribute to the sometimes frustrating and sometimes artistically-numbing commitment of his work to social change.

Martin Lynch is a socialist. His plays, whether pitched towards the orthodox middle-class audiences of Irish theatre or towards new audiences his working career in community action seeks to assist, gnaw away at the oppressive structures of working-class division and its attendant social inequalities. His groundbreaking collaboration on the all-female Charabanc Theatre Company's first production, *Lay Up Your Ends* (1983), *Castles in the Air* (1983) and *Minstrel Boys* (1985) typify that strand of Lynch's writing which is most strident politically and bears often durable fruit. Works such as *Crack Up* (1983) and *Welcome to Bladonmore Road* (1988) attempted to resolve the tensions surrounding the transition from working class to middle class which some were able to secure during the Thatcherite 1980s, even in Northern Ireland; though the plays, while successful at the box office, were not warmly received critically. A mellower and original imaginative response to working-class tradition was charted in *The Stone Chair* (1989), written for and with the people of the Short Strand district in Belfast, which opened unexpectedly in the Grand Opera House to the kind of packed and raucous audience which recovered something of the energy of Lynch's earliest playwrighting ventures of the late 1970s, such as *They are Taking Down the Barricades*. The result was one of the most exhilarating evenings in the history of the Ulster theatre and a defining moment in the development of contemporary community creativity in Belfast. The desire to tell a story, the creative acts of play-making and the willingness to adopt a role at a higher volume than reality in order to tell a truth, gave rise to a possession by the people of the very mechanics of the stage itself, conventionally the zone from which they felt most excluded. Martin Lynch's role in claiming the theatre in that way for people unfamiliar with it cannot be over-estimated; and has secured for him a place of respect across the communities in Belfast.

But Lynch's activities on and off the ball over the last 15 years tend to obscure both the 'youth' of his imagination and his very real dramatic achievements of the period. His is a developing art, worked from a literate community drama movement, through early espousal by the north's voracious artistic establishment, to the point at which the plays collected in this volume stand to be judged—the point at which a play such as *Pictures of Tomorrow* puts an already substantial career into relief.

His career must be viewed against the background of the history of the drama in Northern Ireland. Unlike most dramatists or writers, he has chosen Belfast as his writing environment. He has stayed here. His work, more clearly than any of his contemporaries, is rooted in the vernacular poetics of Belfast working-class life—by this is meant that chronicling of Belfast urban experience found in Joseph Tomelty, Denis Ireland, Padraic Fiacc and, above all, in Sam Thompson. These writers mark out the creative hinterland in which Lynch moves instinctively, with a sureness of touch, and with an understanding increasingly sophisticated and decisively modern. It is Sam Thompson's ghost, indeed, which haunts the disconcertingly timeless gantries of *Dockers*; but it is also haunted, significantly, by Elia Kazan's masterpiece of optimistic individualistic revolt, *On the Waterfront*—an infusion of the 20th-century's fantasy factory into the traditional epic of Belfast life which is both exciting and an element impossible to imagine in the conception of Thompson's *Over the Bridge*. If it was brave on Lynch's part to attempt to revisit an environment as notorious as waterfront politics, it is no less exciting to find, as forebears of John Graham, not only Davy Mitchell of *Over the Bridge*, but John Proctor of *The Crucible* as well as the ultimate contender, Terry Malloy. In *Dockers*, the Belfast dockside vernacular (only incidental to Thompson's play) is relished—it is itself a character, and like so much of the north's drama, the telling dramatic effects are in dialogue rather than action. This is both a strength and a weakness. If there is nothing in *Dockers* as theatrically showstopping as the off-stage murder of Davy Mitchell or the return of the dead sons in Tomelty's *All Souls' Night*, it is because the detail being worked out is that of characters in dialogue and in ideas, rather than in implicit moments of silent drama; and also because such character detail brings with it genuinely promising comic possibilities which Lynch pursues with rigour. This is a play influenced by and imbued with the values of a previous generation; but the pastness of that experience can only be marked by an affection made manifest as comedy. The greatness of Davy Mitchell in the tragedy of *Over the Bridge* is matched in *Dockers*, not by John Graham, but by Buckets McGuinness—a character whose ancestors are found, not in the pieties of Ulster tragedy, but in the anarhic character of Barney Brudge in Tomelty's *Barnum was Right*.

The finally-successful play of *Dockers*, achieving a comedy out of tragic principles, is a success for the resilience and flexibility of a form of drama, distinctive to the north of Ireland, which has proved both popular and imaginatively satisfying. The play's failings, however, include a character of principle, John Graham, whose imaginative conception is, given the playwright's avowed agenda of socialist activism at the time, much less vivid and much more prosaic than that of the wastrel scrounger sideshow.

In this context, *The Interrogation of Ambrose Fogarty*, marking Lynch's exposure to modern political drama, particularly that of Dario Fo (whose work Lynch has adapted), is important. Again, though this play comes to grips with the incidents of political violence in the north, the focus is resolutely on character; and, in Willy Lagan, Lynch has created a vulnerable comic figure whose counterpoint to Ambrose Fogarty's consciously-ambiguous posturing is almost always under control and at the service of the action. In contrast with the large forces of *Dockers*, *Ambrose* is an intimate work, the quickfire humour and interrogations mirroring and deflecting each other, and exposing latent and explicit violence at their intersections. Lagan—like traditional Ulster comic creations in his ability to elicit aggression and turn it to his advantage, and in his essential 'goodness' despite manic personal traits—is a paradigm of the innocent in everyone, in Ambrose and his interrogators now and in their previous 'civilian' lives, suddenly brought to book by harsh authority. But he is also a deliberate refugee from another world (and another dramatic world), stumbling from a life of soda farls, aged mothers, two-up-two-downs and bottles of porter, into contemporary police brutality. His bewilderment at the ritualised, 'theatrical' violence peculiar to the interrogation room is a confrontation of the values of an older Ulster dramatic convention with a very new, very different world of social and political upheaval, where the threatened, implicit conflict of 'the Orange and the Green' has already taken place, is no longer on the horizon of the drama but is its very theme.

Again, Lynch employs an idiom familiar to his audiences and his own experience to stretch its medium in contact with the incongruous. The political message of the play, blunt though it is, is expressed with more effect and emotional power in the twin fates of Lagan and Fogarty than in explicit statements or editorial. Fogarty is more restrained than John Graham, and paradoxically more rounded, more sympathetic and more heroic, and is the template northern protagonist for the 'troubles' to their close— turning up in a variety of guises throughout the 80s and 90s in the plays of Lynch himself and even, at some distance, in the bizarre person of Kenneth McAllister in Marie Jones' *A Night in November* (1994). But it is Willy Lagan whose conception endures in the memory and in this character Lynch embodied the confused, happy spirit of the truly innocent victim of violence the 'people' always are, even when guilty.

The 'people' in Lynch's plays are invariably masculine. There are women characters—notably Theresa Graham in *Dockers* and Josephina in *Pictures of Tomorrow*, both of whom play pivotal and heroic roles of a type—but the contexts in which they operate and the functions they perform restrict their fulfilment as characters. This is a weakness common in contemporary northern Irish mainstream drama—perhaps only Stewart Parker, because his imaginative territory was not contiguous with northern Irish politics or the social structures current in that region, managed to convince in his evocation of female figures. But it is true that the chosen ground of Graham Reid and Martin Lynch, as of Brian Friel and, surprisingly, of Christina Reid as well, militates against a conception of female characters as anything other than matriarchs, sirens or surrogate male heroes. In Lynch's work, despite serious attempts in other of his plays, this remains an abiding problem and one which will ultimately have to be solved in the progress of his art.

In this regard, *Pictures of Tomorrow*, a classic of modern Irish theatre, displays a heartening expansion of Lynch's dramatic brief. For the first time in his work, the major themes are approached obliquely and primarily through action, though the dialogue achieves a new level of lyricism unfamiliar in his vernacular outings. It is the first play of a mature vision, and its maturity is won from the scarring of ideological disillusionment and the formal exhaustion of the playwright's own traditional methods. The themes too have changed—there is still idealism and aggressive class politics but cast in the past tense; the central concerns are adaptability, survival and optimistic resignation, summed up in the title originally intended—*Manos Arriba* ('Hands Up'). It is also a play in which Lynch deals with characters both much older and much younger than himself, a challenge to empathy to which he rises with aplomb. The locale has changed also—crucially the curtain rises on a London flat, the familiar environs of the Belfast working-class caught only in boyhood memory and the diehard politics of Hugh. There is, too, a new dramatic flexibility in the use of flashback and a quite complex time-frame in which younger selves confront their elders both literally and metaphorically. Lynch has learned quickly and at depth from the Friel of *Dancing at Lughnasa* and, most fruitfully, from the McGuinness of *Observe the Sons of Ulster Marching Towards the Somme.*

For the first time, the vision is epic, the themes of disillusion and renewal embracing a much wider range of political and human ambition than before in the playwright's work. Though *Pictures* is both more lyrical and less mannered than his other plays, Lynch does not aspire to the status of soothsayer poet— some might say, the ultimate career move for an Irish dramatist—which has descended on Friel, McGuinness and Thomas Murphy. Lynch is too urban and too aware of the incompleteness of experience to relax into Irish Catholic melancholia. There is, in *Pictures,* a sense of what simply can not be retrieved—there is no afterlife for the idealism or the energies of the Spanish Civil War and its values any more than there is any renewed vigour or role for the disabled Ray or the childish Hugo. What there is, however, is a recognition of the necessity of change, epitomised in Lynch's final evocation of 'the green shoot waiting for the flower', a discreet quotation from the radical Ulster poet and dissenter, John Hewitt, which closes the play. The work is resolved, not by the moving recitation of the names of the dead—a trope at the heart of Irish nationalist and communist ritual alike—but by the dying fall of old age and acceptance: a uniquely human recognition. It is this willingness on the playwright's part to yield ideology to the requirements of a humane imagination without sacrificing the valid and wayward passion of politics that augurs so well for the future of his art, rendering the early chapter of his career, which closes here, such a fulfilling and intriguing one.

Damian Smyth
1st January 1996

DOCKERS
(1981)

Dockers was first performed at the Lyric Players Theatre, Belfast, on 12th January 1981. It was directed by Sam McCready. The cast was as follows:

John Graham	Oliver Maguire
Theresa Graham	Stella McCusker
Buckets McGuinness	Louis Rolston
Leg McNamara	J.J. Murphy
Hughie McNamara	Ian McElhinney
Danny-boy McNamara	Peter Quigley
Jack Henry	George Shane
McKibben	Mel Austin
Jimmy Sweeney	Mark Shelley
Sarah Montague	Leila Webster
Mary-Ann McKeown	Maureen Dow
Barney	Michael Gormley

The play is set in 1962. The location is the Sailortown district of Belfast.

ACT ONE

SCENE ONE

The scene is an employment schooling-shed for dockworkers. It is desolated, barren and grey. Along the wall is a three-foot high wooden platform, protected by a steel crush barrier. A group of dockers enters casually, some engaged in conversation and some reading newspapers.

JOHN: I don't care. If you're drivin that winch, Leg, you'll not get me down in the houl of that boat.

LEG: I've never caused an accident in my life.

JOHN: It's not for the want of tryin.

LEG: You ask your da who's the best winchman he ever saw.

JOHN: I'd believe you, but millions wouldn't.

[*The dockers are standing beside or near the platform.*]

LEG: Just ask your da.

[*A docker enters, in a slight hurry.*]

BUCKETS: Well, young Graham, what's goin?

JOHN: Ach, Buckets, what about ye? Aye, there's a fair bit of work this mornin. As far as I hear, the Ghent boat's in.

BUCKETS: Oh, give that a wide berth. What's Sweeney at?

[*The foreman,* JIMMY SWEENEY, *enters with* JACK HENRY, *the union chairman.* SWEENEY *jumps up on the platform.* HENRY *exits.*]

JOHN: Beg stuff.

BUCKETS: That's no good, either. What about your man?

JOHN: Fruit boat. But he's finished at twelve and has his own gang.

BUCKETS: Is Wicked Moustache out this mornin?

JOHN: Aye, he's over there, but he's at beg stuff, too.

BUCKETS: In the name of Jasis, is there nothin else? Every time I go near a beg boat, I'm bad with m'chest for days after it. Friggin grain! No good for the drinkin, y'know.

JOHN [*mockingly*]: When was the last time you were at a beg boat?

BUCKETS: Who? What? I wisht I'd a pound in m'pocket for every beg boat I'd worked at down the years. What are you slabberin

about anyway? You're only a meal-hour round the dock. What? The likes of you givin me bettins?
JOHN: I'm only havin you on, Buckets. Here, away over there. The Headline has a handy wee Timber boat in.
BUCKETS: What da buck ... get away ... bucksake! Timber boats!
JOHN: I don't know why you got outta your bed a'tall this mornin.
BUCKETS: Nor do I. I'm away up to the corner to wait on Barney's openin. I'll see you later.
JOHN: Okay, Buckets, see ya. [BUCKETS *turns to go, then stops.*]
BUCKETS: By the way, young Graham, I hope you're not thinkin I'm walkin away from work. Not a'tall. I'm just givin the non-union men a chance to get a day's work. [*He smiles.*]
JOHN: Get away of that with ye, Buckets. [BUCKETS *walks towards exit.* JOHN *shouts after him*] I'm gonna tell your oul woman you didn't weigh in for work this mornin!
BUCKETS: No, tell your own ma about the time your da lost his pay packet down the toilet in Du Barry's!
JOHN: At least my da earned a wage!
BUCKETS: Ya don't call me Shitey Pound Note!
JOHN: Ach, away on to hell of that with ye!
BUCKETS: Shitey Pound Note! [*He exits shouting*] Aye, tell your ma about the time your da lost his pay packet down the toilet in a brothel! Shitey Pound Note!

[JOHN GRAHAM *shakes his head and smiles.* JIMMY SWEENEY, *the foreman, speaks to a man standing directly below him.*]

SWEENEY: Are we ready to start, McKibben. It's after eight nigh!
MCKIBBEN: Wait and I'll go and see if there's anybody still comin down the road.

[MCKIBBEN *walks up to the exit and looks into the distance. He turns back and shouts as he is half-way across.*]

MCKIBBEN: Alright! Away yiz go!

[*The men quickly bunch up against the crush barrier directly under* JIMMY SWEENEY. *The foreman, quite selectively, picks and chooses which men he is employing by handing each man a small disc. As a man is selected, he exits.*]

SWEENEY: Right, Kelly! You! O'Neill! You! McNamara! Quinn!

[MCKIBBEN *then pushes his way forward to the front of the platform, by which time the remaining men are jostling each other, with arms outstretched.*]

MCKIBBEN: Come on, men! Stand back and give him a chance. Do

yiz wanna make exhibitions of yourselves? Come on!
[MCKIBBEN *places himself directly below the foreman.*]
SWEENEY: McKibben! And Graham! That's it!
[SWEENEY *jumps down and quickly exits.* HUGHIE MCNAMARA *enters the shed as* JOHN GRAHAM *is about to exit.*]
HUGHIE: Nothin left, John?
JOHN: Nope. You can see for yourself. There's forty or fifty first-preference union men without work.
HUGHIE: So, no work for us non-union men the day again.
JOHN: The work's not there—
HUGHIE: John, I'm gettin fed up standin outside that gate every mornin while yous all get the pick of the work. I've only got four days in three weeks.
JOHN: What can you do when the work's not there?
HUGHIE: Open the books and let me into the union.
JOHN: I think there's a meetin about that today.
[*They both turn and walk towards the exit.*]
HUGHIE: Well, you've got on to the union committee for the first time, John. We're all expectin some changes.
JOHN: Who do you think I am, Houdini?
[*They exit.*]

SCENE TWO

The scene is at the dockside. JOHN GRAHAM *and* MCKIBBEN *enter pushing a hand-truck. A heave, made up of six bags of grain rests on the truck. A hook is lowered from the ship. The men hook on the heave which then disappears off stage. Leg McNamara's voice is heard off stage.*

LEG: Houl on down there a minute!
MCKIBBEN: Don't tell me that winch's broke down again!
JOHN: Looks very like it.
LEG: Need any ropes down there?
MCKIBBEN: Never mind the ropes! Get that winch movin till we get away outta here!
LEG: What do you want me to do? I'm only drivin the thing, I didn't build it!
JOHN: I thought you knew all about winches!

LEG: Ach, away and laugh at your ma!

[MCKIBBEN *sits down on the truck.*]

MCKIBBEN: We'll never get away the day.

[LEG MCNAMARA *enters. He wears thick, oily gloves.*]

LEG: It'll not be long till it's fixed, lads. Candyapple Docherty's helpin the ships's engineer to fix the winch. [*He laughs.*]

MCKIBBEN: We'll never get away the day.

JOHN: What time is it, Leg?

LEG: Nearly eleven a'clock. Is there much cargo left?

JOHN: Only another half-a-dozen heaves, no more.

LEG: That's not so bad.

MCKIBBEN: If that winch wouldn't keep breakin down, we could've been away long go.

LEG: There's the two of yiz shop stewards. Away and do something about it.

JOHN: There's a bit of a difference between bein a shop steward and a ship's engineer.

LEG: Oh, it's alright. Here's the union chairman. Jack Henry'll get things movin. What about ye, Jack? [JACK HENRY *enters.*]

HENRY: What's wrong here?

MCKIBBEN: Winch's broke down, Jack.

LEG: For the umpteenth time.

JOHN: But we shouldn't be too long. There's only another half a dozen heaves left.

HENRY: If the winch gets fixed! That's what's wrong with too many people at this dock. Easy come, easy go. This is all work and we've had to fight hard and sore to get it over the years. Sometimes I think some of you dockers don't know the half of it.

JOHN: What should we know, then?

HENRY: Well, for a start, there's two unions round here and it hasn't always been easy to keep the lion's share of the work away from themens.

JOHN: You mean the Protestant section?

MCKIBBEN: They're based in England and our union's based in Dublin.

JOHN: But why has no one ever found a solution to the problem of two unions at Belfast docks?

HENRY: There's always been two unions. That's the way things are and always will be.

Dockers

MCKIBBEN: I think the solution's simple. Always do a deal with the employers beforehand, so that we get any disputed work, even if it means doin the job at a cheaper rate. At least it ensures we get it.

JOHN: And you regard yourself as a trade unionist?

MCKIBBEN: Why not?

JOHN: Because any trade unionist can see that the present situation, whereby the employers can play the work off two unions, wouldn't arise if we were one, strong union. Catholic dockers and Protestant dockers. That's common sense.

HENRY: Common sense, my arse. Our job goes no further than to protect the rights of our members. Against the Protestant union, if that's necessary.

JOHN: But they're trade unionists, too. Two unions at Belfast docks defeats the very purpose of organised labour. Larkin didn't ask anybody's religion when he led the workers of Belfast to bring the city to a standstill in 1907. How it ever got to the stage of two unions I'll never know.

MCKIBBEN: Because they're Protestants and we're Catholics.

JOHN: But we're all dockers.

MCKIBBEN: That's got nothin to do with it.

LEG: Maybe somebody should approach the other crowd about all of us coming together.

HENRY: What do you know about anything?

LEG: I was only makin a suggestion, Jack.

HENRY: That's another thing. Too many people have too much to say round here. We're all followers of our union founders, Larkin and Connolly, but we have to be practical.

[*Enter* BUCKETS MCGUINNESS.]

BUCKETS: What's all the yellin about? Is the new Committee fightin among themselves already? Is the new member causin trouble? Have you been spakin up, John Graham?

MCKIBBEN: Shut up, McGuinness, what do you know?

BUCKETS: Shut up, m'bollocks! What? You? I'm round this dock long before you, your da or anybody belonging to you. [MCKIBBEN *attempts to go for* BUCKETS, *but* HENRY *waves him back*] Oh, he wants to bate me for sayin the wrong things. It would annoy you to think the dockers is askin questions for a change. Questions like will the Committee be able to handle John Graham?

JOHN: Scrub it, Buckets!

BUCKETS: Or as I heard one docker say the other day, 'Can we now expect to see the union return to what it used to be under Jim Larkin and Connolly?'

LEG: But Connolly's union we are and us Belfast dockers'll carry on with the worst wages and conditions in any port, British or Irish.

HENRY: Watch it, Leg. You're luckin a son into the union.

[LEG *is extremely embarrassed.*]

BUCKETS: That's what I like about our union. They would never be personal about union affairs. Well, I can say whatever the hell I like. I have no sons, nor do I crawl to anybody for work. What? I wouldn't lower myself.

MCKIBBEN: There's neither work nor want in ye.

BUCKETS: For once in your life, McKibben, you're right. If I had the inclination to work I'd have to lick the arse of people like you and I'd rather stand up in Barney's any day firin liquor into me. If work was any good, the wealthy would be doin it.

MCKIBBEN: You're only a drunkard.

BUCKETS: A happy drunkard. And I'd rather be a happy drunkard than a sweat-arsed, work-drunk, mealy-mouthed, nothin-to-show-for-it dock labourer. Leg, I want to see you about a few shillins.

HENRY: That suits you, McGuinness. C'mon, McKibben, to we see what's wrong with this winch. By the way, Graham, there's a union meetin at dinner-hour, to decide on whether or not to open the union for more members.

[*Exit* MCKIBBEN *and* HENRY.]

BUCKETS: There goes our two union leaders. There's more brains in a bucket of skins.

LEG: Did you hear Henry to me? Jasus, you'd think I was askin for somethin I'm not entitled to. A man should be able to spake his mind even if he wanted twenty sons into the union.

BUCKETS: I thought you had a son in, Leg.

LEG: The eldest lad, Hughie, he shoulda been in. The union books closed two days before he left school and he's pushin thirty nigh.

JOHN: Is that how long it is since the union books were open? You wouldn't think it?

LEG: It is strange the way the dock works. You can't get in unless you're in the union and you can't get into the union unless you're da was a docker before ye.

JOHN: I'm sure it seems a bit unfair to the outsider.

LEG: The outsider! What about my sons? My Hughie's workin non-union round here nigh for years and me 33 years round the place.

BUCKETS. That's because certain union men have no sons and don't want the books open and you know it, Leg.

LEG: I know it only too well and the whole dock's talkin about it. They've left it that long nigh that men's gonna be fightin over who gets in and who doesn't. As well as Hughie, Danny-boy's luckin in. He's only 22, but he insists that he should get the button cause he's gettin married.

JOHN: The oldest son always gets the button.

LEG: Easier said than done. I don't know what I'm gonna do.

[*Enter* HUGHIE MCNAMARA.]

HUGHIE: Da! Da, did you hear there's gonna be a union meetin the day about openin the union books?

LEG: I heard alright.

HUGHIE: Well, c'mon with me, da, till I get my name down.

LEG: Take your time, Hughie. Give is a chance to get the thing sorted out.

HUGHIE: What do you mean, take m'time, da? I'm waitin years for this and you tell me to take m'time?

[*Enter* DANNY-BOY.]

DANNY-BOY: You better not. I want that button.

HUGHIE: I'm the oldest son, it's mine.

DANNY-BOY: I need the money, I'm gettin married. Right, da?

LEG: Of course, you're gettin married, Danny-boy, but Hughie is the oldest between the two of ye.

DANNY-BOY: What? Are you makin differences nigh between your own sons? He's better than me?

LEG: I'm not, I'm not!

DANNY-BOY: That's alright. I'm no good. As long as I know the way of it.

LEG: It's not that way a'tall.

DANNY-BOY: What way is it, then?

JOHN: You've got it all wrong, Danny. Your da's only doin his best. As you know, it is the usual system round here that the oldest always has first option.

DANNY-BOY: Oh, yiz are all against me nigh!
LEG: No, we're not, we're just—
DANNY-BOY: Just nothin! Da. I want a decision from you. Nigh! I'm savin up to get married. I need to know.
HUGHIE: You're not on.
DANNY-BOY: Neither are you.
JOHN: Look, why don't the two of yiz leave it for a while, sit down later and discuss the whole thing quietly with your da?
LEG: That's what I've been tryin to tell them.
HUGHIE: There's no discussin about it. *I'm* the oldest.
DANNY-BOY: Who do you think you are?
BUCKETS: Hold on a minute, lads. There's a very simple way round this.
LEG: What are you talkin about?
BUCKETS: Toss up.
JOHN: You couldn't do that.
HUGHIE [*sarcastically*]: Toss a bloody coin.
LEG: No, that's no way to sort it out.
BUCKETS: Well, if anybody can come up with a better idea, let's hear it? [*Silence*] Right then, let's toss. Heads or tails, Danny-boy?
LEG: I don't like the idea of this.
BUCKETS: It's not your idea, it's mine. Luck, this way both sons have an equal chance. Have yiz no sense? What? Otherwise, there'll be blood and snatters. Call, Danny-boy?
DANNY-BOY: Heads.
BUCKETS: Right! All's it needs is a bit of common-sense. Up it goes.
[*He tosses the coin up in the air. The others stand intently as he lifts it off the floor*] I'm afraid it's tails, Danny-boy. And the new holder of a button in the Dockers union is ... Hughie McNamara.
DANNY-BOY: I'm not wearin that, da. No toss of a coin's keepin me outiv work.
HUGHIE: You were bate fair and square.
DANNY-BOY: M'da's gonna decide who gets it, not that. N'that right, da?
HUGHIE: Crawlin to your daddy nigh? Ya wee boy ye.
DANNY-BOY: I'm no wee boy.
HUGHIE: You're a big chile.

Dockers

LEG: C'mon, Hughie, that's enough.
HUGHIE: He's a big baby.
LEG: I said knock it on the head.
DANNY-BOY: I'm warnin you, Hughie
HUGHIE: Aye, you'd break a lot of delph.
DANNY-BOY: Da!
  [DANNY-BOY *steps forward aggressively, fists poised.* HUGHIE *responds likewise.*]
HUGHIE: C'mon, try it ... son!
LEG: Hughie!
JOHN: Scrub it, lads.
HUGHIE: He's only a wee boy.
DANNY-BOY: Am A?
  [DANNY-BOY *throws a punch.*]
LEG: Jesus Christ, stop it!
  [*The two brothers wrestle and end up rolling on the floor, while* LEG *and* JOHN *attempt to separate them.* BUCKETS *discreetly exits as* JOHN *eventually manages to pull* HUGHIE *off* DANNY-BOY.]
HUGHIE: Don't you think this is over. I'll make you sorry for that!
  [HUGHIE *walks off.*]
DANNY-BOY: Any time!
LEG: Shut up, for Jasis sake, will ya?
JOHN: That's out of order, Danny. You wanna catch yourself on.
  [MCKIBBEN *enters.*]
MCKIBBEN: What's goin on here?
LEG: Nothin. Right, you! [*To* DANNY-BOY] Aren't you workin in the next hatch?
DANNY-BOY: Aye.
LEG: Well, get back to it. If Jimmy Sweeney sees you standin about here, you'll be sacked.
DANNY-BOY: I'm goin.
LEG: And let that be the end of it. Imagine two brothers fightin each other?
  [DANNY-BOY *exits.*]
MCKIBBEN: What is goin on here?
JOHN: Leg's sons were fightin over who's gettin into the union.
MCKIBBEN: I've said it all along. The books should never be opened.
LEG: I can't do anything about it, Harry. Both of them needs work.

MCKIBBEN: The might get a quare shock if none of them gets in. [*Enter* JIMMY SWEENEY.]
SWEENEY: C'mon a that, w'yiz! We haven't all day to get this cargo shifted. I've anor hatch on this boat to luck after. [LEG *exits.* JOHN *lifts the shafts of the truck and begins to move off, followed by* MCKIBBEN. LEG *hurries off towards the ship*] C'mon, yiz are workin for yourselves here!

SCENE THREE

BARNEY MCGIVERN *is on duty behind the bar of his public house. Dominated by an old-fashioned wooden counter, the pub is anything but luxurious. At one end of the bar is a small enclosed snug, while a six-foot high partition at the other end hides a single standing place at the bar.* BUCKETS MCGUINNESS *is standing at the bar with the proverbial glass of wine at his fingertips.* THERESA GRAHAM *enters.*

THERESA: Sorry I'm late, Barney, but I didn't know the time goin in this mornin. Hiya, Buckets.
BUCKETS: What about ye, Theresa daughter?
BARNEY: Never worry, girl, never worry.
THERESA: That's what's wrong with me, I worry too much. There was me runnin the feet off myself to get John Graham's dinner ready and him never showed up for it. I'll go for the pies nigh, Barney, and clean the place up when I come back. Will that be alright?
BARNEY: Please yourself. I'm not particular one way or the other.
THERESA: I wonder where John is to this time?
BUCKETS: Probably still at the first meetin of the new shop stewards committee. You're married to a top man in the union nigh.
THERESA: Oh, don't I know? That's all I've heard from him since he was elected last week. It's all you get from you get up in the mornin till you go to bed at night. Union, union, union! Will I get the usual two dozen, Barney?
BARNEY: Should be enough, Theresa.
THERESA: Right, I'll see yiz later then.
BUCKETS: Cheerio.

[THERESA *exits.* BUCKETS *drains his glass and looks at* BARNEY.]

BUCKETS: Barney a ... I'm not very strong at the minute, do you a ... do you think you could work me a drink on strap?

BARNEY: Not on your life. At least not until you pay me the bill you've already run up.

BUCKETS: But sure, there's a rubber boat due in ...

[SARAH MONTAGUE *enters from the snug and walks to the bar.*]

SARAH: Is there no sign of your woman yet, Barney?

BARNEY: Not yet.

SARAH: I don't know why she goes near that pawn. He gives her no more than buttons.

BUCKETS: Ah nigh, go on Sarah Montague. If you were handed one odd boot and a clock with no hands on it, you wouldn't pay out either.

SARAH: Who's talkin to you? Didn't your missis try an pawn a paintin of Robert Emmett?

BUCKETS: What was wrong with that?

SARAH: Nothin. Except she painted it herself. Give is a wee gin, Barney. [MARY-ANN MCKEOWN *enters from the street*] Where the hell were you?

MARY-ANN: Oh Sarah dear, you don't know the trouble I've had this day. When I got up this mornin, that lazy blurt wouldn't go out to his work without his five Woodbine. Then our Rosie came round luckin the loan of a pound. God, Sarah, I hadn't got it to give to her. Not this week anyway.

SARAH: But did you go up to the other place? Give is a wee sherry as well, Barney.

MARY-ANN: Don't mention it. Tryin to get money up there's like tryin to tell a Protestant King Billy's horse wasn't white.

SARAH: Well, that's not as bad as tryin to tell a Papist that Patrick Pearse used bad language nigh an again.

BUCKETS: Would you listen to the two of them. I don't know how yous two sit in that box without tearin the hair out of one anor.

[SARAH *lifts her drink.*]

SARAH: As long as you and your likes aren't there, Buckets McGuinness, we'll do alright. C'mon, Mary-Ann, I think we should discuss our financial matters in private.

MARY-ANN: Whatever you like nigh, Sarah, it's all the same to me.

SARAH: You'd think the proprietor of this establishment would be more careful who he let into this public house. Dacent customers could be offended. [*Exit* SARAH *to snug.*]

MARY-ANN: Don't take any heed of her, Buckets son, she's only a oul nark.

BUCKETS: Don't worry, I don't. [MARY-ANN *exits to snug*] Well, there you are nigh, Barney. Them two's away to discuss their financial matters in private. Ha, the laugh of it. Half bloody Sailortown knows their financial matters and more. I heard two shipyard men from Ballymacarrett at the dogs last night talkin about the money the owe Sarah Montague.

BARNEY: Ah, she's not the worst. There's moneylenders in this town, as you well know, who'd watch you dyin in the street afore they'd lend you something, if you weren't clear with them.

BUCKETS: Aye, and them the best chapelgoers in the city. Well, I'm gonna put that to the test, Barney. I owe Sarah Montague 18 shillins this long time and I'm gonna put the hammer on her nigh. [BUCKETS *goes over to the snug*] Sarah! Sarah Montague, could I spake to you for a minute?

SARAH [*shouting from the box*]: Go away. You still owe me 18 shillins!

BUCKETS: But Mrs. Montague, I was wantin' to talk to you about that very thing! [SARAH *enters, very stern looking as usual*] Mrs. Montague, I a ... well, I had nothin to lift this week and the wife's luckin a few hapens ... but there's a timber boat due in tomorrow and I'm a cert to be over the hatch for Big O'Connor, so I'll have at least two days pay to lift next week.

SARAH: You're a confounded liar!

[*She turns to exit, but* BUCKETS *grabs her by the shoulder.*]

BUCKETS: Mrs. Montague, I swear on our Paddy's life, I'll pay you back next week.

SARAH: Sure, your Paddy's one fut on the grave as it is ...

BUCKETS: Luck, Mrs. Montague, I'm tellin you the God's honest truth, Big O'Connor always gives me a job over the hatch at a—

SARAH: You can Big O'Connor me till you're blue in the face. The answer is NO! [*She exits and slams the door behind her.* BUCKETS *slowly returns to the bar.*]

BARNEY: Bad luck, Buckets.

BUCKETS: And you said she wasn't the worst. Barney a ... Listen, give is one wine and I'll fix you up on Thursday?

Dockers 31

BARNEY: Man dear, you're the limit. I can't!
[*Enter* SARAH.]
SARAH: Here's a pound, you, and if that isn't paid by Thursday, along with the 18 shillins, you've had it!
BUCKETS: Ach, thanks very much, Mrs. Montague. Sure you know you'll get every penny of it as soon as the wages office opens on the the dot. Thanks.
SARAH: Thursday!
[SARAH *exits. Buckets' face lights up. He kisses the pound note.*]
BUCKETS: Make that a double wine, Barney. And a ... bring her over her usual.
BARNEY: I told you she's not the worst.
BUCKETS: Naa. But she's still an oul—
[LEG MCNAMARA *enters*] Ach, bully Leg, what about ye? What are ye havin?
LEG: Bottle a stout. Where'd you get the money? It must be ... the day the two of us got into the union together, since you last bought me a drink. Mind thon day up in Hannigan's Bar? You vomited all over North Queen Street.
BUCKETS: Give over, Leg. Take a bottle of stout an shut up. Will you take a halfin?
LEG: No, this'll do me. M'head's bustin. I was on the whiskey all last night round in Peter's. I don't suppose any of the Dock Committee's been in yet?
BARNEY: Not yet. What is it, problems?
LEG: Did he not tell ye? The two sons was fightin' down at the boat this mornin over which one of thems gettin into the union.
BARNEY: I don't believe you!
BUCKETS: Ach, what are you worried about, isn't it all settled nigh? Didn't I handle the whole thing like a master?
LEG: It was you that started them fightin. Barney, he tossed up a coin an all hell broke loose.
BARNEY: Sure, Leg, you shoulda known better than to let Buckets McGuinness near anything.
BUCKETS: Is that the thanks you get for tryin to be helpful. It is sorted out, isn't it?
LEG: Some chance.
BARNEY: You've problems there, Leg.
BUCKETS: Not as bad as mine. I've to get Sarah Montague 38 shillins by Thursday.

BARNEY: Did I not hear you tellin her you were goin to be workin at a timber boat?

BUCKETS: For Jasis sake, Barney! How long do you know me now? There's a timber boat due in alright but, if you catch me near it, give me a good boot up the arse and chase me home. No! No, don't chase me home. That's where the wife is. I owe her money as well. [BUCKETS *slaps* LEG *on the shoulder and has a good laugh at the idea*] You're never safe no matter where you go. I often wonder where we'd all be the day if our oul lads hadna been dockers. If I could a just changed the K for a T things mighta been different as a doctor's son.

LEG: You've no guarantee.

BUCKETS: Maybe you're right. Maybe we're not so badly off the way we are.

LEG: We've John Graham on the committee nigh, maybe we're on the threshold of a new era. A new period of change.

BARNEY: Nobody'll ever change the dock, it's too set in its ways.

LEG: Oh, I don't know. Young Graham's a lad of some ability and he's a very determined kid. Hasn't he spent the last five years to get where he is nigh against stiff opposition?

BUCKETS: Is right. But there's a certain element who have the habit of turnin the most conscientious union man into an employers' lickspittle overnight. Luck, I'll tell you what I'll do. Where's that oul photo of the first Union Executive with Larkin and Connolly in it?

BARNEY: I think it's down there somewhere.

BUCKETS: Give is it up here. [BARNEY *bends down below the bar and comes up with an old framed photograph which he hands to* BUCKETS] Nigh that somebody with a bit of wit is shop steward in the Irish Transport and General Workers' Union, Docks Section, we might see a return to the union these men helped to build. [BUCKETS *walks to the end of the bar where he takes down a calendar and replaces it with the photograph*] Up ya go and I hope to Jasis we can keep ye up there with the help of John Graham.

LEG: As long as he doesn't bow the knee to no employer or no union hench-men, he'll have our full backing. Mines anyway.

BUCKETS: Well, time'll tell the story. Here, Leg! [BUCKETS *holds up his empty glass*] It's your turn to buy this downtrodden, underpaid dock labourer a drink. [*Speaking politely*] I'll have a wine please, thank you.

LEG: A wine, Barney, and a bottle of stout for myself. Hey, I wonder will John call in afore he goes home. I'm bustin to know if the books is gettin opened.

BARNEY: I'd imagine he'd be in shortly. The meetin'll hardly last all day.

BUCKETS: They're probably cuttin the water outiv him. I didn't wanna say it in front of his wee girl, but he'll have a rough time with the Jack Henrys of this world.

LEG: Well, there's an awful lot of men's pinnin their hopes on him.

BUCKETS: I hate to say it, but the might as well pin their hopes on the Vatican givin some of their priceless paintins to the starvin people of India. I hope I'm wrong. [JOHN GRAHAM *enters.*]

LEG: There's the man himself.

BUCKETS: What about ye, son?

JOHN: Dead on, lads. Give us a bottle of stout, Barney.

BARNEY: Alright, John.

LEG: Well, how did the first meetin go? Did yiz decide on openin the books?

JOHN: Just about. I don't think there'll be too many gettin in, though.

LEG: Is that right?

JOHN: Is it Hughie you're puttin in, then?

LEG: I don't know what to do.

JOHN: Still fightin, are they?

LEG: Wouldn't you know.

JOHN: That's bad. Is there no way of sortin it out? Since Buckets' magic formula didn't exactly have them shakin hands.

LEG: I'll have to think of something.

JOHN: Do you think it might help if I had a word with Hughie?

LEG: Would ye, John?

JOHN: I'm not sayin I'll solve the problem, but I'll have a yarn with him anyway.

BUCKETS: And I could have a talk with Danny-boy. [LEG *glares at* BUCKETS] For Jasis sake, Leg, to luck at you, you'd think I was the devil himself.

LEG: Just stay outiv it!

BUCKETS: I know Danny-boy well—

LEG: Haven't you done enough damage? Just stay outiv it!

[SARAH *and* MARY-ANN *enter from the snug.*]

SARAH: What nigh is all the shoutin about?
BUCKETS: Nothin much. Leg and me give two Brethren from York Road Orange Lodge a bit of a kickin last night and we were just debatin who done the most damage.
SARAH: Huh! You wouldn't have the guts to luck sideways at an Orangeman, never mind lift your hand to two of them. Do you want anor sherry, Mrs. McKeown?
MARY-ANN: Whatever you like nigh. It's all the same to me, Sarah.
SARAH: But it's you that's gonna be ... Ach, it doesn't matter. Give is a gin and a sherry, Barney.
BARNEY: A gin and a sherry comin up.
MARY-ANN: Do you know what I was thinkin, Sarah?
SARAH: How am I supposed to know what you're thinkin, unless you tell me?

[BARNEY *sets up the drink.*]

MARY-ANN: I was thinkin maybe I should take a wee hot whiskey instead.
SARAH: But sure I ... Oh, it wouldn't be you. You may change that, Barney.
BARNEY: No problem. I'll bring it over to you.

[SARAH *walks into the snug, followed by* MARY-ANN *making faces behind her back.*]

BUCKETS: You know, givin drink to them two's a waste of time.
LEG: How?
BUCKETS: They never get drunk.
BARNEY: As long as the keep spendin.
JOHN: They've too much talkin to catch up on ...

[THERESA GRAHAM *enters excitedly.*]

THERESA: Is John Graham here ... Oh God, John, there's been an accident at the dock!
JOHN: What happened?
LEG: Was there anybody hurt?
THERESA: Mr. McNamara, it was your young fella.
LEG: Danny-boy!
THERESA: Yes, Danny-boy.
LEG: Jesis, Mary and Joseph!
THERESA: But I don't think he's badly hurt. Just something with his arm.
LEG: Where is he nigh?
THERESA: Oh, he's away to the hospital an all.

LEG: Are you sure it was just his arm?

THERESA: I was talkin to Scrub A'Nail in Pilot Street. He said he was workin along with him and he seemed to think he wasn't too bad a'tall.

LEG: I may go up to the hospital anyway. Which one is it, do you know?

THERESA: The Mater.

JOHN: Aye, you might be as well goin on up, Leg, and seein him anyway.

BUCKETS: Do you want me to go along with ye?

LEG: I'll be alright.

[LEG *exits.*]

JOHN: How did this happen, Theresa, did you hear?

THERESA: Aye, Scrub said it was an overloaded heave fell on him in the houl of the boat.

JOHN: Oh. Overloadin heaves? That's Jimmy Sweeney again. He was bossin that boat.

BUCKETS: There's bosses round here and they'd put three times the begs into heaves if they could get away with it.

JOHN: Aye, and dockers who'd do it without a word of protest.

BUCKETS: All to get away that wee bit earlier.

BARNEY: It couldn't be safe standin under a bundle of begs when it's swingin up in the air above ye. Especially if they're overloaded.

THERESA: God, I near died when I heard there was somebody hurt at the dock. My heart was in my mouth thinkin it was this fella. Know the way you always think the worst.

BARNEY: It's been a right fright for you. It seems to me there's far too many accidents at that dock. It's a wonder there isn't more killed.

THERESA: Like everything else. They'll wait till some poor unfortunate bein gets killed and then they'll do something.

BUCKETS: It wouldn't be the first. I mind the day we stood and watched a man sinkin slowly in the houl of a grain boat.

JOHN: Why didn't yiz get in and get him out?

BUCKETS: There was any amount of us in the houl, shovellin hell for lyre. But the more we shovelled, the more he sank. And we couldn't pull him out, his head woulda left his shoulders.

THERESA: Oh my God!

BUCKETS: We even had time to get a priest down to give the poor man the last rites. A slow, slow death. That was the first and last time I ever saw a crowd of dockers standin weepin into their caps.

JOHN: It's hard to believe, Buckets, yiz couldn't get him out.

BUCKETS: I know, but it's true. You ask any of the oul dockers.

THERESA: Don't be goin on, yiz'll have me more worried than I am already. I don't know how yiz stick it!

JOHN: We're not gonna stick it any longer. I've already had it out with the union about safety regulations at the dock and I'm gonna insist on some action against Jimmy Sweeney.

BUCKETS: There's planty of dockers has a thing or two to say about him. Sure, there's not a man about the place would have a drink with him. He sits his life alone in the canteen takin his tea and then slinks about the job spyin on the men. Would you do it, eh? Not a bit of wonder the talk about him.

JOHN: About him, Buckets, but not to his face and that's what's wrong. His name'll be top of the agenda tomorrow mornin. That's the first thing I wanna see stopped. Overloadin heaves. We don't want any more accidents.

[JIMMY SWEENEY, *the foreman, enters. Amidst silence, he walks straight over to the single place behind the partition at the end of the bar. He orders a drink. All eyes turn on* JOHN GRAHAM. *He takes a deep breath and steps out into the middle of the bar.* THERESA *attempts to restrain him.*]

THERESA: Not nigh, John.

JOHN: It's alright, Theresa, it's alright. Sweeney! Jimmy Sweeney, I wanna have a word with you!

[SWEENEY *takes his time appearing.*]

SWEENEY: Whadaya want, Graham?

JOHN: I'm lettin you know, I'm raisin your name with the committee first thing in the mornin. You've been responsible for an injury to a young docker.

SWEENEY: Sure, he was only a non-union man.

JOHN: That's immaterial. I'm raisin your name.

SWEENEY: Do whatever the fuck you like!

JOHN: I'm warnin you, you'll not get away with it.

SWEENEY: Luck, I didn't sling the heave, so don't come slabberin to me, Graham. Blame the dockers who made up the heave.

JOHN: You were the boss. You told them, three extra begs in each heave.

SWEENEY: Crap! Nigh, will you go away and give my head peace?
JOHN: That's exactly what I won't do. There'll be no peace for you while I'm on the committee.
SWEENEY: I'm tremblin. [SWEENEY *exits behind the partition.* JOHN, *seething with anger, turns and pauses before exiting hurriedly.*]
JOHN: C'mon, Theresa, before I lose my temper!
[*As* JOHN *and* THERESA *are about to exit,* LEG *enters with* MCKIBBEN.]
LEG: Oh, John, Danny-boy's alright. Harry here tells me he only sprained his arm.
JOHN: That's good. Maybe Harry'll do something about *him*!
[JOHN *and* THERESA *exit.*]
MCKIBBEN: What's wrong with him?
BUCKETS: He's only after having a row with Jimmy Sweeney about the accident.
MCKIBBEN: Aye, Graham'd know all about accidents. I better have a word with Jimmy. [MCKIBBEN *exits behind the partition.*]
BARNEY: I'm glad to hear the lad's alright, Leg.
LEG: Aye, it's nothin to worry about. He'll be out of the hospital afore six a'clock. One of the begs fell on his arm.
BUCKETS: Coulda been his head.
LEG: I know. McKibben's havin a word with him about it nigh. I can't have that bastard Sweeney. [*McKibben's voice is heard.*]
MCKIBBEN: Barney! Give Jimmy a bottle and a halfin.
BARNEY: Right you be.
BUCKETS: Havin a word with him's right. He's fixin himself up for a job in the mornin. That's a union man for ye.
LEG: Ach, I suppose I should've known.
BUCKETS: You've always known, Leg. The only man who'll try and stand up for the dockers nigh is John Graham. He didn't half give it to Sweeney here a while ago.
LEG: John shoulda hit the glipe. I wish I was young again, there'd be two John Grahams.
BUCKETS: Aye, you'd shite coalbrick if you'd a square-arsed hole!
[SWEENEY *and* MCKIBBEN *enter, moving towards the exit.*]
MCKIBBEN: It's the dockers' own faults. Half of them doesn't even know how to sling a heave.
SWEENEY: You can say that again. Hey, McNamara!
LEG: What's that, Jimmy?
SWEENEY: I'm startin a gang for the Dutch boat in the mornin. I need a man for over-the-hatch.

LEG: Well, I'll be out in the mornin, Jimmy. Is there much cargo?
SWEENEY: Enough to get us four days outiv it.
LEG: That's dead on, Jimmy, I'll be out. See you in the mornin.
[As SWEENEY and MCKIBBEN are about to exit, LEG calls SWEENEY to the side.]
LEG: Oh Jimmy! Forget about that accident. I know it was nothin to do with you. The young lad's right as rain anyway.
SWEENEY: Well, you better tell that other Comanche Graham that. And when you're at it, tell him I said very few foremen like to employ agitators.
MCKIBBEN: And I'll be raisin *his* name at the next meetin.
SWEENEY: It's changed times round here, when wee lads is gonna bate ye. [*They exit.*]
BUCKETS: Up the workers, Leg, eh?
LEG: Whadaya on about?
BUCKETS: Two John Grahams?
LEG: Buckets, you must take the work when it's goin.
BUCKETS: So, while John Graham's goin round fightin for the likes a you, you're cuttin the feet from below him?
LEG: Luck, it wasn't me invented the system round here. That's the way it's always been.
BUCKETS: It is corruption.
LEG: That's life. I'm fed up tellin our Hughie. Trade unions, militancy, fightin talk and all the rest of it's only for buck-ejits. At the end of the day, it's all about puttin bread on the table. The childer can't eat speeches.
BUCKETS: Scrub the union then?
LEG: It's alright John Graham talkin about the union, but the union doesn't pay my wages. You have to luck after number one. Nobody's gonna come throwin loaves a bread at ye. Anyway, I may get up to the house and let the missus know about Danny-boy. That'll be another blurtin and cryin match.
BUCKETS: You're lucky it wasn't his head.
LEG: I know. See ya later. [LEG *exits.*]
BUCKETS: Barney, did you ever hear of the Kamikazzi pilots durin the war? Watch this. [*He walks towards the snug.*]
BARNEY: Where are you goin?
BUCKETS: I owe the wife three pounds and I have to go home sometime. Here goes. Sarah! Mrs. Montague, could I have a wee word with you?

SARAH: Have you got my 38 shillins?
BUCKETS: Yes! [*His face winces as the publican looks astounded.* SARAH *enters.*]
SARAH: Where is it?
BUCKETS: Well, I don't exactly have it on me at the moment ... but [SARAH *turns to go, but he grabs hold of her arm.*] ... what I mean, Mrs. Montague, is ... I have a brand new suit in the pawn. The wife only bought me it at Easter. The best a sweg it is. Nigh, if you could lend me three pounds sterling to lift it, I could then sell it to you. You could then take the three pound and the 38 shillins outiv it and since the suit's worth a good tenner, you'd only owe me five pounds two shillins. Nigh, don't worry. I'd give you plenty of time to pay me.
SARAH: How the hell did you work that one out?
BUCKETS: The suit, Mrs. Montague, the suit. It's a foreign make, worth twenty pound to you.
SARAH: What do you mean, foreign?
BUCKETS: Made in Douglas, Isle of Man. Nothin but the best.
SARAH: I'm sure. There's no way I'd give you this money if I didn't think there was a suit there. But here, take that three pound and get me that suit back here straight away.
BUCKETS: Fifteen minutes, Mrs. Montague, I'll not be any more than 15 minutes. [SARAH *exits.*]
BARNEY: I don't know anybody that can get money off her like you. But here, you may rush up and lift that suit afore the pawn closes.
[BUCKETS *takes a long drink.*]
BUCKETS: What suit?
[*He exits.*]

SCENE FOUR

The scene is the Graham home. It is a small, terraced kitchen-house. No illusions of grandeur, but neat. JOHN GRAHAM *enters carrying a tray containing a teapot, cups, sugar etc. He switches on the television and sits down.*

HUGHIE: John! Are you there, John?
[HUGHIE MCNAMARA *knocks on the door and enters.*]

JOHN: Come on in, Hughie.

HUGHIE: Did you hear about the accident to our Danny-boy? He's in hospital.

JOHN: I did, aye. Wanna cup of tea? [*He hands* HUGHIE *a cup of tea.*]

HUGHIE: Thanks, John. An overloaded heave fell on his arm.

JOHN: Jimmy Sweeney, you mean.

HUGHIE: That's a bastard. We'll have to do something about him, John. Our D-B could be lyin dead the day.

JOHN: How is he anyway?

HUGHIE: I phoned up. He's alright. Gettin out shortly, the said. Have you a wee drop of sugar, John?

JOHN: Sorry, Hughie. Here.

HUGHIE: John, what are we gonna do about foremen like Sweeney? And our union leaders aren't much better, McKibben and Jack Henry.

JOHN: Did you know that Sweeney was once on the committee?

HUGHIE: I didn't know, but from what I hear, that seems to be the way too many of the committee have went over the years.

JOHN: Simple. Most of the guys who go on the committee have no politics.

HUGHIE: You reckon politics is essential to be a shop steward?

JOHN: You need politics to go into front-line conflict with the employers. If you don't know the wider picture, them boys can charm you inside out.

HUGHIE: I'd like to see them tryin it with me.

JOHN: Could you resist the offer of a well-paid, regular job? 'Cause that's the first tactic the use to get rid of the best shop stewards.

HUGHIE: How would you handle that type of bribe?

JOHN: Well, for a start, it wouldn't come as a surprise to me. I know what I'm doin at the bargainin table. I know I'm representin workers. And I know what the men on the other side of the table represent. Themselves, profit, money in the bank. Hughie, unless you're conscious of that goin in, you're a batin docket.

HUGHIE: That sounds great, John, but not everybody understands that.

JOHN: Not a bit a wonder. Because we're all brain-washed with the platitudes and phrases the employers come off with in their newspapers. [JOHN *mimics an upper-class voice*] 'We want to provide jobs for the community ... our main concern is to provide a service.' It would make you sick to listen to it when you know that an employer sets up to do one thing—make money—nothin more and nothin less.

HUGHIE: But some of the committee do their best.

JOHN: A lot of nice, well-meanin guys become shop stewards. But it's like getting into the ring with Sonny Liston. They've no chance of winnin.

HUGHIE: Well, as you say, our union leadership doesn't seem to have any great politics.

JOHN: Not only do they not have any Labour politics, but they'll resist anything radical at every turn. Larkin and Connolly, how are ye!

HUGHIE: I don't suppose McKibben and Henry are too happy about you?

JOHN: There's been nothin said to me. But McKibben has told a couple of dockers that if Graham comes off with any 'red talk', as he puts it, I'd be for the chop.

HUGHIE: McKibben's bad news.

JOHN: He's only the message-boy. Jack Henry pulls the strings.

HUGHIE: Do you think there's ever any chance of Henry ever improvin?

JOHN: I don't know. He's not an expert on exactly what dynamics influence the world of high finance, but he's not stupid either.

HUGHIE: He must know changes are long overdue at the dock.

JOHN: Yes, but the question is, will it suit him to bring them in?

HUGHIE: Time will tell. Which reminds me what I called round for. It's time you lent me that book you promised. *The Ragged Trousered* something ...

JOHN: Oh yes, I forgot about that. It should be over here somewhere, I think. [JOHN *begins to search a small bookshelf while* HUGHIE *stands watching the television*] Are you readin anything at the moment?

HUGHIE: You'll never guess.

JOHN: I give up.

HUGHIE: *Lady Chatterly's Lover.*

JOHN: Very nice, but hardly what you'd call enlightenin stuff.

HUGHIE: But in a way it is, John. I lap up the idea of a gamekeeper touchin for the Lady of the Manor. Just like my ambiton to have a skelp at Princess Margaret. Know what I mean. Pauper meets princess and all that stuff. It definitely sharpens the mind about the class thing.

JOHN: Bringin sex into politics as usual. No, I can't see that bloody book, Hughie. I'll have a better luck for it later on.

HUGHIE: Well, you can throw it round to me.

JOHN: Tell me this, have you given any more thought to the button thing?

HUGHIE: It's all sorted out.

JOHN: And?

HUGHIE: It's D-B's. That is, if he's not sickened by the accident.

JOHN: Really?

HUGHIE: Well, when it boils down to it, he does need it more than me.

JOHN: That's a good decision. Your da'll be pleased.

HUGHIE: He doesn't know yet. That's where I'm goin nigh. [THERESA GRAHAM *enters*] Ach, the very woman I'm wantin to see.

THERESA: There must be something wrong when you wanna see me.

HUGHIE: Oh, there's nothin wrong. It's just that I'm a ... I'm in the finals of the Jivin Competition in the Plaza this Saturday and I was wonderin, I mean, if it's alright with you, John, I was thinkin maybe, you'd partner me.

THERESA: Me! God save is! What happened Sheila McKenna, did she get fed up you trampin all over her toes?

HUGHIE: I never tramped on a partner's toes in my life. But I fell out with her after the semi-finals.

THERESA: What happened?

HUGHIE: She wanted me to go to chapel with her.

THERESA: Ahh, that's nice.

HUGHIE: Don't have me usin bad language! Once a wee girl round this way thinks she's goin steady with you, the first thing she asks, is for ye to go to chapel with her. If you fall for that, it's confession the followin week. Here's me to myself, 'Hughie, son, give this woman a by-ball!' What do you say, John, eh?

JOHN: Nothin.

HUGHIE: You must agree.

JOHN: I'm sayin nothin, Hughie.

THERESA: He knows better. John always says that when the

Catholic Church has the mothers of the country, they've got everybody else.

JOHN: Hughie, you're a witness. I never said a word.

HUGHIE: Right, end of argument. Back to the point. Are you gonna partner me on Saturday night, or what?

THERESA: Don't be silly. It's years since I was even at a dance.

HUGHIE: Aye, but you were good. Sure you won the competition two years in a row. Eh, John?

JOHN: It's up to her.

THERESA: No, Hughie, I don't think so. My dancin days is over. The only dancin I do nigh is dance attention to a husband and two kids. But it was nice of you to ask, Hughie. I still say Sheila McKenna is your best bet.

HUGHIE: I told you I'm fed up with her and, anyway [*whips out his comb and proceeds to comb his hair*], if you really wanna know the truth, I got shot of her because she kept wreckin m'hair.

THERESA: Go on, ya fool ye.

HUGHIE: But who am I gonna get?

JOHN: Have you tried Sarah Montague?

HUGHIE: It's not a wake I'm goin to. I suppose there's nothin else for it. I may go and make that phone call.

JOHN: What phone call?

HUGHIE: Connie Francis.

THERESA: What are you on about?

HUGHIE: Who? Me and Connie Francis has a wee thing goin together. She asked me over to California the last time I was talkin to her.

JOHN: And why didn't you go?

HUGHIE: I told her I was too busy. I was workin the weekend at the South African boat. I'm away.

THERESA: You couldn't believe a word comes out of your mouth.

JOHN: Listen, Hughie, I'll have a good luck for that book and send it round to you.

HUGHIE: Okay, see yiz.

THERESA: Cheerio, Hughie. [HUGHIE *exits.*] That's a goodin, eh! Dance with him in a jivin competition!

JOHN: Sure you know Hughie McNamara. [JOHN *returns to the bookshelf. He is on his hands and knees.*]

THERESA: What's wrong, have you taken to a fit of prayin?

JOHN: What? No, I'm luckin for a book I was gonna lend Hughie.

THERESA: More bloody politics.
JOHN: So what?
THERESA: Do you never get enough? Did Mary come round with the kids?
JOHN: Do you see them?
THERESA: I'm only askin.
JOHN: Frig it! Did you see that book?
THERESA: What book?
JOHN: *The Ragged Trousered Philanthropists.* It's a thick book with a red cover. By Robert Tressell.
THERESA: The ragged what?
JOHN: Ach, it doesn't matter.
THERESA: You don't have to eat the nose of me.
JOHN: I'm luckin for a book I left down right there, only yesterday, and nigh it's missin.
THERESA: Luck, John Graham, if you're in bad form over what's goin on at the dock, don't take it out on me.
JOHN: What? Who mentioned the dock?
THERESA: Don't try and kid me. You laugh and joke with Hughie McNamara, but I know when there's more on your mind than a book.
JOHN: Okay, so what?
THERESA: So what? It's time we had a talk about this whole thing.
JOHN: Some other time.
THERESA: No, John, nigh.
JOHN: Haven't you still to go round to get the kids outta Mary's?
THERESA: That can wait.
JOHN: Alright. So what are you sayin?
THERESA: Pack it in.
JOHN: What?
THERESA: I want you off that committee.
JOHN: I'm only on to it.
THERESA: And luck at the trouble it's caused already.
JOHN: But that's what committees are for. So that people can talk and avoid trouble.
THERESA: I want you off it, John.
JOHN: I can't, Theresa. There's things I need to do.
THERESA: Like what?
JOHN: Plenty.
THERESA: Alright, tell me. Tell me what it is that's so important

that you absolutely need to do.
JOHN: Luck, Theresa. I work at the dock. Nigh, all's I want to do is work in reasonably acceptable conditions and for a decent wage that will be enough to feed me and you and the kids. Nothin more and nothin less.
THERESA: And what about the rest of them? If they aren't shoutin, why do you have to?
JOHN: The rest will shout. Given time.
THERESA: So, in the meantime, you're gonna do enough shoutin for everybody? While they're all sittin in pubs laughin behind your back?
JOHN: I don't care who's laughin at me. Somebody has to step out from the crowd.
THERESA: Oh aye! Oh aye, you're the big fella in the big picture. John Graham's gonna change in a fortnight what's been goin on since before he was born?
JOHN: Theresa, you're bein unreasonable. I just wanna play my part. Honestly and to the best of my ability.
THERESA: What about the rest of them?
JOHN: If I can make the dockers think a bit more about their own situation, as time goes on I think I can get a bit more support.
THERESA: That all sounds very nice, but what about the likes of Harry McKibben? God forgive me for sayin it but he's no good. If my father was alive the day, he'd have a heart attack to think you were sittin on the same committee as him.
JOHN: I can't let that come into it.
THERESA: Why? Does my family not mean anything to you?
JOHN: It's union business, Theresa.
THERESA: And what do you call what he done to our Vera?
JOHN: I understand that, but it was a long time ago.
THERESA: Don't you ever think for one minute that we'll forget it.
JOHN: Theresa. The fact that Harry McKibben was seein your Vera while she was still at school and then left her in trouble can have no bearin on the present situation.
THERESA: But he was ten years older than her. Ah no! It doesn't matter any more. We should all forget that Vera isn't here anymore. Her young life lost havin that bastard's baby and nigh you're sittin on the same committee as him!
JOHN: I have to, for Jasis sake, I have to!

THERESA: You don't have to!

JOHN: What do I do, then? Walk away? Walk away over something that happened nearly twenty years ago? Something that doesn't directly concern me?

THERESA: Doesn't concern you?

JOHN: It doesn't!

THERESA: Then I don't matter anymore?

JOHN: I didn't say that.

THERESA: And the kids.

JOHN: How, in the name a God, did you work that one out? My children do concern me. You concern me. This house concerns me ... very, very much. But—

THERESA: But what?

JOHN: I need to do what I'm doin at the dock!

THERESA: That's just my point! You think more of that than you do of me and the children.

JOHN: Don't talk stupid!

THERESA: I'm not talkin stupid and I've had enough. I've had it up to here of you!

JOHN: Do you think I'm havin great fun? I'm just as sick of you as you are of me!

THERESA: Get out then!

JOHN: You get out! [*They both stand in acrimonious silence. Finally,* JOHN *speaks*] Theresa. [*No reply*] Theresa. Just let me get on with it, will ya? [*Still no response*] I know it means you and the children sufferin. But we will all benefit from it in the long run. I know what it means to you, but I could never answer to my conscience if I lived out thirty years at the dock in silence. Just to eke out the same miserable existence that m'da and all the other dockers have lived through. Only to retire early with a bad back, a bad chest and a weak heart. Theresa, I just couldn't do it.

[*Silence.*]

THERESA: I wouldn't want you to.

JOHN: What?

THERESA: I wouldn't want you to. I couldn't live with it myself. I'm sorry, I've been selfish.

[JOHN *goes over to her and puts his hands on her shoulders.*]

JOHN: No you haven't.

THERESA: I have.

JOHN: You haven't. You were only doin what you thought best for your children.

THERESA: And you.

JOHN: I know that. [*He turns* THERESA *round to face him.*]

THERESA: And anyway.

JOHN: Anyway what?

THERESA: I don't want to finish my days sittin across the fire from an old, cantankerous, retired husband in bad health. [*They both smile.*]

JOHN: I can't guarantee you won't. Can you guarantee me that I won't end up bein nagged to the grave by a silly, dotin oul woman?

THERESA: No, I can't.

JOHN: That makes it evens. [*They kiss.*]

THERESA: You will promise me one thing, John?

JOHN: What's that?

THERESA: That if you don't help to change things at the dock, say ... within a year or two, you'll get out before they hurt you? [JOHN *breaks away.*]

JOHN: Don't be silly. No one's gonna hurt me.

THERESA: You know it can happen. It's happened to other people who said the wrong things.

JOHN: If it satisfies you any, yes, I'll get out if I don't make any realistic headway inside ... how long did you give me?

THERESA: A year or two and no more.

JOHN: That's not very long ... but it's a deal. Right?

THERESA: Right, but—

JOHN: But, but, but! Will the said Theresa Graham, *née* McAllister, give the said Mr. John Joseph Graham, her fullest co-operation and understanding in his pursuit of better wages and conditions at the deep-sea docks, in the borough and town of Belfast?

THERESA: I will, m'Lord.

JOHN: Case dismissed. [*They both laugh*] Nigh, where the hell is that book.

THERESA: Right, I'll go round for the kids, then, before our Mary takes rickets.

JOHN: Don't be sittin round there all day.

THERESA: Don't worry, I won't. I'm happy. In fact, I'll be dancin on air all the way there and back.

JOHN: Watch the buses!
[THERESA *exits.* JOHN *goes on a thorough search of the room for the book. Presently, the door is rapped loudly and* JACK HENRY *and* MCKIBBEN *enter in an angry mood.*]
HENRY: What did you say to Jimmy Sweeney?
JOHN: What are you talkin about?
MCKIBBEN: You know fine well what we're talkin about. You threatened another member of our union a while ago.
JOHN: I what!
HENRY: That's right. We've been told you threatened Sweeney that you'd get him.
MCKIBBEN: For supposedly causin an accident at a boat.
JOHN: That's a lie! I never threatened anybody. We did have words, yes.
HENRY: Words! You listen to me, Graham.
JOHN: No, you listen to me. For a start, you have no right to walk into the privacy of my home to brow-bate me. I never threatened anybody and I don't care whether you believe me or not.
MCKIBBEN: Don't push your luck, Graham, or I'll flatten you where you stand.
JOHN: You punchin won't change my views. Give it a rest.
[MCKIBBEN *steps forward menacingly.*]
HENRY: Leave it! That won't be necessary ... yet! Nigh, listen, bucko, you're only—
JOHN: I told you, you've no right to—
HENRY: Listen! Shut up and listen for once! You're only on the committee a meal-hour. If you have any ambitions of stayin on it, you're doin all the wrong things.
MCKIBBEN: And shut your trap or I'll shut it for you.
JOHN: I spoke to Jimmy Sweeney about an accident at his boat. I am a committee man and—
HENRY: I don't wanna hear that nigh, but you better have a good explanation in the mornin. [HENRY *and* MCKIBBEN *turn and walk to the exit.*]
JOHN: What is this? [*Both men stop.*] The Mafia?
HENRY: You'll see.
[*They exit.*]

[*Black-out.*]

ACT TWO

SCENE ONE

The dockers enter by the schooling-pen. JIMMY SWEENEY *jumps up on the platform, while* JACK HENRY *stands to the side.*

LEG: Nothins the same anymore, John, son. Young people want more out of life nigh. I don't know where it's all gonna end.
JOHN: Maybe it's just beginnin.
LEG: God forbid. Hey, I wonder what Sweeney's at?
JOHN: No idea. [LEG *speaks to* SWEENEY *while* MCKIBBEN *looks down the road.*]
LEG: Dutch boat, John. C'mon, we'll stand in.
MCKIBBEN: Alright, away yiz go!
   [*The men surge up against the barrier.*]
SWEENEY: Right! You! And you! Lindsay! Quinn! Murphy! You and you! [MCKIBBEN *moves to the front of the platform.*]
MCKIBBEN: Come on, lads, stand back.
SWEENEY: McKibben! And McNamara and that's it!
   [SWEENEY *jumps down and exits with* HENRY. *As most of the dockers exit, the remaining few stand about chatting.* LEG *stops beside* JOHN *on his way out.*]
LEG: Jasis, I don't know how I got that. [*Looking at his disc*] He must be short of a man for over-the-hatch. [JOHN *shows little or no reaction*] I'll a ... I'll get on down to this boat. I'll maybe see you later in Barney's.
JOHN: Yeah, sure Leg, see you in Barney's. [LEG *exits.* JOHN *stares blankly in front. Presently* SWEENEY *enters followed by* HENRY.]
SWEENEY: Right, yousens! I need two extra men to do a bit of loadin in the Chapel sheds. [*The three remaining men walk forward, including* JOHN GRAHAM] Okay, you and you! That's it! [SWEENEY *strides off.* GRAHAM *and* HENRY *exchange blunt stares, before* HENRY *walks off.* JOHN *stands disconsolate, before sitting down on the platform to read a newspaper. In a moment,* BUCKETS MCGUINNESS *enters, somewhat inebriated.*]

BUCKETS: Ah, young Graham, I thought for a while there I was late. Isn't it good to be early for a change. You know, us trade unionists, know like, us class-conscious types, we have to weigh in early and not give the bosses a chance to stick the boot in over time-keepin. Like, if I dropped my high standards, they'd sack me as quick as the swally their Holy Communion. Is there ... is there something wrong? What ails ye?

JOHN: Ah, I'm alright, Buckets. Dead on, dead on.

BUCKETS: Here. [*Takes a bottle of wine from his inside pocket*] Take a wee drop of that. It'll liven you up, kid.

JOHN: No, you're alright, thanks. [BUCKETS *takes a drink himself.*]

BUCKETS: You know, it's marvellous what a drop of drink'll do for ye. When Churchill tuck a drink he fancied himself as a bricklayer. It's true. He built walls all over Downin Street, blocked up doorways, windys, the lot. When he retired as prime minister, the had to employ demolition men to let them into 14 rooms. That's true. Every word of it. A sister of my cousin's brother-in-law used to work for him. Aye, you need to be either mad or drunk to get on in this world. Or both. That's why the Rasputins, the Hitlers and the Churchills got on so well. Whereas, if you're sober and sensitive, your brain's permanently wrapped in barbed-wire. And every time your emotion responds to what you see round ye, the barbed-wire sticks in hard. [*He takes a drink of wine*] I'm neither sensitive nor sober and thank thee, Lord, for this sweet life. [*He holds up the bottle towards the sky in jubilation*] I'm havin great fun. Hey! Where in the name a Jasis is everybody? It's not a holiday, is it? [*He sets the bottle down behind him.*]

JOHN: What?

BUCKETS: I said, where is everybody, where's the work?

JOHN: You're a bit late. Everybody's schooled and away to work n'all.

BUCKETS: I don't believe ye. What! That oul clock of ours must be runnin slow again. That means I'll have to spend another day in Barney's. Who was it decided that I should be brought into the world in Sailortown? Who was it decreed that m'own da should give me my first drink at 13 years of age? Why the hell amn't I a steady, chapel-goin pillar of the community? Who was it picked me to be me? [*He picks up his bottle of wine only to find there is no wine left*] Who was at m'bottle of blow?

JOHN: Nobody only yourself.
BUCKETS: Right, then, Barney's it is. Where are you for?
JOHN: Round to the canteen for a cup of tea before the union meetin.
BUCKETS: Not workin?
JOHN: Naa. Sweeney deliberately cut the ears off me.
BUCKETS: Shootin your mouth off?
JOHN: Probably.
BUCKETS: Henry behind it?
JOHN: Probably. That's what this meetin's about. There's gonna be a row over what I'm supposed to have said to Sweeney. Imagine, it's gonna be that's—
BUCKETS: Listen, listen, lis ... en! Never go round crabbin cause you're gettin the water cut outiv ye.
JOHN: I'm not crabbin. I'm just sayin. The union's puttin the hammer on me so I'm goin round here to squeal the place down.
BUCKETS: Watch that. Don't make the mistake of turnin union activity into union wreckin.
JOHN: But there's problems inside the union.
BUCKETS: And would you tell me what union hasn't got problems? Just never let that divert you from the real thing, the struggle with the employers. On every issue, luck to put the onus on the employers. They own you, me, the newspapers, the city, the dock, everything. Ownin means responsibility. Don't take it off them for the wages they pay out.
JOHN: That's all easier said than done. If they won't face up to the employers, they'll have to face up to me. And if they want a row, I'll give them it.
BUCKETS: And who'll win?
JOHN: I don't care who wins. I'll let them know they've been in a fight.
BUCKETS: You're bate!
JOHN: What?
BUCKETS: You're bate before you start with that kind of talk. 'I don't care who wins.' That's the talk of a boxer who knows he's gonna take a dive before he gets into the ring.
JOHN: I didn't mean it like that. It's just that ... I'm gettin frustrated ... fed-up.
BUCKETS: Stick it out, kid, stick it out. The future depends on you.

You wouldn't like to think that in twenty years time, things were just as bad for the dockers, just because you got fed-up and made a pig's-arse of things. C'mon, we'll get away outta here. [*They walk towards the exit*] Are you sure you weren't at this? [*He shakes the bottle.*]

JOHN: For Jasis sake.

[*They exit.*]

SCENE TWO

BARNEY *is behind the bar of an otherwise empty public house.* SARAH MONTAGUE *and* MARY-ANN MCKEOWN *enter.*

SARAH: I'm tired tellin ye, tired tellin ye! If he doesn't go out to work, throw him out on his backside.

MARY-ANN: I wisht I had the heart to do it.

SARAH: You're very foolish, I wouldn't put up with it.

MARY-ANN: Sarah, it's alright you talkin, but I'm married to the man nearly twenty years. I may see it out nigh.

SARAH: Bein married to him doesn't mean you've to lift him and lay him. You wanna catch yourself on.

MARY-ANN: Sure, if I didn't luck after him, he'd walk out and leave me. He's done it before, as you well know.

SARAH: Aye, but you'd wee childer then. Yours is all grew up nigh. Let him run on wherever the hell he likes.

MARY-ANN: But, sure, where would he get his grub? God knows the trouble he'd get into on his own.

SARAH: I'm wastin my time talkin to you, wastin my time. Do you know what your trouble is, Mary-Ann McKeown? You're still fond of him. That's your trouble. Still fond of him. Barney! Was Buckets McGuinness in here yet?

[BARNEY *appears unsure.*]

BARNEY: Oh a ... no ... no, I haven't saw him this mornin.

SARAH: Just as I thought. He's hidin from me. C'mon, missus, we'll try the other one up at the corner. A frog never wanders far from the water!

[MARY-ANN *stands puzzled.*]

SARAH: What's wrong with ye nigh?

MARY-ANN: I coulda swore I saw him comin in here earlier on.
SARAH: That man of yours has ye away in the head. Are ye comin?
MARY-ANN: Oh yes, Sarah, I'm comin alright, I'm comin. I've to get the messages in for his dinner.
SARAH: Sometimes I wonder. Did you never think of gettin him put away in a home? That's what he needs. His arse well warmed!

[*The two women exit chatting. From the other end of the bar,* BUCKETS MCGUINNESS *enters from the toilets, doing up his fly. He walks across the bar rather unsteadily and proceeds to go asleep at a table decorated with various glasses and bottles of drink.* BARNEY *comes over to clear some of the empty glasses at Buckets' table. He shakes* BUCKETS.]

BARNEY: Come on a that w'ye, man. Waken up! Your woman was in here luckin you.
BUCKETS: What! Where! You'd do what!
BARNEY: How did you get into that state? It's not even dinner-hour yet and you're stupid drunk.
BUCKETS: I don't drink. I mean ... I need a drink. Give is a wine.
BARNEY: Give you a wine! Sure, you can't even lift your chin to finish what's in front of you. Will I throw this out? [BUCKETS *shakes his head furiously*] Well, you don't seem able to drink it, so what'll I do with it?
BUCKETS: Just ... throw it round me. [BARNEY *returns to the bar.*]
BARNEY: Oh, I shoulda known better than to waken a man up from the horrors of drink. You'd better get away outta here afore she comes back.

[BUCKETS *makes his way to the bar.*]

BUCKETS: This drinkins no good. I take far too much of the stuff. I'm definitely goin round to St. Joseph's to take the pledge.

[SARAH MONTAGUE *enters. She throws* BARNEY *an accusing glance.*]

SARAH: Buckets McGuinness, where's my money?
BUCKETS: What money are you talkin about?
SARAH: Don't you what money me. I want four pound eighteen shillins right this very minute.
BUCKETS: What? [*He looks round behind him*] Are you sure you've got the right person?
SARAH: As sure as every July has a Twelfth, I'm sure. C'mon. Where's the three pound you got to lift the suit out of the pawn?
BUCKETS: Oh! That money! [*Rummages through his pockets in*

pretence] Why didn't you say it was that money? I haven't got it. But! But there's a spud boat due in this week and I'll definitely get a few days outiv it, Mrs. Montague, definitely.

SARAH: First, it was a timber boat, nigh it's a spud boat. Do you think I'm not wise?

BUCKETS: Of course, you're not ... I mean ... You're a wise oul bastard, no I didn't mean that ... I meant my wife's an oul bastard. Because, Mrs. Montague, I had every hapney I owed you in this trouser pocket last night afore I went to bed. But, like a dishonest Florence Nightingale, the bloody woman rifled m'pockets durin the night, and left me with not even the price of five Woodbine. Nigh, would you credit that?

SARAH: I wouldn't credit anything concernin you.

BUCKETS: Know what she wanted the money for? Food! To buy bloody food! What a waste of hard-earned money. I wisht I'd a woman that shared my interests in life.

SARAH: I do. Money! And I want it nigh!

BUCKETS: I haven't got it.

SARAH: Right, then, that definitely means trouble for you. That's the last you'll get and you know what that means. Send us in a wee gin, Barney. [*Exit* SARAH *to snug.*]

BUCKETS: What the hell am I gonna do nigh? That's the Bank a Monty Carlo well snookered.

BARNEY: That's your problem, if you wouldn't luck on a pound note as a drinkin voucher, you'd be a bit better off.

BUCKETS: I've always said that.

BARNEY: Said what?

BUCKETS: I've always argued round this dock that the should pay us out in drinkin vouchers.

BARNEY: That way, your wife'd never see a hapney.

BUCKETS: I can't get anybody to understand that. Anyway, I may try and get a few days work from somewhere this week. [*Enter* LEG] Here, Leg, is the spud boat in yet or do you know when it's due?

LEG: Are you on your geg? The spud boat pulled outta here for Cyprus dinner hour yesterday, cargo discharged an'all. If you hurry, you might catch it. Off the coast of Portugal. [LEG *laughs.*]

BUCKETS: It's no laughin matter, Leg. This oul hure's luckin her money an I haven't a match.

Dockers 55

LEG: As per usual. I may buy you another drink. Barney, a bottle a stout and a wine.
BUCKETS: No! No! I'm away, Leg. I have to go.
LEG: What! You're refusin your medicine? That doesn't happen often.
BUCKETS: It's not often I owe her the guts of a fiver.
LEG: Well, where are you goin?
BUCKETS: Where do you think? To luck for another money-lender to pay her back. [*Exit* BUCKETS.]
LEG: Well, Barney, how's things? Has any of the committee been in yet?
BARNEY: Not so bad, Leg. No a ... none of them's been in yet, but it's still early.
LEG: Aye, I suppose it is. I was up in the Union Rooms with the young lad payin his fee. I'm just waitin on the committee endorsin his name.
BARNEY: I was glad to see Danny-boy gettin his button. He's a hell of a nice kid. But you want to keep him away from that fella that just walked out there or he'll end up the same way as many another young fella that went round the dock. Bad company, bad habits and afore you know it, Skid Row. It's alright bein a coat-puller at Bucket McGuinness' age, but when you luck at some a the young men, you'd wonder what has them the way they are.
LEG: The casual system, Barney. One week you're like Paul Getty and the next you're bummin it. I'll have to watch the lad. But, then again, it won't be long till he's married and I'll have no say in the matter. He'll have his own life to lead then. But I think he's sensible enough. He'll luck after thon wee girl well. Sure the were up luckin at a house there last week and I think they're gonna buy it.
BARNEY: And it's not many can buy a house afore they're married.
LEG: 'Tis not. But she's workin and with him gettin a button and that, they've everything planned. The two a them, God spares them, 'll be married afore Christmas. [*Enter* JOHN GRAHAM] Ach, billy John, how'd the meetin go?
JOHN: It didn't go. Give is a beer, Barney.
LEG: What do you mean?
JOHN: I mean there was trouble.

LEG: Why, what happened?

JOHN: They put me on trial over Danny-boy's accident. It wasn't *how* did this accident happen, it was *why* did you threaten Jimmy Sweeney.

LEG: What did you say?

JOHN: I proposed that Jimmy Sweeney, as foreman of that boat, should be suspended pendin an inquiry into how there was 13 begs in the heaves. Jasis, they near ate me!

LEG: And didn't accept it?

JOHN: Didn't accept it? All hell broke loose and it ended up with me callin McKibben a lickspittle and walkin out. Leg, I'm not luckin for trouble but I really think I had no alternative.

LEG: Oh, it's gonna be blood and snatters from here on in. And you saw the way Sweeney left you standin in the pen this mornin. How or why he licked me, I don't know. Tell is, was Danny-boy's name cleared for the union?

JOHN: It was, aye. His and another ten were cleared.

LEG: That's great. Danny-boy'll be pleased to hear that. But where does that leave you, John?

JOHN: Disgusted with the whole bloody lot of them.

LEG: Are you gonna pack it in?

JOHN: I don't know. I'm fightin a lone battle. I need more support.

LEG: And how are you gonna get that?

JOHN: Well, the May Day march is comin up this Saturday and if I can get as many dockers to that as possible, it'll maybe reawaken something in them.

LEG: There's never many usually turns out for it, John.

JOHN: Don't I know. They'd rather march in their hundreds on St. Patrick's Day, commemeratin a friggin myth, than march as part of the workin-class movement through the streets of their own city. It's the same old story in Ireland. Socialism versus the Saints. And here we are, the only Third World country in western Europe, and the Saints is winnin hands down. Will you be there yourself?

LEG: Ah God, Jasis, no, John. I couldn't march with my leg. But I never used to miss it years ago. You'll have some trouble gettin McKibben and company there. [HUGHIE *and* DANNY-BOY *enter. Danny-boy's arm is in a sling*] Oh luck what the wind blew in. Is that boat finished?

HUGHIE: Aye, I got away early. There was only 200 ton in it. So I thought I'd go up and take Danny-boy out for a drink.
JOHN: How's the arm?
DANNY-BOY: A wee bit sore, but I'll live.
JOHN: You were lucky. By the way, you're in the union.
HUGHIE: Heyyyyyy! [*Slaps* DANNY-BOY *on the back*] No problem, our kid. You're made nigh.
DANNY-BOY: That's great. I think that calls for a celebration. Da, buy is a drink?
LEG: I knew that was comin. Barney, two bottles a beer.
JOHN: Well, son, how does it feel to be a fully-fledged member of the union?
DANNY-BOY: Terrific. I just hope the work comes along.
HUGHIE: It better come along. Danny-boy needs every penny he can earn.
JOHN: So do we all.
HUGHIE: Aye, but Danny-boy needs money quick, don't you D-B? Tell them.
LEG: Tell is what? [DANNY-BOY *is embarrassed.*]
HUGHIE: Tell them, Danny.
LEG: Well?
DANNY-BOY: I'm bringing the weddin forward, da.
LEG: Forward? When to?
DANNY-BOY: Very soon.
LEG: How soon?
DANNY-BOY: Not this Saturday, but next! Susan's expectin. She's due in a coupla months.
LEG: Holy Christ!
HUGHIE: Isn't that great, da?
LEG: Aye, great, I mean no, no!
HUGHIE: That's what we called in here for. We were wantin to see you, Barney, about bookin upstairs for the reception?
BARNEY: No problem. It's there for yiz.
LEG: Does your mother know about this?
DANNY-BOY: Yeah, she knows all about it.
HUGHIE: There was a wee bit of blurtin and cryin but she came round in the end and we all had a good laugh. [*Enter* MARY-ANN MCKEOWN *from the street*] Da, it's no use askin any more questions. Danny-boy's girl's pregnant and he has to get married quick. And that's all about it.

[MARY-ANN *lets out a squeal and rushes towards the snug.*]

MARY-ANN: Sarah! Sarah! Do you hear that? Sarah! [*As she disappears into the snug, her voice is heard. The others gape after her in bewilderment*] God, Sarah, did you hear that? Are you not listenin to what's goin on round ye?

SARAH: What ails ye, woman?

MARY-ANN: That young fella McNamara has some wee girl in the family way and has to marry her. They're standin out there talkin about it right nigh. [*Enter* SARAH *and* MARY-ANN.]

SARAH: Right, which one of yiz done it?

HUGHIE: It's our Danny-boy here, Mrs. Montague. He's blowin the fuse.

SARAH: He's what?

HUGHIE: Gettin happily harried, know?

SARAH: Oh, he is, is he? And is this right about the wee girl bein pregnant?

HUGHIE: Dead right. Maybe twins.

SARAH: Where's she from?

DANNY-BOY: Limestone Road

SARAH: Do you mean she's a Protestant?

DANNY-BOY: Church of Ireland.

MARY-ANN: God love and protect is.

SARAH: Are you turnin?

DANNY-BOY: I don't know yet.

LEG: He won't be.

SARAH: Nobody's talkin to you. When's the weddin?

DANNY-BOY: Saturday week.

SARAH: You'd need to make up your mind, son. Have you even decided what the childer's gonna be?

HUGHIE: Some a them might be girls and some a them might be boys. [*Laughter.*]

SARAH: What are you laughin at, greasy hair? A dacent girl wouldn't venture near you for a kiss, never mind to get pregnant. [*They all laugh except* HUGHIE *and* SARAH] Well, whoever gets married these days needs luck and you'll need all you can get. Give the boys a drink, Barney.

[*The men all cheer.* SARAH *pays and walks towards the snug with* MARY-ANN. DANNY-BOY *calls after her.*]

DANNY-BOY: Oh, thanks very much, Mrs. Montague, that was very nice of you. I was wonderin, Mrs. Montague, if you would do me a wee favour. I'm not luckin the loan a money nigh. Just ... just a wee favour between you and me.

MARY-ANN: Maybe he wants you to do Matron of Honour, Sarah.

SARAH: Would you like to mind your own business?

MARY-ANN: Whatever you like nigh, Sarah, it's all the same to me.

DANNY-BOY: No, I wondered if you would, as a special favour for me gettin married, like, a sort of weddin present, would you not give Buckets McGuinness a bit more time to pay back the money he owes you?

SARAH: Have you been drinkin wine?

LEG: Ach, go on Sarah, it'll do you no harm.

HUGHIE: C'mon a that w'ye.

SARAH: Not a chance!

JOHN: Do it for Danny-boy.

MARY-ANN: Maybe you should, Sarah. He's not a bad oul crater.

DANNY-BOY: Just this once, Mrs. Montague. Poor oul Buckets. He's runnin round distracted about it. Just a couple of weeks?

[SARAH *turns and walks towards the snug.*]

SARAH: He doesn't deserve it. You can tell him, for I'm not.

DANNY-BOY: Thanks, thanks, Mrs. Montague. [*The two women exit to the snug.*]

BARNEY: If I hadna saw it with my own eyes, I wouldn't believe it. First, she buys the bar a drink and then she reprieves Buckets McGuinness. She couldn't be well.

JOHN: Stranger things have happened.

LEG: Here, I'm away back to work. Put that one over for me, Barney. I'm over the hatch for this man Sweeney and you daren't be late.

JOHN: Right, Leg, see you later on.

HUGHIE: See ya, da.

[LEG *moves towards exit.* DANNY-BOY *moves after him.*]

DANNY-BOY: Da! Da, you're not against me gettin married, are ye? Like, you're not annoyed or anything?

LEG: What age are you nigh, Danny-boy?

DANNY-BOY: Twenty-two.

LEG: For Jasis sake, I was married with two childer by the time I was 22. Of course, I'm not annoyed. [*He puts his arm around Danny-boy's shoulder*] In fact, me and your mother'll do all we can to put the weddin over. You can depend on that. Thon's a nice wee girl you have. Luck after her. I'll see yiz later.

DANNY-BOY: See ya, da.
[LEG *exits.*]
BARNEY: Listen, John, I'm away upstairs for a minute or two. Give is a shout if somebody comes in.
JOHN: Work away, Barney. [BARNEY *exits*] Right. Nigh that I've got you two men together, what about the May Day parade on Saturday? Are yiz marchin?
DANNY-BOY: What parade?
JOHN: The May Day parade.
HUGHIE: What time's it at, John?
JOHN: Eleven a'clock.
DANNY-BOY: When did you say it was?
HUGHIE: Saturday, ya ejit ye!
DANNY-BOY: And what's it for?
JOHN: It's what's known as International Workers' Day. It's the day when workers from all over the world march through their towns and cities in solidarity with the cause of Labour and the trade union movement.
HUGHIE: I couldn'ta put it better myself.
JOHN: While we're marchin through Belfast, we know that thousands, in fact millions of men and women are walkin through the streets of London, New York, Moscow, Paris, Madrid, you name it. That's the day the organised workin class is on the march.
HUGHIE: Organised is right!
JOHN: This year we're tryin to get as many dockers as possible to turn out.
DANNY-BOY: Well, I definitely couldn't go on it. M'da has me lined up for a job with Sweeney, workin the weekend. Like, I have to weigh in. I need the money badly.
HUGHIE: I'm workin the weekend, too, but I've arranged to get away on Saturday mornin for the march and get back to the boat as soon as it's finished. And then I've to get away to the Plaza that night.
DANNY-BOY: Aye, but you're not workin with Jimmy Sweeney.
HUGHIE: I'm in the next hatch with McKenna and he's as bad. I just told him straight, I was goin to the march.
JOHN: I don't think Danny-boy's in a position to rear up at any boss with him just into the union, Hughie. It's the casual system round here, remember?

HUGHIE: Well, nigh that you mention it. I read an article in the paper the other day about some of the unions in England talkin about scrubbin the casual system and askin for a guaranteed fall-back pay when there's no work in.

JOHN: Yeah, I read that myself and the sooner the better. This casual system round here is unique within organised labour.

HUGHIE: It's ancient.

DANNY-BOY: What's wrong with it?

JOHN: Don't tell me, Danny-boy, you see nothin wrong with what goes on in that schoolin pen every mornin. Grown-up men shovin and pushin each other for whatever's goin.

DANNY-BOY: That's the way it's organised.

JOHN: That's not organised life, Danny, that's anarchy. The strongest survive, the weakest go to the wall. It's anarchy alright, but you won't hear their mouthpieces puttin it over like that. No, they use words like hard work, endeavour, enterprise, initiative.

HUGHIE: Too right. Educated bastards. That's what's wrong with us, we're not educated enough to twist big words and meanins round to suit ourselves. Like the merchants the pour out of Oxford and Cambridge.

JOHN: Yeah, it's a nice wee set-up, isn't it? Do you know that almost every single Cabinet since the war has been made up of these Oxford and Cambridge characters?

HUGHIE: Aye, what chance had we got, goin to Earl Street school?

JOHN: That's it, Hughie, the dice are stacked against ye, even before you're born.

DANNY-BOY: Because of where you're born?

JOHN: Definitely. We'll never have an influence in government and it all starts with the education set-up.

HUGHIE: If we did, there'd be changes. The Plaza wouldn't be so dear for a start. There'd be changes alright.

JOHN: And since the people who go to Oxford and Cambridge come from the middle and upper classes, try and guess what side they'll be on when they get into government?

DANNY-BOY: All's I wanna be's a docker.

HUGHIE: You're wastin your time, John. He's as thick as two short planks. D-B, do you know that John's been gettin into rows over your accident?

JOHN: We'll just have to wait on him findin out for himself.

[BUCKETS MCGUINNESS *enters. He appears to be not in such a good mood.*]

DANNY-BOY: Ach, there you are nigh, Buckets. Where were you? [BUCKETS *is silent.*]

JOHN: Ah, the boul Buckets doesn't luck in the best of form. I better get offside before he starts throwin punches. I'm away down to the canteen to drum up some support for the march. See yiz later, lads. Y'alright, Buckets. [JOHN *laughs as he exits.*]

DANNY-BOY: Buckets, what's wrong with ya? Hey, we've got good news for you.

BUCKETS: What? Sarah Montague's been run over be a bus?

HUGHIE: Even better.

BUCKETS: What? The bus reversed back over her again?

DANNY-BOY: I'm tellin ye, Buckets, all your troubles are over.

BUCKETS: You mean the wife's dead?

HUGHIE: No. Danny-boy worked the article for ye. You'll be a happy man when you hear this story.

BUCKETS: I couldn't for the life a me listen to any wee stories. I'm not in the form for it. I musta been knocked back by every moneylender in Belfast the day.

DANNY-BOY: Where were you?

BUCKETS: Where wasn't a? I was all round Sailortown, York Street, up the Falls, the Shankill. I even ended up in the City Hall.

HUGHIE: What were you doin in the City Hall?

BUCKETS: Tryin to register m'self as a charity. [BUCKETS *takes a glass and leans over the counter, helping himself to some wine.*]

DANNY-BOY: And what'd the Lord Mayor say?

BUCKETS: He wasn't bad about it. Very understandin'. He says, 'Buckets, I've known you a long time'.

DANNY-BOY: You mean you know the Lord Mayor of Belfast?

BUCKETS: Know him? Me and him has a long association together with a very worthy charity. Dr. Barnardo's Home.

HUGHIE: How's that?

BUCKETS: He was Honorary President and I was reared in it. And I'm tellin ye I was down seein him and he was very understandin about it. He takes me out to the front door, away from the other councillors, and he says to me, 'Buckets, I've known you a long time and you know me, right?' I says, 'That's right, Mr. Lord Mayor, you know me well, very well indeed'. He says, 'I

know I do. Nigh fuck off outta here afore I get you arrested'.
[HUGHIE *and* DANNY-BOY *laugh*] The cheek a him. Jasis, I mind
him when he only owned one shop!

DANNY-BOY: But, listen, we were talkin to Sarah Montague.

BUCKETS: Fraternisin with the enemy? The shot men like you in the last war.

HUGHIE: It concerns you, Buckets.

BUCKETS: Luck, I don't wanna hear nothin about that oul embezzler the day. I'm just about sick hearin the woman's name. [SARAH MONTAGUE *enters*] And I couldn't care less about her or her few shillins. It was only happens when I was able to work down the houl of a boat.

SARAH: What's that about my money?

BUCKETS: I said, bollocks you and your money, you oul hurebeg! You'd think I was goin to run outta the country to see you. What?

SARAH: And I thought I was doin you a good turn.

BUCKETS: Doin who a good turn? At five shillins in the pound, that's daylight robbery. [HUGHIE *and* DANNY-BOY *are embarrassed.*]

SARAH: Four pound, eighteen shillins. I want it for Saturday. Every brown penny!

[SARAH *storms out of the bar.* BUCKETS *shouts after her.*]

BUCKETS: You've some chance!

DANNY-BOY: Buckets!

HUGHIE: You've got it all wrong!

BUCKETS: I'd go to jail first. What! Dick Turpin wore a mask!

DANNY-BOY: Buckets! I spoke to her the day and she agreed to give you another two weeks to clear your slate.

BUCKETS: You'll not make little outta me! Who! Four pound, eighteen shillins didn't rear me! What did you say?

DANNY-BOY: Will you for frig sake listen! We all spoke to Mrs. Montague on your behalf and she agreed to let the money go for a while.

HUGHIE: A few weeks, she said.

BUCKETS: Ah Jasis! I don't believe yiz.

DANNY-BOY: Frig, that's what we were tryin to tell you all along.

HUGHIE: But you wouldn't listen.

BUCKETS: Why me? Why was I out kickin futball when the brains was bein given out?

SCENE THREE

The Graham home. THERESA *is putting on her coat and scarf and is about to leave. She looks for her shopping bag.* JOHN *enters.*

THERESA: No work this mornin?

JOHN: None.

THERESA: Oh, before I forget. M'mammy wants us to go to her house on Saturday and to start the wallpaperin.

JOHN: Does she?

THERESA: She has the wallpaper in a fortnight nigh and you know she's nobody to do it for her.

JOHN: Sure thon place isn't worth paperin. It's fallin down round her.

THERESA: She does her best.

JOHN: And anyway, I'll be at the May Day march on Saturday.

THERESA: Ach, John.

JOHN: Make it the following weekend.

THERESA: Saturday and Sunday?

JOHN: Saturday and Sunday.

THERESA: That's good. I'll call in and let her know.

JOHN: What about some dinner, missus?

THERESA: I'm goin. I'll not be long. If Eamonn comes in out of school give him a plate of cornflakes till I get back. I'm away ... Oh, here. Do you know what he said to me this mornin as I was puttin him out to school?

JOHN: No, what?

THERESA: He said when he grows up, he's goin to be a school-teacher.

JOHN: A school-teacher! What put that into his head?

THERESA: I've no idea, but he seems to like school. Very good at doin his homework and that.

JOHN: But a school-teacher?

THERESA: John, I'd love our Eamonn to stay on at school and become a school-teacher.

JOHN: Theresa, he's only ten years of age. It's early yet.

THERESA: But why can't he?

JOHN: There's ... there's a whole lot of reasons. There's the 11-plus for a start. He has to pass that. And anyway, as he gets older he'll feel out of it, if he's the only one of his mates still studyin, while they all go on to the dock, or go to sea or something.

THERESA: Or the bru! Whatever happens, I don't want him to go to the dock.

JOHN: At the end of the day, that might be all there is.

THERESA: It won't be. I'm gonna make sure he gets as good an education as there is goin.

JOHN: Aye, the same as you got. You can't even spell Dick and Dora. [JOHN *laughs.*]

THERESA: At least my head isn't buried in books all the time. And anyway, our teacher told us at school that we would get married and have babies.

JOHN: And am I sorry you tuck her advice.

THERESA: Huh! I don't know where you'd be the day without me. You hadn't an arse in your trousers till you married me.

[*The door is knocked and* HUGHIE MCNAMARA *enters.*]

HUGHIE: I hope I'm not interruptin nothin.

JOHN: Not a'tall, Hughie, come on in.

THERESA: No, come on in, Hughie McNamara. Get yourself well up to the fire there and put your feet up along with King Farouke. It's a man's life alright.

JOHN: That's what you'd like us to think. I'll get you a start on a beg-boat this week nigh, if you want. [*Both men laugh.*]

THERESA: Tell is this, Hughie. Did you make it up with Sheila McKenna for the dancin competition on Saturday night?

HUGHIE: It's all arranged.

THERESA: And?

HUGHIE: I'm partnerin Connie Francis and I fixed her up with Buckets McGuinness!

THERESA: Funny.

HUGHIE: No, I'm only sleggin. I've agreed to dance with her on one condition. That she just has to wreck m'hair once and I'm walkin off the floor. [*He checks with his hand to make sure his hair is in place.*]

THERESA: I'm glad to hear that. Make sure you pay her in.

HUGHIE: Are you mad? Her da ownin the newspaper stand in Royal Avenue and you want *me* to pay *her* in? I'll meet her inside as usual.

THERESA: And you're all set to win then?

HUGHIE: Not as confident as I would be if you were partnerin me.

THERESA: No chance. But, you know, I think I would like to go to a dance one of these days.
HUGHIE: Throwin hints, John.
JOHN: I never heard a word.
THERESA: No, seriously. I miss them days. Gettin all done up for the dances. The make-up, the hair-dos, high-heels and everything. And the fun we had when a crowd of us went into the town together. The butterflies and the whole atmosphere. It used to be great. I do miss them days. Especially the dancin. I used to love dancin with Miser O'Hare. He could really dance.
JOHN: If you really want, maybe we could go and watch Hughie on Saturday night.
THERESA: Yeah, maybe we should. Cheer him on.
HUGHIE: Fancy a swing nigh?
THERESA: What?
HUGHIE: Put me through m'paces for the competition? That's a great idea. C'mon.
THERESA: You couldn't dance here, Hughie, it's too ... [*She looks at* JOHN *apprehensively.*]
JOHN: Yiz might as well. Yiz are both mad.
HUGHIE: Right, c'mon girl, let's have ye. Put on a record there. [JOHN *and* HUGHIE *clear a dancefloor.*]
THERESA: And I have just the record for you, Hughie. [THERESA *is at the record-player.*]
HUGHIE: What is it?
THERESA: Wait'll ya hear. [*Music starts.*] 'Stupid Cupid'!
HUGHIE: Connie Francis!

[HUGHIE *and* THERESA *then go through a flashy jiving routine, cheered on by* JOHN. *At the end of it,* THERESA *flops on to a chair exhausted.*]

THERESA: Oh, that's enough for me. I'm not able for it anymore. I'm out of breath.

[JOHN *and* HUGHIE *replace the furniture.*]

JOHN: Very good. That was first class.
HUGHIE: I never even got warmed up.
THERESA: Nobody'd believe it. Wait'll I tell m'ma that I was jivin with Hughie McNamara in the middle of the kitchen, in the middle of the afternoon.
HUGHIE: Make sure and tell her your husband was here.

THERESA: Don't worry, she might think I'm mad but she definitely knows I'm not blind.
HUGHIE: Cheek! [*They all laugh as* THERESA *exits.*]
JOHN: Well, Hughie, you seem to be in top form for Saturday night.
HUGHIE: Book me, man, book me!
JOHN: What?
HUGHIE: Give me the message, book me. *The Ragged Trousered* thing. What do you think I came round here for? The book!
JOHN: Oh, I have it waitin on ye.
HUGHIE: It's about time.
JOHN: There you are.
HUGHIE: Nigh, wait'll I tell you what I have for you.
JOHN: What? A brand new hook for the one you broke on me?
HUGHIE: No! A brand new book on Elvis! John, It's a cracker. Tons of photos. Photos that have never been printed before. You know, in the army and that. I haven't finished it yet, but you're the first one that's gettin it after me.
JOHN: I can't wait.
HUGHIE: I knew you'd like it, John. Nigh. Another wee thing just as important I have to tell you.
JOHN: You're full of news the day.
HUGHIE: Well, I wanted to let you know that me and our Dannyboy have been talkin about the whole union thing and we have decided to give you our full backin.
JOHN: I thought I had that already.
HUGHIE: Aye. [*He clenches his fist*] But we're talkin about that!
JOHN: What?
HUGHIE: Don't be lettin on to be stupid, John. We've worked it out that the way things is goin up to nigh, these guys is gonna give you the push to get you outta the way.
JOHN: That's nonsense, Hughie.
HUGHIE: A wee bit of rough stuff's never happened before, like?
JOHN: Maybe in the old days. Luck, Hughie, I know what they're up to. But the threat of Harry McKibben doesn't scare me, and that's all it is at the moment, a threat.
HUGHIE: Well, let's meet threats with threats. Just to let them know you're not on your own. I've been in one or two rows before and with our D-B and yourself, we'll let them know what the score is.

JOHN: Hughie. Wait a minute. You've got it all wrong. I don't want to fight with anybody. I'm not ascared of anybody, but that's just not the way I wanna go about things. I think I can win by fair argument and persuasion.

HUGHIE: That's too airy-fairy.

JOHN: Maybe so, but that's me. Good or bad, that's me.

HUGHIE: Do you think I couldn't handle McKibben?

JOHN: I'm sure you could. But I think I can handle him, too. Within the confines of the union.

HUGHIE: Are you sure?

JOHN: Definitely. I appreciate your offer, Hughie, but if there's gonna be any skulduggery, and I honestly don't think there will be, let it come from them. Let the dockers see them for what they are.

HUGHIE: But the dockers know them for what they are and none of them wants to do anything about it. M'own da's the biggest lickspittle goin.

JOHN: It's only his way of survivin.

HUGHIE: He shouldn't grovel.

JOHN: I don't blame him for grovellin. The older men are hooked. We need to luck towards the younger lads comin into the union, like your Danny-boy. That's where the changes'll come.

HUGHIE: That's probably why they're so reluctant to open the union books.

JOHN: That's part of it.

HUGHIE: I don't suppose I'll ever make the union nigh.

JOHN: You never know. We're into the sixties nigh. The economy's on the way up and if the union and the employers push for the proper development of Belfast Port, then with all the increased trade, the should be needin a lot more dockers.

HUGHIE: But will that happen?

JOHN: Time will tell. In twenty years time, we'll be able to luck back and judge. In the meantime, McNamara, make sure you're out of your pit on Saturday mornin for the march.

HUGHIE: You've a cheek. I was the first— [*There is a loud rap on the door.* JACK HENRY *and* MCKIBBEN *immediately enter.*]

HENRY: I'm here to notify you that, as a result of your behaviour at the meetin today, you are suspended from the union committee until further notice.

JOHN: You have no right to do that.
HENRY: I have every right.
JOHN: Does that include invadin the privacy of my home?
HENRY: We couldn't find you anywhere else.
JOHN: Well, I'd prefer if you didn't come here and I thought we'd already agreed on that.
HENRY: You had to be notified.
JOHN: Was my suspension passed by the whole committee?
HENRY: It was passed by me and that's enough.
JOHN: I'll check that in a union rule book.
HENRY: There are no union rule books.
JOHN: I'll get one from head office.
MCKIBBEN: Keep your nose outta head office or I'll knock it off.
HUGHIE: Would you like to try it?
JOHN: Hughie!
MCKIBBEN: What's this got to do with you, McNamara?
HUGHIE: Plenty.
JOHN: Hughie, I warned you to stay out of this.
HENRY: Union affairs don't concern you.
HUGHIE: My brother's accident concerns me and yous should be doin something about it.
HENRY: It was his own fault.
HUGHIE: Ballicks!
MCKIBBEN: Keep that up, McNamara, and you're only markin your own card.
HENRY: Alright, leave it. He doesn't concern us. But you do, Graham. You'll receive notification of my decision in writin and you'll be asked to appear in front of the next committee meetin. In the meantime, keep your mouth shut.
MCKIBBEN: Or I'll shut it for you.
HUGHIE: You'll not do it with your mouth.
JOHN: That's enough, Hughie. I told you I don't want things done that way.
HUGHIE: Sure they've suspended you.
JOHN: I'll deal with that. That's my problem.
HENRY: I'm glad you're showin some respect, Graham.
JOHN: Common sense, Jack.
HENRY: I'll see you at the meetin. [THERESA GRAHAM *enters.*]
THERESA: Oh, John, did you ... see ... sorry, I didn't realise there was anybody here.

HENRY: We were just goin. [*The two union men exit.*]
JOHN: Nobody'll believe it.
THERESA: Believe what? What were they doin at my door?
JOHN: Suspendin me from the committee.
THERESA: What?
JOHN: Who would believe that our union does its business through illegal suspensions and physical threats to its members?
THERESA: You're suspended? What for?
JOHN: Forget it.
HUGHIE: For bein a real shop steward, that's what for.
JOHN: Hughie, you let me down there. You know Jack Henry'll use that against me.
HUGHIE: Use what?
JOHN: He'll accuse me of havin henchmen.
HUGHIE: But he's walked around with henchmen for 15 years.
JOHN: That's not the point.
THERESA: John Graham, I want you to tell me what exactly's goin on here?
JOHN: I told you, it doesn't matter.
THERESA: It does matter. We've talked all this out, remember? What happened, Hughie?
HUGHIE: Oh, I was just headin off, Theresa. It's not for me to say anything, one way or the other. I'll see you later, John.
JOHN: Aye. Oh, here, Hughie. Don't be walkin out without your book.
HUGHIE: I near forgot that! I'll see yiz. [HUGHIE *exits.*]
THERESA: Well?
JOHN: Well what?
THERESA: What happened here? What did you mean when you said physical threats? Harry McKibben?
JOHN: That's nothin.
THERESA: No, that's nothin. He'll just beat you to a pulp one of these days, but that's nothin.
JOHN: Luck, I thought we'd already agreed to let me get on in peace with union affairs?
THERESA: Yeah, but we also agreed that, if things went wrong, you'd get out.
JOHN: It's not that bad yet.
THERESA: No, it's just terrific. Harry McKibben's—

JOHN: Will you give over about Harry McKibben! Nigh, let's get this straight. What I do at the dock is my business. You stay out of it!
THERESA: I'm your wife! How can I stay out of it, even if I wanted to?
JOHN: 'Cause I'm tellin you to.
THERESA: And I'm supposed to stand around passively while they break you in two?
JOHN: I told you. Nobody's gonna break me in two. I can handle it. Just leave me alone!
THERESA: You're not on your own to be left alone. You've a wife and two children in there somewhere.
JOHN: Don't make it any harder.
THERESA: I'm not. I'm just lettin you know that you've more than yourself to think about.
JOHN: You're goin over old ground.
THERESA: I need to. What about all that talk over Eamonn's education? What's he gonna do if his father ends up punch-drunk and broken? Or worse?
JOHN: For the last time, I'm doin this for the children. It's so that we can be in a better financial situation to help with Eamonn's education.
THERESA: John, you're all fancy talk. Big ideas. The future! Someday! What about nigh!
JOHN: What about nigh?
THERESA: That's what I'm askin.
JOHN: Don't you ever give over? Can I not get a wee bit of peace in my own house?
THERESA: It's not a matter of that.
JOHN: What is it a matter of?
THERESA: Talkin.
JOHN: I'm fed up talkin. [*He grabs his coat.*]
THERESA: We don't talk enough.
JOHN: I think we do. [*He moves towards exit.*]
THERESA: Where are you goin?
JOHN: Timbucktoo!
  [*He exits.* THERESA *looks distressed.*]

SCENE FOUR

BARNEY *is flicking through the pages of a newspaper at the bar of his empty public house. Presently, the pub door opens and* BUCKETS MCGUINNESS *sticks his head inside.*

BUCKETS: Psst! Psst! Barney! [BARNEY *looks over*] Is Sarah Montague here?
BARNEY: No, the coast is clear. [BUCKETS *enters.*]
BUCKETS: Thank God for that. You know, it's gettin out of order. Give is a wine, Barney? There's not a pub in the whole a Sailortown I can have a peaceful drink in, without havin to luck over my shoulder for moneylenders.
BARNEY: It's you that borrowed the money.
BUCKETS: Unfortunately.
BARNEY: Maybe, someday, they'll go out of fashion.
BUCKETS: It couldn't come soon enough. I don't think it'll be too long afore hire purchase takes over from your back-street moneylenders as the Saviour of the Workin Class.
BARNEY: Do you think so?
BUCKETS: Jasis, I remember the day our neighbourhood first discovered hire purchase. Buck Alec, I think it was, who first caught on to the fact that you could get a brand new wireless outta one of the big shops downtown for one and thruppence.
BARNEY: Was that not only the deposit?
BUCKETS: And that was all the got. Boy, our district didn't half liven up. When you walked down the street, the doors and windys were lyin wide open to the world with the latest music blarin at top volume.
BARNEY: What did the shops do when nobody made any more payments?
BUCKETS: Ah, God, it was terrible. Would you believe me that within month the whole district was like a morgue. The shop came out with the peelers and tuck the whole lot back. I don't think the war was a bigger shock.
BARNEY: Well, tell me this and tell me no more. Did you square up that money for Sarah?
BUCKETS: As from here and nigh, I've decided I'm givin her nothin. Not a light is she gettin a me.
BARNEY: You'll not get away with it.

BUCKETS: You know, Barney, everything in life has its advantages and disadvantages. Every single thing. Her advantage as a moneylender is the interest she charges. Her disadvantage is men like me not payin her back.

BARNEY: I don't care what you say, when she comes through that door, you'll be expected to pay up. She only give you to Saturday and that's today.

BUCKETS: It's as good a day as any for it.

BARNEY: For what?

BUCKETS: For kickin Sarah Montague's teeth down her throat. [*Enter* SARAH *and* MARY-ANN *from the street*] And hittin her a good boot up the arse! [BUCKETS *sees* SARAH *enter. He quickly swings round facing her*] Ach, the very woman I want to see. [SARAH *stops and holds out her hand*] That's what I've come to tell you about, Sarah, Mrs. Montague. I've something to tell you about that.

MARY-ANN: He's at it again, Sarah.

BUCKETS [*at* MARY-ANN, *speaking softly*]: I'm speakin to Mrs. Montague. About the four pounds, eighteen shillins.

SARAH: No abouts!

BUCKETS: Will you listen to me, missus. It's about your oul lad.

SARAH: What? What about Sam Montague?

BUCKETS: If you'll only listen to me for a minute, I'll tell ye. Nigh, this'll come as a surprise to you. Do you wanna sit down?

SARAH: Hurry up!

BUCKETS: Well, I was drinkin with your husband last night in the White Lion. Nigh, afore I go any further, I'm gonna ask you a question. Did your oul fella come in with an overcoat on last night or did he not?

SARAH: What of it?

MARY-ANN: He's only tryin to get away from the point, Sarah.

BUCKETS: Would you kindly refrain from interrupting, Mary-Ann McKeown. Nigh, was the coat not brand new and did it have the name of a Dutch tailors on the inside?

SARAH: What's all this got to do with the money you owe me?

BUCKETS: That, Mrs. Montague, is precisely the point. I don't owe you anything. You owe me money.

SARAH: What?

MARY-ANN: I told you, Sarah. You shouldn't have listened to him.

BUCKETS: Go you and bollocks yourself! You see, I touched for that overcoat at the Dutch boat yesterday and sold it to your Sam for six quid and he told me to get the price of it of you. Nigh, I hated sums at school, but if you take the money I owe you away from the price of the coat, you owe me one pound two shillins, I think.

MARY-ANN: Oh my God, Sarah! [SARAH *stands in stunned silence.*]

BUCKETS: I'm not in any hurry for it, mind you. You'll have plenty of time to pay it since me and you has a long-standin business arrangement. And no interest whatsoever.

MARY-ANN: What are you gonna do, Sarah? Are you gonna pay him?

BUCKETS: Take your time, Mrs. Montague, as I said. I'm fairly strong at the minute and I can wait for it.

SARAH: C'mon, Mary-Ann, I may go round and see this oul gabshite. Are ya comin?

MARY-ANN: Whatever you like nigh, Sarah. It's all the same to me. [*The two women walk towards the exit.*]

SARAH: Wait till I get my hands on this carried-away oul fool.

MARY-ANN: You couldn't houl out to that, Sarah.

SARAH: Loves himself, he does. Tasty Sam. Him on the pension, too. I'll overcoat him when I get home. [*The two women exit.*]

BARNEY: How do you do it, man?

BUCKETS: That's it, Barney, the don't call me Buckets McGuinness for nothin.

BARNEY: Come to think of it, why do the call you Buckets? That's a wild name.

BUCKETS: It was all to do with an Indian boat. [*Enter* LEG MCNAMARA] Ach, billy Leg, what about you? What are you havin?

LEG: A bottle of stout.

BUCKETS: I'm just tellin Barney here about why the call me Buckets.

LEG: Ah, that one. Well, you may tell it some other time. Barney, the lorry's just pulled up outside.

BARNEY: Heavens, I've forgot to leave the empties out the back. I'll do that nigh.

LEG: Do you wanna hand?

BARNEY: Not a'tall. I'll not be a minute. [BARNEY *exits.*]

BUCKETS: Take your time. [BUCKETS *walks in behind the bar, takes a long drink from a bottle of wine before filling a glass*] What are you havin, Leg?

LEG: Leave me out of it. If he catches you at that, you'll be a sorry man.
BUCKETS: If. [BUCKETS *comes out from behind the bar as* JIMMY SWEENEY *enters.*]
SWEENEY: Is McKibben here?
LEG: Hasn't been in yet.
SWEENEY: Must be round in Benny's. [*He turns to exit.*]
LEG: Oh a Jimmy! Is the lad along with you the day?
SWEENEY: He is, aye. And he doesn't know his hook from his hand.
LEG: I know, I know. [*He is embarrassed*] Will the get Sunday out of it?
SWEENEY: And Monday. [SWEENEY *exits.*]
LEG: Right, Jimmy. Thanks.
BUCKETS: Isn't it as well John Graham's not here. That'd be all we need. A shoutin match to liven things up.
LEG: Aye, and this International Workers' Day.
BUCKETS: I forgot about that. The march is this mornin then.
LEG: That's what I'm surprised at. I'd a thought it woulda passed this way b'nigh.
BUCKETS: Well, I haven't seen it. [BARNEY *enters*] Barney, sure the parade hasn't passed this way yet?
BARNEY: Not that I've seen. It usually comes down Whitla Street and goes along Garmoyle Street, before finishin across the street there.
BUCKETS: I'm sure there's one or two thirsty men walkin.
LEG: I wonder what the turn-out was like.
BUCKETS: I'm sure they're not as big as they were in my day.
LEG: Ach, give over. You're like myself. You could count on the fingers of one hand the many times you marched.
BUCKETS: Sure, never mind. You don't have to be a priest to say prayers and we don't have to go marchin to be workers. So, let's drink a toast to the workers, Leg. We mighten be able to march anymore, but we're still proud members of the Irish Transport and General Workers' Union.
LEG: Right.
BUCKETS: To the union!
LEG: To the union! [*They both stand and drink a toast. A brass band is heard*] That sounds like it nigh.
BARNEY: That's it alright. [*The music gets nearer.*]

BUCKETS: I must have a wee luck. It's the least you can do. [*He walks over and holds open the front door, looking outside. He is joined by* LEG *and* BARNEY] Oh, there's a brave crowd.

LEG: Can you see any of our fellas?

BUCKETS: I can't even see the union banner.

[HUGHIE MCNAMARA *appears and makes his way past the men into the bar. They all follow him inside as* BUCKETS *closes the door.*]

LEG: Oh, here's two-ton, fightin Tony Galento. Are you not supposed to be at work?

HUGHIE: Don't worry, I'm only in for a quick bottle before I go back. Bottle of beer, Barney!

LEG: Is none of the committee comin over?

HUGHIE: I'm sure they will. There's still speeches goin on, so I nipped away a wee bit early since I've to go back to work.

BUCKETS: And McKibben and Henry turned up?

HUGHIE: Yep. Themens and John Graham paradin side b'side. You'd think everything was just dead on.

LEG: Isn't it?

HUGHIE: How could it be?

LEG: But sure didn't I hear that Graham's suspension was lifted at the last meetin and nigh you say they were friendly enough on the march. Everything must be alright.

HUGHIE: The only reason John's suspension was lifted was because he brought it to the attention of head office.

LEG: I'm sure Henry and McKibben weren't too happy about that.

HUGHIE: You better believe it. As I said, they're paradin side b'side at the minute, but how long that'll last is anybody's guess.

BUCKETS: I've seen it all before.

HUGHIE: Don't worry. John's got plenty of backin nigh.

LEG: Which reminds me. What's this I hear about you givin lip to McKibben?

HUGHIE: So what?

LEG: So what! Who do you think you're talkin to? Because I've a bad leg, don't think I wouldn't think twice about bringin m'hand across your jaw!

HUGHIE: Okay, da, you win. Give it a rest till I finish my drink.

LEG: Just cut out the oul cheek. And keep out of McKibben's road.

HUGHIE: Alright, alright, I'm sorry. Do you wanna bottle of stout?
[JOHN GRAHAM, JACK HENRY *and* MCKIBBEN *enter, rather noisily.*]
JOHN: And did you see the hack of oul Banana Reilly tryin to carry the union banner? Swayin all over the place he was. [*They all laugh.*]
HENRY: No doubt he'd a few drinks before the parade, knowin Banana.
MCKIBBEN: At least he turned up, not like some people. [*He is looking at* BUCKETS.]
BUCKETS: And listen to who's talkin, Karl McKibben Marx himself! Specially resurrected from the dead to lead the Belfast workin class to victory. I want the Finance Minister's job when you take over.
JOHN: And what qualifications have you?
BARNEY: Well, when he can outwit the likes of Sarah Montague over money, there must be some genius there.
[*The men laugh.* MCKIBBEN *calls a drink. More jokes are made as* HUGHIE MCNAMARA *takes* JOHN *to one side.*]
HUGHIE: Well, John, how is everything?
JOHN: Dead on, great.
HUGHIE: Are you sure?
JOHN: Of course.
HUGHIE: No problems?
JOHN: No.
HUGHIE: You don't want me to hang around?
JOHN: For God's sake, Hughie.
HUGHIE: Right then, I'll get back to work.
JOHN: Don't be workin too hard.
HUGHIE: I bet you when I come by here at five a'clock, you'll be sittin here drunk.
JOHN: No chance.
HUGHIE: See ya, then. See ya, da!
LEG: Right, Hughie son!
[HUGHIE *exits.*]
BUCKETS: Who, Fargo A'Nail! I'll never forget the day he was caught walkin out of the dock gates with a load of apples and oranges and even onions on him.
LEG: They sent for the peelers, didn't the?
BUCKETS: Aye, the Bulkies locked him in a room by himself until the cops came and the couldn't believe it when the couldn't

find one single apple, orange or onion on him. He'd ate the lot! Skins and all!

LEG: And the had to let him go.

JOHN: Right, I'll tell you what. Since we're sort of celebratin the day, why don't you give us a song, Buckets?

HENRY: Aye, c'mon McGuinness, liven things up.

JOHN: We've all heard you singin before. C'mon.

BUCKETS: I don't sing.

JOHN: Buckets. One song to start it off.

BUCKETS: Alright then, but only one.

LEG: That's the man.

MCKIBBEN: Away ya go.

[BUCKETS *steps forward and proceeds to sing* 'Days Gone By', *to the air of* 'I'll Tell Me Ma'.]

Where I come from was right n'rough
We didn't always get enough
Times were hard but we got along
Stickin together and singin a song

Nobody shunned a tale of woe
People were friendly and nice to know
A neighbourhood steeped in joy and tears
Do you remember the bygone years.

Horses and carts and tramway lines
Annoyin the peelers with finger signs
A jam-jar in to a picture show
Kissin Mae West from the middle row.

Mitchin school for dockside games
Sneakin on ships till the sailors came
Bacon cuttins and hairy pig's-feet
Kickin futball in Nelson Street.

Do you remember those days gone by
A way of life we don't know nigh
People will tell you the times were bad
But they were the best bloody years I ever had.

[*They all applaud, as* SARAH *and* MARY-ANN *enter from the street.*]
SARAH: Buckets McGuinness, could I have a word with you?
LEG: Oh-oh!
[SARAH *walks downstage and* BUCKETS *follows. She opens her purse and puts some money in his hand.* BUCKETS *is astounded, as* SARAH *and* MARY-ANN *exit to the snug.*]
BUCKETS: I don't believe this.
MCKIBBEN: What have you been doin to deserve that?
JOHN: You must owe that wee woman a fortune b'nigh.
BARNEY: Yiz have got it all wrong. Sarah owed Buckets that money. N'that right, Buckets?
BUCKETS: No, Barney. I still owe her four pound eighteen shillins.
LEG: That's what I thought.
BARNEY: But what about the overcoat you sold her Sam?
BUCKETS: I never sold her Sam any overcoat. He bought it off a Dutch sailor in the bar.
BARNEY: Then why did you tell Sarah he bought it off you?
BUCKETS: To get rid of her.
BARNEY: Oul Sam musta been very drunk
BUCKETS: That's what's happened. That's it! [*He starts laughing*] Oul Tasty Sam's been that drunk, he hasn't remembered who he bought the overcoat off. [*He slaps the money on the bar counter as they all cheer*] Give everybody a drink, Barney! [*He holds up his glass*] Here's to my good friend, Sarah Montague. Well, gentlemen, how'd the march go?
MCKIBBEN: It was a great march.
HENRY: Very good turn out.
JOHN: Not enough dockers, though.
MCKIBBEN: We'll get them out next year. Right?
[MCKIBBEN *holds out his hand to* JOHN. *They shake.*]
JOHN: Right.
MCKIBBEN: Listen. Let's drink a toast to the union.
BUCKETS: We've already done that.
MCKIBBEN: Well, we couldn't do it often enough. To the union!
ALL: To the union! [*They drink.*]
MCKIBBEN: And to International Workers' Day. [*They drink again.* JIMMY SWEENEY *and* DANNY-BOY *enter*] Ah, there's Jimmy. C'mon to we have a drink, Jimmy.
DANNY-BOY: Hi, da.

LEG: Barney, give the lad whatever he wants there, will ye.
JOHN: Right, nigh that Buckets has done his piece, let's have Harry McKibben for a song! [*Cheers and applause*] Right, Harry, let's have ye.
MCKIBBEN: Okay, okay. I'll sing a rebel song. [*Cheers.*]
HENRY: Go ahead, Harry.
 [MCKIBBEN *proceeds to sing* 'Kevin Barry', *but after only a verse* SARAH MONTAGUE *and* MARY-ANN MCKEOWN *enter from the snug.*]
SARAH: What's all the singin about, eh? Jasis, isn't it funny yiz only remember about the Republic with drink in yiz.
MCKIBBEN: Ah, give over, you weren't exactly decorated in the cause of Ulster.
SARAH: No, but I could sing about it a lot better than that.
JOHN: Right. C'mon, Sarah, you give us a song then.
LEG: That's a girl, Sarah.
BUCKETS: Give is ... 'Pennies From Heaven'. [*They all laugh.*]
SARAH: I was gonna sing 'The Sash', but I'll sing another good loyalist song instead.
MCKIBBEN: Okay, just this once. Let's hear it.
HENRY: Barney, you don't mind an Orange song on your premises?
BARNEY: Not a'tall.
JOHN: Right, a wee bit of order to we hear the woman singing. You're on the air, Sarah.
MARY-ANN: Do you want me to sing along with you, Sarah?
SARAH: In the name a Jasis, Mary-Ann McKeown, have some respect for yourself and your religion. Sit there and shut up!
MARY-ANN: Whatever you like nigh, Sarah, it's all the same to me.
 [*They all laugh as* BUCKETS *joins in with* MARY-ANN *in saying her oft-repeated line, as above.* SARAH *proceeds to sing* 'The Green Grassy Slopes of the Boyne'. *In the middle of it,* BUCKETS *grabs her and dances round the bar with her, as does* JOHN. *The others laugh and cheer. They applaud as she finishes.*]
MCKIBBEN: Very good, Sarah, very good. You know we all have to live together in this city with our two religions.
HENRY: There's got to be toleration, respect for the other man's point of view.
MCKIBBEN: Yes, toleration is the key word.
JOHN: Definitely. Nigh that Sarah has sung, it's my pleasure to call upon the chairman of the union for a song. [*Applause.*]
MCKIBBEN: Away you go, Jack.

MARY-ANN: Give is 'The Oul Bog Road'.
HENRY: No thanks. I don't know any songs. All's I know is hymns. No, instead I'm sure the youngest man on the committee could give us a song or two. John Graham! [*Applause.*]
MCKIBBEN: If he can sing as well as he can talk, he'll be alright.
LEG: Give is one of them latest ones.
HENRY: It's his own pleasure, nigh, his own pleasure.
JOHN: Well, I'd like to sing one song. And since this is International Workers' Day, I'd like to sing a workers' song.
BUCKETS: C'mon, John, ya boyo!
JOHN: This song was written by an Irishman, Jim Connell, one of the many Irishmen who've had to go abroad luckin work.
MCKIBBEN: All because of England, mind you.
SARAH: You leave England out of this.
MCKIBBEN: Sure wasn't it England left Ireland the way it is. Men had to go away to get work.
SARAH: C'mon, Mary-Ann, if we're gonna be insulted over our religion, we'll get away out of this.
MARY-ANN: Whatever you like nigh, Sarah, it's all the same to me.
BUCKETS: Excuse me, Mrs. McKeown, but I understood you were of the Roman Catholic persuasion?
MARY-ANN: So a am.
BUCKETS: And you've been insulted?
MARY-ANN: Will you stop tryin to complicate things. If Sarah wants to go, I'm goin with her.
BUCKETS: If Sarah stuck her head in the fire, would you do it too?
MARY-ANN: No, I wouldn't.
SARAH: Are you comin or what?
MARY-ANN: Whatever you like nigh, it's all the same to me.
[*All the men mimic* MARY-ANN *before the two women exit to the street.*]
MCKIBBEN: Right, back to the song. C'mon, John, I always liked an emigrant's song. You were sayin?
JOHN: This one's not exactly an emigrant's song. This Irishman had obviously travelled a great deal and found that not only is the Irish workin class gettin a raw deal, but so were the English workin people and the French and the Germans and so on. So he wrote this song. [*He begins singing*]

> The people's flag is deepest red
> It's shrouded oft our martyred dead ...

[MCKIBBEN *stands bolt upright, Henry's face draws and* SWEENEY *puts down his drink.*]
> And ere their limbs grew stiff and cold
> Their heart's blood dyed its every fold.

MCKIBBEN: Hey! Cut that crap out, Graham! [JOHN *glances round at* MCKIBBEN, *but carries on singing.*]

JOHN: So raise the scarlet banner high
> Beneath its folds ...

MCKIBBEN: I said cut that crap out! [JOHN *stops singing*] We don't want to listen to none of that Communist shit!

SWEENEY: And we're not goin to.

HENRY: Change the song, Graham!

JOHN: But it's a workers' song. This is Workers' Day and we're union men.

MCKIBBEN: It's Commie shit!

JOHN: You can put whetever interpretation you want on it, but I feel like singin it.

MCKIBBEN: Not round here you won't.

HENRY: Change the song, Graham.

JOHN: I thought you all believed in toleration. Remember? A while ago every man's view must be allowed for. Even your bigoted minds gave way to the singin of a Protestant song. It's all very well to play at bein trade union leaders, but when the true concept of Labour is raised, our leaders are terrified. Is that what's happenin here? Is it not? My Labour song offends Labour leaders?

HENRY: You don't know the half of it! You have no idea what went into buildin our union over the years.

JOHN: You built it?

HENRY: I put 25 years into it. How long have you put in?

JOHN: Twenty-five years of what?

HENRY: Twenty-five years of plenty and I'm fucked if I'm gonna stand round and let troublemakers like you wreck it.

JOHN: Who's wreckin?

HENRY: You're wreckin! How come nobody else is shoutin their heads off? I don't know but I think one complainer out of a thousand men is a good record. A bloody good record!

JOHN: And why do they not complain, eh? Do you think the all enjoy shovin and pushin each other like animals in that pen every mornin?

HENRY: What are you suggestin?

JOHN: You know damn well what I'm suggestin.

HENRY: You've made one remark too many, Graham.

JOHN: And what? You're gonna throw me off the committee? Don't worry, your days'll soon be over, Jack. The older dockers were easy meat, but there's younger men comin after me and they won't accept the oul ways.

HENRY: Don't have me laughing. [HENRY *chuckles.*]

MCKIBBEN: Why don't you take yourself off and spew that silly crap over somebody else?

SWEENEY: Aye, away and sing your 'Red Flag' round in the Labour Club.

[BUCKETS *walks forward and takes* JOHN *by the arm.*]

BUCKETS: Aye, John, let it go this time. Let ignorant men have their way.

[JOHN *shrugs him off.*]

JOHN: I've started it here and I'll finish it here. [*He resumes singing*]

> Look round the Frenchman loves its blaze
> The sturdy German chants its praise ...

MCKIBBEN: I warned you!

[*He lunges forward on to* JOHN, *knocking him on to the floor.* LEG *takes* DANNY-BOY *to the side, away from the disturbance.* JOHN *carries on singing.* MCKIBBEN *pulls him back by the hair and kicks him repeatedly.* JOHN *folds up, but again starts singing.* HENRY *gives the nod and, this time, both* MCKIBBEN *and* SWEENEY *trail him outside, where a further beating takes place. Presently, the two men enter.*]

MCKIBBEN: He had that comin to him.

HENRY: What? Take that from a gaunch like that? No sweat.

SWEENEY: Right, that's him sorted out. Let's have a drink. What are you havin, Leg?

LEG: What? Oh a ... a bottle of stout, Jimmy.

SWEENEY: Danny-boy?

DANNY-BOY: Glass a beer, thanks.

SWEENEY: Buckets?

BUCKETS: Nothin, nothin for me.

[*Suddenly, the doors burst open and* THERESA GRAHAM *enters. She makes straight for* MCKIBBEN.]

THERESA: You bastard! [*She slaps him on the face.* MCKIBBEN *draws his fist back, but refrains*] You no-good, cowardly, stinkin, bastard! You waited patiently on your chance, didn't ye, Harry McKibben!

MCKIBBEN: He asked for it.

THERESA: And I'm sure it didn't take much. The fact that he breathes a'tall is enough to annoy you.

MCKIBBEN: He's an agitator!

THERESA: And what does that make you?

MCKIBBEN: A better man than him.

THERESA: You wouldn't make a patch for John Graham's arse. He's a better man than you'll ever be.

MCKIBBEN: He's a communist.

THERESA: Well, God knows there must be something to recommend it, if ignorant men like you's against it.

HENRY: Would you not be better goin on home?

THERESA: When I'm good and ready. And don't you stand there, Jack Henry, b'the way it's all nothin to do with you. You've a lot to answer for. [*She glares around the pub*] Yiz all have a lot to answer for. Whether yiz did the batin or turned your backs, yiz are guilty, each and every one of yiz.

[LEG *takes her by the arm.*]

LEG: C'mon, Theresa girl, that's enough. [*She steps away from him.*]

THERESA: When I think of the times I told him he was wastin his time. I told him the dockers weren't worth it, but he thought yiz were. There's a thin line between idealism and blindness, but it was no use talkin.

MCKIBBEN: Go away and take him with you.

THERESA: Don't worry, we're goin, but don't be thinkin yiz have seen the end of John Graham, for yiz haven't. He might as well see it through nigh. He'll be through them dock gates on Monday mornin, should I have to carry him myself.

MCKIBBEN: You just might have to carry him back through again.

THERESA: How can you be so full of badness, Harry McKibben? Why don't you leave us alone? First it was our Vera and nigh it's my husband. How far do you wanna go?

LEG: Let it go nigh, Theresa.

THERESA: Why doesn't he leave us alone? He's never satisfied unless he's hurtin somebody. [*She points outside*] He'll be back on Monday mornin. I'll make sure of it. Should I have to carry him myself. [*She exits.*]

SWEENEY: That's women for ye. Here, Jack, yiz'll have to co-op a man on to the committee.
HENRY: Ah, that should be no problem. We can forget about him.
MCKIBBEN: C'mon, we'll sit down here outta the road.
HENRY: Aye, we could be doin with a bit of peace and quiet.
SWEENEY: Send us in three bottles a stout, Barney. [*The three men exit to the snug*] [*Off-stage*] Did you know that Smith & Coggins are luckin a new foreman this week?
MCKIBBEN: The must be gettin a fair bit of work.

[*There is a prolonged silence in the bar.*]

BARNEY: Isn't that a terrible carry-on?
BUCKETS: Desperate. Give is it across the card, Barney. [BARNEY *proceeds to set up a bottle of stout and a whiskey.* BUCKETS *walks over to the end of the bar and takes down the union photograph from where it had been hanging on the wall. He throws it in the bin*] That's another young man ruined b'the dock. And it wasn't drink done it this time. [*He knocks back his whiskey*] I mustn't have enough drink in me. The barbed wire's cuttin lumps outta me.

[*Lights.*]

THE INTERROGATION
OF AMBROSE FOGARTY

(1982)

The Interrogation of Ambrose Fogarty was first performed at the Lyric Players' Theatre, Belfast, on 27th January, 1982. It was directed by Sam McCready and designed by Stuart Stanley. The cast was as follows:

Ambrose Fogarty	John Keenan
Willie Lagan	Ian McElhinney
Stanley	Oliver Maguire
Peter	Derek Halligan
Jackie	George Shane
Sergeant Knox	Michael Gormley
Constable Davy McFadden	Brian Hogg
WPC Yvonne Lundy	Susie Kelly
Captain Levington	Ben Benson

Set in a police station in west Belfast in the mid-1970s, the play covers a three-day interrogation period.

ACT ONE

The scene is a busy police station in west Belfast, Northern Ireland. At stage-left, there is a cell and a door for another cell. The station reception area occupies stage-right, while an interviewee room dominates the centre of the stage. At the reception area desk SERGEANT KNOX *is typing out a report. Behind him,* WOMAN POLICE CONSTABLE YVONNE LUNDY *and a plain-clothes policeman,* JACKIE, *are standing in a doorway, apparently watching television. The crackling of the station communications radio at the back wall dominates occasionally.*

RADIO: Echo Tango Eight One. Echo Tango Eight One to Bravo Hotel, over. Echo Tango Eight One. Echo Tango Eight One to Bravo Hotel, over.
YVONNE: Echo Tango Eight One, send, over.
JACKIE: I hate that pansy bastard Russell Harty!
RADIO: Registration number Juliet, Oscar, India—five, nine, zero, seven. It would seem that there are three occupants, over.
YVONNE: Roger. Keep in touch with the DSO.
RADIO: Roger, out.
 [*A plain-clothes policeman,* PETER, *enters.*]
PETER: There's that report, Sergeant Knox. Have it checked out.
KNOX: Will do, Peter.
PETER: Oh, by the way, what's the latest on the situation outside?
KNOX: It would appear the main riot's over. We're down to about the last two dozen die-hards.
PETER: Any arrests?
KNOX: None so far.
PETER: The major seems to have handled things well.
KNOX: Well, he's near the end of his tour, so he's seen it all before.
PETER: Almost a veteran, eh? [*Exits.*]
KNOX: Yvonne! [YVONNE *presents herself*] Put out a call to the vehicle nearest that location and have it checked out.
YVONNE: Right.

JACKIE: Yvonne, come on and see the antics of this. He can't get the envelope opened!

YVONNE: Sorry, Jackie, I'm busy. [*Speaks into radio*] Bravo Hotel, Bravo Hotel to Bravo Hotel One One, over.

RADIO: Bravo Hotel to One One, send, over.

YVONNE: Would you check out a report of a single shot heard in the Cavendish-Oakman Street area, over.

RADIO: Will do. Do we know if there are any army patrols in that location? Over.

YVONNE: No army patrols. Roger, out. [*Returns to the doorway.*]

JACKIE: That man is one silly nincompoop!

[*The phone rings.* KNOX *answers.*]

KNOX: Hello ... Yes ... If you call at 3 p.m. tomorrow, Mr. Donnelly, someone will attend you ... Right ... Cheerio.

[*He puts the phone down. Presently some shouting is heard from offstage at the main entrance to the reception area. A head appears at the entrance, on the floor. The face is grinning broadly. As we see just a little bit more of the head and shoulders, an army captain swings into view with the legs of the body, and proceeds to trail it across the floor, kicking at it as he does so. The body is* WILLIE LAGAN. *He is holding on to a brown paper parcel which is under one arm while he waves with the other. Unbelievably, he is still grinning. He shouts and whistles. Willie's whistle is more a kind of tuneless hissing noise than a real whistle.*]

CAPTAIN: Shut up! Shut up, mate!

WILLIE: No problem, no problem. [*Whistles.*]

CAPTAIN: I said, shut your beak!

WILLIE: Get 'em up, move 'em out! [*Whistles again, then roars with laughter. The* CAPTAIN *drops Willie's legs.*]

CAPTAIN: Now get up, you lunatic.

[WILLIE *turns over to a sitting-up position.*]

WILLIE: Lunatic, lunatic—ahhh! I like it, I like it. [*Grabs the Captain's baton.*] Here, shake hands.

CAPTAIN: I'll make you stand up. [*He proceeds to draw a baton and beat* WILLIE *once or twice before* KNOX *rushes out from behind the desk.*]

KNOX: Just a minute, just a minute, Captain, that's quite enough.

CAPTAIN: He won't get up!

KNOX: He'll not be able to get up if you keep that up. [*Physically steps in between the* CAPTAIN *and* WILLIE] Let's have you on your

feet, Sir. [*Helps* WILLIE *up by the arm.*] That's better. Now what's all the trouble about?
WILLIE: He hit me a dig, a dig.
CAPTAIN: I'm placing this man under arrest for taking part in a riot.
KNOX: Well, if you don't mind me saying so, Captain, he doesn't exactly look like a normal teenage rioter.
CAPTAIN: Well, he fucking well is. I want him charged.
KNOX: What were the circumstances?
CAPTAIN: He was observed throwing bottles of beer, and when we charged forward we placed him under arrest.
WILLIE: That's lies, all lies.
CAPTAIN: I saw you with my own eyes!
WILLIE: I'm not talking to you, talkin' to this man, okay shut up.
KNOX: All right, all right!

[*A call comes through on the radio.*]

YVONNE: Sergeant Knox! Constable McFadden requires assistance at the door to bring in a prisoner.
KNOX: Right. Would you do that, Captain?

[*The* CAPTAIN *moves to leave.* WILLIE *laughs.*]

WILLIE [*whistling*]: Hold on, hold on! Where's my ... [*Whistles and mimics guitar-playing*] guitar, guitar?
KNOX: Do you have some property belonging to this man?
CAPTAIN: Yeah, it's outside. [*Steps off and returns with a guitar.*]
KNOX: I'll take it. [KNOX *takes the guitar and sets it down beside him. Exit* CAPTAIN.]
WILLIE: Magic, magic. That's mine, that's mine. Try and guess who give me that. Don't know, don't know? Cash, Cash, Johnny Cash, big, star, good singer, good singer. [*Sings.*]

> I hear that whistle blowin',
> It's comin' down the line
> I ain't seen the sunshine
> Since I don't know when
> 'Cause I'm stuck in Folsom Prison
> And time keeps draggin' on ...'

KNOX: All right, that's enough, I believe you, Johnny Cash gave you it, all right.

[WILLIE *holds the guitar up and kisses it.*]

WILLIE: I love it, I love it. That's my wife, my wife.
KNOX: Right now. I want some details from you. What's your name?

WILLIE: My name? Willie Lagan, Country-and-Western singer, that's me.

KNOX [*writing down the details*]: Lagan. Where do you live, Willie?

WILLIE: With my mother. [*Laughs.*]

KNOX: I didn't ask you who you live with, I asked you where you lived.

WILLIE: The Lower Whack, Lower Whack.

KNOX: The what?

WILLIE: Lower Whack, the Lower Falls, know ... [*Whistles*] am ... a Grosvenor Place.

KNOX: What number in Grosvenor Place?

WILLIE: Ninety-five.

KNOX: Ninety-five, Grosvenor Place. Now, what's all this about you being involved in the rioting?

WILLIE: I don't know, no idea, not me.

KNOX: Where exactly were you arrested?

WILLIE: Exactly?

KNOX: Exactly.

WILLIE [*whistles as he points downwards, then swoops his hand down and grabs his own private parts*]: Right there! Right there! Your man, General Montgomery, him, him. He grabbed me by the swingers. Sore, fuckin' sore.

KNOX: No, no, hold on. Where were you standing when you were arrested?

WILLIE: Springfield Road corner, know just outside Beacon's Bar, right there. I never done nothing!

KNOX: Outside Beacon's bar at the junction of the Falls and Springfield roads?

WILLIE: Magic, that's it, that's it.

KNOX: What were you doing there in the middle of a riot?

WILLIE: Just going home, on my way home. I was just walking ... [*Whistles*] down the Falls Road and [*Whistles, hand down at his privates again*] arrested! I wasn't even—

KNOX: No, now hold on a second. Start from the start. What were you doing in that area in the first place?

WILLIE: Right, okay. From the start, the beginning, Adam and Eve, okay. I was ... [*whistles and imitates the actions of playing the guitar*] playing in the wee Dwyer's Club.

KNOX: That's the Dwyer's Club in Leeson Street?

WILLIE: That's right, that's right, me, me. Every Sunday afternoon. Me, Willie Lagan, Country-and-Western singer. Live on stage, live, live! [*Sings*] 'I'm tired of crying, and all your lying ...' Finished ... [*Whistles*] got x-rayed, know, money, and fucked off ... [*Whistles*] nipped. Up to the sister's, called up.

KNOX: Where's your sister's?

WILLIE: Cavendish Street ... [*Whistles*] round the back. Sister gave me some soda farls, soda farls for my mother. I was walking home and ... [*Whistles.*]

KNOX: Yes, but did you throw any bottles of beer at the soldiers?

WILLIE [*laughs*]: Good joke, good joke. Is there no bar in here, no bar? [*Laughs.*]

KNOX: Somehow or other I don't think you're the sort that would throw away a bottle of beer for any reason. Right. I'm afraid I'll have to lock you up until we get to the bottom of this. If that soldier insists on pressing charges you could be in trouble. Let's go.

WILLIE: Guitar, guitar, that's mine.

KNOX: Right. You can take that with you but not a sound, hear!

WILLIE: Okay, okay. [*Lifts his guitar. He is led to a cell and locked up by* KNOX. *In the meantime,* CONSTABLE DAVY MCFADDEN *arrives with* AMBROSE FOGARTY *by the arm, escorted by the* CAPTAIN.]

DAVY: Where's Sergeant Knox?

YVONNE: He's just gone to the cells with a prisoner.

DAVY [*To* AMBROSE]: Right. Sit down there, would you please. [AMBROSE *sits down. The* CAPTAIN *stands beside him*] Give a buzz upstairs and tell the quare fells the prisoner's here.

YVONNE [*buzzes*]: Ah, Detective Scally, the prisoner's here ... Right. [*To* DAVY] Put him in an interview room, there'll be somebody down right away.

DAVY: Okay. C'mon. [AMBROSE *stands up*] Thanks Captain, I'll take him on in. [DAVY *escorts* AMBROSE *to the interview room.*]

CAPTAIN: Hey, Yvonne, tell us what colour your knickers are.

YVONNE: I've none on.

CAPTAIN: Way-hey! That's what I like to hear. A girl that's ready for action.

YVONNE: You don't know what action is, Captain.

CAPTAIN: Why don't you show me the ropes?

YVONNE: I'm not in the habit of wasting my time.

CAPTAIN: Na, you're more hung up on that fat bastard of a police constable that just walked out there.

YVONNE: I beg your pardon.

CAPTAIN [*mimicking her voice*]: I beg your pardon. [*Laughs.*]

YVONNE: If you can't hold a conversation without making fun of people, then you'd better not try in the first place.

CAPTAIN: I'm sorry, it wasn't me and I'll never do it again. [*Then moves closer and leans on the desk right beside* YVONNE] Listen, Yvonne, darling, how would you like an offer you couldn't refuse?

YVONNE: Like what?

CAPTAIN: Like you and me going out one of these nights, eh?
[*She moves away to the radio as a message comes through.*]

YVONNE: I can't. I work. Golf Charlie Eight One, to Bravo Hotel, send, over.

CAPTAIN: What do you think I'm doing over here? Pheasant shooting?

[*As the* CAPTAIN *exits,* JACKIE *enters the interview room, camera in hand.*]

JACKIE: Right, who have we here?

DAVY: Prisoner Fogarty.

JACKIE: Ah, Ambrose Fogarty. I've waited a long time to meet you.
[*Nods to* DAVY, *who leaves.* AMBROSE *is silent.*]

JACKIE: What's wrong, Ambrose? Not in the mood for talking? I see. Well, we'll leave all that till later. In the meantime, some formalities. [*Harshly*] Stand up! [AMBROSE *stands up.* JACKIE *lifts a small blackboard*] Full name, Ambrose?

AMBROSE: Ambrose Fogarty.

[JACKIE *chalks this on blackboard.*]

JACKIE: Date of birth?

AMBROSE: 4th of the 11th, '53

JACKIE: Religion?

AMBROSE: None.

JACKIE: None at all? [AMBROSE *shakes his head*] Well, for these purposes I'll just put down RC. Okay? Now just hold that like a good man and we'll get some nice wee pics of you. [*Places the board in Ambrose's hands up against his chest.*] That's it, up a little, fine. [*As he moves back to take the photograph,* AMBROSE *lowers the board down by his side.*] Hold it up to your chest.

AMBROSE: No.

JACKIE: What do you mean, 'No'? Hold it up!

AMBROSE: I'm not doing it.

[JACKIE *walks over to* AMBROSE.]

JACKIE: Listen, Bonzo. You're not in a position to say what you're doing and what you're not doing. Now just hold that board up to your chest [*Physically positions Ambrose's hands on the board*], and no oul' nonsense out of you. [AMBROSE *drops the board on the floor.* JACKIE *glares at him*] All right, we'll do it without the board. [*Moves back in position*] Look into the camera, Ambrose. [AMBROSE *turns his head to the side and scratches the side of his head with the opposite hand*] What are you playing at?

AMBROSE: I'm not having my photograph taken. Under the terms of the Emergency Provisions Act 1973, you need a certificate signed by a police officer no lower in rank than a Chief Inspector before you can take a prisoner's photograph.

JACKIE: Is that right? Well, let me tell you something, mate. You're not sitting at no Civil Rights meeting now. Nor standing at a street corner. You're in a police station, arrested as a suspect terrorist, and as such you have no rights. Now keep your hands down by your side and look into this camera.

AMBROSE: I'm not doing it.

[*As* JACKIE *positions the camera,* AMBROSE *covers his face with his hand.*]

JACKIE: Right! [*Puts the camera down*] We'll see about that later on. Stand over by that desk. [AMBROSE *obeys*] I'm going to take your fingerprints. [*Organises some items on the table*] Give me your right hand. [AMBROSE *remains silent and motionless*] I said, give me your right hand. [AMBROSE *shakes his head determinedly.* JACKIE *grabs his arm.* AMBROSE *pulls it back*] Look, don't make this difficult for yourself. You can co-operate with me now, or I can call in half-a-dozen soldiers to physically take your prints. Which way do you want it done?

AMBROSE: I don't want to have my fingerprints taken. It's against the law.

JACKIE: You know quite a lot about the law.

AMBROSE: Enough to know that to have my photograph or fingerprints taken you need a Chief Inspector's certificate.

JACKIE: Is that so? Right. If that's the way you want to play it, fair enough. If you're going to act the smart Alec, just remember that you have three long days and nights ahead of you. If you want to mess us about, just think what we can do to you over three days. [AMBROSE *remains silent*] But then you seem to be a cocky character. Reckon you'll daddle through this, eh? Do you, Ambrose? [AMBROSE *shrugs his shoulders*] Well, let me let you into a wee secret. We allowed you to run about too long. Now, we have you by the goolies. All our evidence collected. Signed, sealed and delivered. You'll not walk out of here this time. Now c'mon till I bring you to your cell. You'll have to get used to life in an eight-by-four box. We'll get your photo and prints later on. No hurry. In fact, Fogarty, there's no need to hurry anything anymore, where you're concerned. Let's go. [JACKIE *and* AMBROSE *go out into the main reception area.* KNOX, *by the radio, is discussing a point with* DAVY.] Sergeant, put this man in a cell, please.

KNOX [*To* DAVY]: Put him in Cell Two.

DAVY: Right. [*Takes* AMBROSE *by the arm.*]

JACKIE: Oh, ah, Fogarty. Remember what I said. There's no hurry. No hurry at all. [*Exits.*]

KNOX [*into radio*]: Bravo Hotel to Bravo Hotel Eight One, over. Bravo Hotel to Bravo Hotel Eight One, over.

RADIO: Bravo Hotel, send.

KNOX: Would you go to the assistance of an officer outside the BBC in Ormeau Avenue. Apparently there's a drunk man there who's knocked over two bollards of flowers and he's now kicking at the door of the BBC. You won't believe this, but he says he wants to make an appeal over the air to his wife, who left him last night.

RADIO: It takes all sorts. Roger, out.

KNOX: Roger on that.

[*While* KNOX *has been using the radio,* DAVY *has taken* AMBROSE *to the cells,* DAVY *jangling a bunch of keys. He directs* AMBROSE *to a cell.* AMBROSE *enters and turns.*]

AMBROSE: You wouldn't have a paper on you, mate?

DAVY: Sorry, I don't.

AMBROSE: Could you get me one?

DAVY: We're not allowed.

AMBROSE: Right, thanks.

[*With a loud slam,* DAVY *locks the cell door and takes up a position at the end of the cell block. He sits on a chair beside a table and begins to write on a clipboard.* AMBROSE *stands in the middle of his cell. He looks around. The walls are white, bare, except for one small ventilator up near the ceiling. A light bulb in a round glass casing glares down from high up on a wall. A few grey, army-type blankets lie crumpled on top of a single bed. A solitary chair rests in a corner. He makes a quick check of the cell door, then sits on the chair. He runs one hand through his hair and heaves a disgusted sigh. Presently he jumps up angrily and paces the floor.]*

AMBROSE: Fuck this! Three frigging days in this kip, Jesus Christ! How am I gonna stick this? Fuck it, fuck it, fuck it. Tons to look at on the walls. [*He runs his hand along the wall, then checks under the mattress*] Three days! seventy-two hours! What to hell's it all about? Nobody has said a dickie-bird up to now, except 'All our evidence collected'. What are they on about, what evidence? [*Pause*] What about Gerry? I wonder do they know anything about Gerry? [*Pause*] wonder will I get my bollocks knocked in. They don't bring you in here for nothing. [*Stops suddenly*] That was wild in the house this morning. Christine. Her eyes. You could actually see the terror in her eyes. Thank Christ the kids didn't waken. That soldier was one ignorant bastard. I hope she's got over it. Scrub that. I have to stop thinking about her. Or the children, while I'm in here. From here on in I'm on my own. No distractions. Nobody to worry about, only me. [*He spots the ventilator up on the wall, jumps up on the bed and feels round it. He stops. A crafty grin spreads over his face*] I wonder will I get away with the fingerprints and photographs thing. [*He jumps down from the bed and bursts loudly into song.*]

Heaven knows, it's not the way it should be.

Heaven knows, it's not the way it should be.'

[PETER *and* JACKIE, *talking, enter the interview room.*]

JACKIE: I felt like hitting him a dig in the jaw.

PETER: Not to worry. He knows as well as we do that his prints and pics will be taken. He's putting on a show of confidence.

JACKIE: A show?

PETER: Don't kid yourself. Anybody who finds themselves arrested and thrown in a cell is worried. Worried sick, in fact. Some are just better than others at concealing it.

JACKIE: So you're gonna start this psychological thing, eh?

PETER: That's what it's all about, Jackie. A battle of wits.

JACKIE: I don't wear that crap. A good going-over is more than enough for most of them.

PETER: Yes, Jackie, but the fear of a good going-over is even worse.

It's harder to penetrate a person's mind than their body, but once you do get in, they're yours for the taking.

JACKIE: I'm not so sure about that.

PETER: The essence of interrogation is psychology. Look. When you hear somebody kicking up in the papers about Castlereagh and interrogation methods, what is it you hear? 'Brutality, punched, kicked, beat-up' etcetera. You never hear a word about the real interrogation. I've seen guys walk out of here, wrecked, who never had a finger laid on them. You can be sure Fogarty's walking about that cell with his mind on the boil. Like a bubbling volcano. It's our job to make it erupt.

JACKIE: Have you come across Fogarty before, Peter?

PETER: Not face to face. But I remember during the UWC strike in 1974, I watched him in Leeson Street for over an hour, out the back window of a Ford Transit van.

JACKIE: What was he doing?

PETER: Remember there was a food shortage? Well, he and his mates had got hold of a load of bread and he was distributing it to the people. That's the sort of thing he would be seen doing publicly. Helping the cause by helping the working class and all that stuff.

JACKIE: Do you think he has any idea why he's in here?

[AMBROSE, *in his cell, is lying on his bed. He sits up sharply.*]

AMBROSE: I wonder is it anything to do with the Newry thing? Maxie? That was two years ago. [*Grins*] Huh. That stew was woeful. No, it wouldn't be that. What? What is it? If I knew I could attempt to prepare myself, but I don't frigging know! Oh Christ, watch it, watch it, watch it. Take it easy, take it easy. Don't run away with yourself. Hold it, hold it. I have to hold my nerve. I've three days of this to go through. If I'm losing my nerve now, without a finger being laid on me, what am I going to be like if they start punching me? I wonder how I would react to a dig in the jaw. [*He prods his jaw with his fist*] Strange. I've never been struck in anger by anyone in my whole adult life. Maybe I'll take it all right. You never know. [*He jumps up and paces the floor*] On the other hand, I might end up throwing myself out of an upstairs window like your man from Ballymurphy. Or the fella who they *said* hanged himself in his cell at Castlereagh. Jesus Christ! What would have to be going on to allow that to happen? Reminds me of

Chile. Santiago Stadium. But then again, I might just walk out in three days' time as clean as a whistle. British justice and all that crap. It's the in-between that counts. [*He sits down on the bed*] The not knowing. The uncertainty. The fear. The breaking-point. [*In the interview room,* JACKIE *and* PETER *continue their conversation.*]

JACKIE: Of course he has a breaking-point. The back of his neck!

PETER: You're hell for this physical thing. I really don't think it'll have all that of an effect on this fella.

JACKIE: You let me take him in hand and I'll show him. A good boot in the balls'll bring an elephant down.

PETER: It won't necessarily get him to sign a confession. No, Jackie. Better to let this man spend a lot of time in his cell worrying. The oul' volcano'll be bubbling away. And after each interview the lava'll get hotter and the bubbles higher. [AMBROSE *is lying in his bed, trying to balance the heel of one shoe on the toe of the other.*]

AMBROSE: Anyway, I'm here for a while, so I might as well make the best of it. A newspaper would come in handy. Big Geek said he was allowed newspapers. [*Smiles*] Bastard musta been giving information to them. I wonder should I try and get some sleep? No. They're liable to be watching me. They'd probably wait until I'm in a deep sleep then come and trail me out for an interview while I'm all groggy. [*He stands up and takes his coat off*] Smicker says it happened to him. But you never know when Smicker's telling the truth and when he's imagining things. I don't care. They're not gonna break me. No talking, no signing statements. No nothing. [*He gets down on the floor and starts doing press-ups, then stops abruptly*] I wonder do they feed you in here?

[YVONNE *enters the cells area pushing a catering trolley. She stops beside* DAVY.]

YVONNE: Are you just going to sit there or do I have to squeeze sausages and beans under the cell doors?

[DAVY *stands up sharply.*]

DAVY: Ready when you are.

YVONNE: Sorry for waking you out of your sleep.

[*She pushes the trolley to the first cell door.* DAVY *opens it.* WILLIE *gathers up his things and moves forward to meet him.*]

WILLIE: Is this me, aye? Released, what?

DAVY: Sit down, mate. It's only your lunch.

WILLIE: I don't want no lunch. I want out. Out there. [*Whistles*] What about my soda farls for my mother's tea?

DAVY: Well, you're not getting out just yet, so you'd better sit down and eat.

WILLIE: This is out of order. Cat! Rough McFucking Duff, what?

DAVY: Here, take that. [YVONNE *hands him a plate of food and a cup of tea.*]

WILLIE: Thanks, thanks. [*He winks at* YVONNE] What's your name sweetheart, what's your name? Fancy coming into my apartment for drinks? [*Laughs*] My apartment! I like, I like, I like!

DAVY: Alright, then?

WILLIE: Smashin', smashin'. [DAVY *is about to close the door*] Oh a ... can I see a smart man, briefcase, briefcase, know a solicitor?

DAVY: What for?

WILLIE: I wanna make out a will.

DAVY: What do you want to make out a will for? You're not facing death just yet.

[WILLIE *scoops up some food on a fork and lets it drop back on to the plate again.*]

WILLIE: After I eat this, I will, I will! I'll be dead! [*Whistles*] Jim Reeves! Kaput! [DAVY *closes the door.*]

YVONNE: He should feel lucky he's getting anything.

DAVY: Now, now, don't be so harsh.

YVONNE: Harsh? Rioters and their likes should be burned at the stake.

DAVY: Your daddy wouldn't like to hear you talk like that.

YVONNE: That's why they transferred him to the quieter waters of Donaghadee.

DAVY: That's no way to be talking about a District Inspector in the RUC.

YVONNE: Look, let's have less talk about my father. Open the door.

[DAVY *opens Ambrose's door.*]

DAVY: Lunch. [AMBROSE *gets up and takes the plate and cup.* DAVY *closes the door*] Right. Since we're not talking about your father, let's talk about us.

YVONNE: There's nothing to say.

DAVY: I've got two tickets for a concert this Saturday night.

YVONNE: I know what your concerts are like.

DAVY: Do you remember you said you'd like to see your man, you know the guy that hypnotises people?
YVONNE: Oh, him. Yeah, I'd love to see him. But I'm washing my hair on Saturday night.
DAVY: Look, Yvonne. There's no need to give me answers like that. Fair enough, we haven't seen each other in over two weeks, but there's nothing to stop us trying again.
YVONNE: I'm not sure, David, I don't know.
DAVY: You're not going to say we haven't got on well over the past six months.
YVONNE: No, it's just that ... well ... we don't really have a lot in common, do we?
DAVY: Not that waffle again.
YVONNE: It's not waffle.
DAVY: Alright, so what! You come from the Upper Newtownards Road and I come from the Lower. You live in a big house, I live in a small one. Your father earns twelve thousand a year, mine works in the shipyard. So frigging what!
YVONNE: Keep it down.
DAVY [*lowers his voice*]: Well, so what?
YVONNE [*moving the trolley*]: Look, I better get this back, I'm wanted at the desk.
DAVY: Running away?
YVONNE [*stops*]: If you really want an answer—I'm going out with someone.
DAVY: Who?
YVONNE: You wouldn't know him. [*Exits with the trolley.*]
DAVY [*under his breath*]: Bitch!
[*Immediately, loud singing and guitar-playing is heard from Willie's cell.* DAVY *makes for the cell door.*]
WILLIE [*singing*]:   If I got on my knees and I pleaded with you,
    Not to go but to stay in my arms,
    Would you walk out that door
    Like you did once before?
    This time—be different—please stay.

[*After mixing up the keys,* DAVY *finally enters the cell.* WILLIE *stops singing.*]
DAVY: What's all the racket about? Where the hell do you think you are, a holiday camp? [*Takes the guitar and throws it on the bed.*]

WILLIE: Only singing, only singing!

DAVY: Well, there'll be no singing in here, right? [*He leaves and locks the door.*]

WILLIE: Aye, all right, Quaseemoto! [*Shouting*] If this guitar's broke I'm suing you for all you've got! You big girl's blouse, you.

[PETER *and* JACKIE *are still in the interview room.*]

PETER: Stanley's been around a long time. He used to tell me stories about questioning Republicans in the fifties. He knew them all. Do you know that at one time there was half-a-dozen men in this division that could speak fluent Irish?

JACKIE: It wouldn't be me. I have trouble speaking English.

[STANLEY *enters the room.*]

STANLEY: Did you get all the papers, Peter?

PETER: Right here, Stanley. [*Lifts a folder and lets it drop*] Everything you ever wanted to know about Ambrose Fogarty but were afraid to ask.

STANLEY: Good. You've both read through it?

JACKIE: Interesting reading.

PETER: Not an awful lot of hard evidence, Stanley.

STANLEY: That's nothing new. The facts are. The bank on the Andersonstown Road was robbed Thursday week ago by three men armed with a machine gun and two pistols. Fogarty was logged by an army foot patrol an hour before it in Fruithill Park—half a mile away. We have a statement from a regular contact in the Lower Falls, who says—read out the statement, read it out.

JACKIE [*reading*]: 'I saw Fogarty twice that day. The first time was about half ten in the morning. He seemed to be in a hurry. He got into a red car outside Fusco's chippie on the Grosvenor Road. I couldn't see who the driver of the car was. The second time I saw him was at about three o'clock. He drove by me in a white Datsun Estate at the top of Leeson Street. He was driving very fast. Sean McAlister was in the car with them. I never saw him for two days after it.'

STANLEY: And the bit on the other side.

JACKIE: 'I heard in the pub that McAlister went across the border because he was involved in robbing a bank or something. I never heard anything about Fogarty except that he's been keeping out of the road.'

STANLEY: All right, now. We've three days to get a statement from Fogarty, and, quite honestly, I don't care how we get it. This man has got away with far too much. I want him charged and parcelled off. I want the pressure piled on. Don't give him a chance to think. Pressure, pressure and more pressure. Any questions?

JACKIE: Heavy stuff?

STANLEY: No, no. Go through the usual procedure till we see how it goes.

PETER: It should be fun. He's already refused his photo and prints.

STANLEY: What about that?

PETER: I'm expecting it in half an hour.

STANLEY: Right. Go and get him, Jackie. I'm going to the courthouse. I'll be back shortly.

[JACKIE *enters the cell area.*]

JACKIE: The prisoner Fogarty please, Davy.

DAVY: Whatever you say, Jackie. [DAVY *sets the clipboard on the table and moves to unlock the door.* JACKIE *lifts the clipboard.*]

JACKIE: Fogarty's eating well, then?

DAVY: Yep, he ate everything we gave him.

JACKIE: We'll see if he's still cocky enough to be eating this time tomorrow. [JACKIE *sets the clipboard down.* DAVY *opens the cell door.* JACKIE *steps inside.*]

JACKIE: Come on with me, Fogarty.

[AMBROSE *and* JACKIE *go out towards the interview room.* DAVY *enters the main reception area.*]

DAVY: They have your man Fogarty away for interview, Sergeant.

KNOX: It's started, then?

DAVY: What's he in for, do you know?

KNOX: Don't know and I don't care. God knows, it's hard enough being a policeman and without getting involved in politics.

[JACKIE *and* AMBROSE *enter the interview room, where* PETER *has been waiting.*]

JACKIE: Take a seat there.

[AMBROSE *sits at one side of the table while the two policemen sit on the other. Generally,* PETER *asks the questions while* JACKIE *writes.*]

PETER: Right, Ambrose son, just a few questions till we find out a wee bit more about you. Any other first names other than Ambrose?

AMBROSE: No.
PETER: What about nicknames, any nicknames?
AMBROSE: No.
PETER: Tattoos?
AMBROSE: No.
PETER: Any scars or marks anywhere?
AMBROSE: No
PETER: Address?
AMBROSE: 202 McDonnell Street.
PETER: And your date of birth?
AMBROSE: 4th of the 11th, '53.
PETER: Married?
AMBROSE: Yes.
PETER: Children?
AMBROSE: Two.
PETER: Names.
AMBROSE: Bronagh and Conor.
PETER: Spell 'Bronagh'.
AMBROSE: B R O N A G H.
PETER: Wife's name?
AMBROSE: Christine.
PETER: Wife's maiden name?
AMBROSE: Don't know.
PETER: What? [*Silence*] You don't know your own wife's maiden name?
AMBROSE: I'm not answering that question.
PETER: Why not?
AMBROSE: It's got nothing to do with you or me being here.
PETER: Is that right? We should have your wife arrested and brought in, then? [AMBROSE *shrugs his shoulders*] What about brothers and sisters?
AMBROSE: What about them?
PETER: How many have you?
AMBROSE: I'm not answering that.
PETER: You've got an older brother, James. Now where does he live?
AMBROSE: I don't know.
PETER: You're a liar.
JACKIE: Answer the fucking question, Fogarty!
AMBROSE: I don't know where he lives.

The Interrogation of Ambrose Fogarty

[JACKIE *throws his pen down and makes to get up.*]
JACKIE: Right, I'll fuckin' well make you answer.
PETER: It's alright, alright. [JACKIE *sits down*] Ambrose isn't that stupid. He's a bright fella. He knows what's good for him. Give him a minute or two. [*Silence*] Now, Ambrose, where does your older brother James live?
AMBROSE: I don't know. [JACKIE *throws his pen down.*]
PETER: Why won't you answer?
AMBROSE: Because my brothers and sisters have nothing to do with me.
PETER: Okay, okay. What about sisters? Any married sisters?
AMBROSE: I'm not answering any more questions about my family.
JACKIE: What if we force you to?
AMBROSE: Force all you want. [JACKIE *gets up and stands over* AMBROSE.]
JACKIE: C'mere till I tell you mate. There's bigger men than you's walked in here and walked out with their tails between their legs.
PETER: On their way to the hospital wing of Crumlin Road Jail.
JACKIE: So you better buck up and start answering questions or you'll find yourself in deep trouble very, very soon.
PETER: We don't want to go to all that trouble, do we, Ambrose? I mean, we don't want to call in a half-dozen soldiers to beat the living daylights out of you, do we? We don't want to have to go and pick up your wife and throw her in one of our cells just to find out her maiden name, now do we?
JACKIE: By the way, how do you think your wife'll get on without you? Like, when you're locked up in the Kesh for 12 years, do you think she'll find enough things to do about the house? She wouldn't start running to pubs and discos, would she? Neglecting the two kids and everything?
[AMBROSE *shifts uneasily, agitated.*]
PETER: Have you any married sisters, Ambrose? [*Silence*] Well?
AMBROSE: I'm not answering any more questions about my family.
PETER: Fair enough. [PETER *nods to* JACKIE, *who leaves the room, and waits outside the door.* PETER *stands up, takes out a packet of cigarettes and comes round to sit on the table beside* AMBROSE. *He holds out the packet of cigarettes*] Smoke? [AMBROSE *looks up at the*

packet warily, then at PETER, *then back at the packet. He leans forward and takes a cigarette.* PETER *takes one himself and lights both cigarettes. He draws heavily on the cigarette before casually walking behind* AMBROSE, *kicking aimlessly at imaginary objects on the floor*]
Well, Ambrose, what are we doing with ourselves this weather?
AMBROSE: Whadaya mean?
PETER: I mean, what do you spend your time doing all day?
AMBROSE: Nothing much.
PETER: Do you take a drink?
AMBROSE: What are you getting at?
PETER: Nothing. Listen, Ambrose, I wanna get something clear before we go any further. I'm not trying to trick you into saying something you don't wanna say. I know you're far too shrewd for that oul' game.
AMBROSE: What am I in here for?
PETER: Does it have to be something in particular?
AMBROSE: You tell me.
PETER: It's nothing in particular. Just routine. Wanna cup of tea?
AMBROSE: That other guy said there was evidence against me about something.
PETER: Never listen to him. He just hates people. Do you wanna cup of tea?
AMBROSE: No.
PETER: Are you sure? I can get you one if you want.
AMBROSE: Na, you're all right, this'll do me. [*Holds up the cigarette.*]
PETER: You know, sometimes I get fed up doing this job. I'd love to be able to go to the Ireland match tonight. I always wanted to be a professional footballer anyway. Did you ever play football?
AMBROSE: Aye.
PETER: Much?
AMBROSE: All my life, up until recently.
PETER: Who for?
AMBROSE: Newsboys Club.
PETER: Many's the time I played against them. [AMBROSE *looks up, surprised.*] Remember Boyland? I played for Boyland.
AMBROSE: What age are you?
PETER: That's classified information, but I'll tell you. I was born in 1951.

AMBROSE: And when did you play for Boyland?
PETER: From I was 12 till I was 19.
AMBROSE: Jesus, I musta played against you at some stage.
PETER: When were you born, '53? Probably did. God, I used to hate playing against the Newsboys. All wee tough Fenians from York Street, ready to beat you at the drop of a hat.
AMBROSE: I wasn't from York Street and there was always a couple of Protestants in our team.
PETER: I'm sure we played against each other.
AMBROSE: Nobody'd believe it. Here I am, sitting in a police station, talking to a cop I probably played football against as a teenager? Incredible.
PETER: If you'da known then, you'da probably broke my two legs.
AMBROSE: I was never a dirty player.
PETER: Funny the way people pop up after years. I ran into a character the other day, last Tuesday it was, who used to knock about the dances with me in the 60s. Me and him used to practically live in Romano's. [AMBROSE *looks surprised*] 'Member Romano's?
AMBROSE: I don't believe this.
PETER: What, Romano's in Queen Street? We used to have the wee girls tortured in Romano's. And the Starlight.
AMBROSE: Went there , too.
PETER: Betty Staff's, the Jazz Club.
AMBROSE [*laughing*]: The Jazz Club! What a place. That used to be the drugs centre then, didn't it? Then they opened the Marquee in Hill Street. I bet you don't remember that one?
PETER: About 1966, '67. I was a real mod by then. Fancied myself as Stevie Marriott outta the Small Faces. Remember the haircuts they all had then? The middle shade, combed back from the crown of the head, all spikey.
AMBROSE: That's one thing. I never liked them stupid haircuts. Most of the ones round our way were still only coming round to accepting straight Beatle haircuts. I was always a Rolling Stones man myself. Hair down to there [*Demonstrates*] at one stage.
PETER: The 60s. They were the days. I can honestly say I enjoyed myself then. There was none of the oul' nonsense then, that you get now.
AMBROSE: '69 changed all that.

PETER: I remember the night the trouble broke out on the Falls Road. Know where I was? Driving along the Sydenham by-pass with about ten of us packed into my da's car, when it came on the news. I thought I was hearing things. People actually shooting each other in Belfast?

AMBROSE: I was supposed to be seeing a wee girl that night, from the Shankill Road would you believe. As soon as I saw the mob on the road, that was that.

PETER: Little was I to know that two years later I'd be in the RUC Reserve.

AMBROSE: With your Stevie Marriott haircut?

PETER: Huh. I'm sure you looked well with your long hair, rioting on the Falls Road.

AMBROSE: I did. Funny looking back on it now, but all the rioters in '69 and '70 seemed to be long-haired characters. It musta been a weird sight.

[PETER, *by this time, has casually positioned himself to observe* AMBROSE.]

PETER: What did you do when you got fed up rioting? [PETER *is staring shrewdly at* AMBROSE. AMBROSE *spots the implications straight away and glances up at* PETER, *then looks away.*]

AMBROSE: Whadaya mean?

PETER: Listen, Ambrose, I'm not asking anything that the whole world doesn't know. The young long-haired rioters of 1969 and '70 became the IRA of '71 and '72. Who doesn't know that? [*Silence*] You don't have to be ashamed of it. C'mon, Ambrose, you must have, at least, felt like joining the IRA?

AMBROSE: I didn't.

PETER: Never once?

AMBROSE: No.

[PETER *walks across the room.*]

PETER: Are you afraid in here, Ambrose? [AMBROSE *shrugs his shoulders*] This isn't Castlereagh, you know. And for that matter, I'm not so sure that all that much went on in Castleragh anyway. I mean, if you were to believe half the stories.

AMBROSE: Am I ... am I gonna be beat up in here?

PETER: Why should you?

AMBROSE: Why does anybody get beat up? It's an interrogation centre, isn't it?

PETER: Well, I can put your mind at rest. No, you won't be beaten up. Just co-operate. That's not much to ask. If you haven't done anything, you'll walk out, no problem. You scratch our backs and we'll scratch yours. It's as simple as that. [PETER *opens the door and* JACKIE *enters.*]

JACKIE [*harshly*]: Let's go Fogarty. [AMBROSE *stands up and* JACKIE *motions him to the door.*]

PETER: Bring me the other prisoner. Ambrose? [AMBROSE *stops and looks back*] Did you ever see the wee girl from the Shankill again?

AMBROSE: No.

PETER: Pity.

AMBROSE: Was.

[PETER *nods in agreement.*]

PETER: I enjoyed the conversation.

[JACKIE *and* AMBROSE *go out into the reception area.* DAVY *is chatting to* KNOX.]

DAVY: She wouldn't fancy a soldier, would she?

KNOX: Maybe he's the 'somebody else' she was talking about?

JACKIE: Take this man back to his cell and bring me the other prisoner.

DAVY: Right.

[DAVY *takes* AMBROSE *to the cells, where he locks him up. He opens Willie's door and brings him to* JACKIE. *During this,* JACKIE *chats to* KNOX.]

JACKIE: Well, Sergeant, how are things?

KNOX: At the moment, alright.

JACKIE: Meaning?

KNOX: Meaning, I don't expect things to remain in order in this police station over the next 72 hours.

JACKIE: Ah, you're a worrier.

KNOX: I'm also a policeman.

JACKIE: What do you think I am, a fuckin' traffic warden? I've a job to do. If you happen to bear the brunt of complaints, that's hard luck.

KNOX: If there are any complaints from any of these prisoners, I have my duty to carry out.

JACKIE: You just do that, Sergeant. If I can be of any assistance ...

[DAVY *and* WILLIE *enter.*]

DAVY: Prisoner Lagan.

JACKIE: What? This is the man involved in the rioting? You're a brave hairy-arsed Fianna boy. C'mon with me. [JACKIE *and* WILLIE *go to the interview room.*]

KNOX: Now, if they molest an unfortunate fella like that, they're capable of anything.

PETER [*in the interview room*]: The boul' Willie Lagan. Take a seat there, Willie. [JACKIE *and* WILLIE *sit down*] Well, Willie, what's all this about you leading the rioters on the Falls Road? [WILLIE *sits in silence*] Well? Willie, I am speaking to you. [WILLIE *turns his head away*] What's wrong, have you lost your tongue? Willie! If there's something wrong, why don't you tell us what it is. Why aren't you talking?

WILLIE [*abruptly*]: I'm on hunger-strike.

[JACKIE *and* PETER *look at each other, in humorous disbelief.*]

PETER: What? Did you say hunger-strike?

WILLIE: Until death! The lot! No food, no water, nothing!

PETER: You must be joking.

WILLIE: I'll be a martyr, a martyr in a fortnight. [*Whistles*] Finito!

PETER: Willie, all that we want is for you to tell us what happened that made the soldiers arrest you?

WILLIE: Big funeral, thousands, tricolour over the top of my coffin. Hunger-strike, that's it, that's it!

PETER: Willie, I'm going to ask you one question and I want an answer, or else. Did you or did you not throw bottles at the Army?

WILLIE: Hunger-strike, hunger-strike.

[JACKIE *stands up and places himself behind* WILLIE.]

PETER: Are you still not answering any questions?

[WILLIE *doesn't reply.* PETER *nods and* JACKIE *slaps* WILLIE *on the back of the head.*]

WILLIE: Which particular question was it, which one?

PETER: That's better. Here. [*Hands* WILLIE *a pen and paper.*] Write down on that, everything that happened. Why you threw the bottles at the Army. And sign it at the bottom. [WILLIE *laughs, roars and whistles.*]

WILLIE: I like, I like, I like. [*He beckons* PETER *to shake hands with him.*] Smart, smart. Bamber Gascoigne. I like, I like, I like. Sign a statement!

PETER: Take him back to his cell.

WILLIE: What, what, what! I want out.

PETER: Back to his cell. [JACKIE *stands* WILLIE *up.*]

WILLIE: I wanna see a man with a briefcase, know, a shirt-and-tie job.
PETER: You'll see a solicitor soon enough. Tell the Desk Sergeant to have his questioning handled by someone else. Tell him to give McMinn a buzz.
JACKIE: Right. Come on you.
WILLIE: Here, listen. What about my ma's tea, like?
PETER: What about your mother's tea?
WILLIE: I have the soda farls for her tea in my cell. What'll I do, what?
JACKIE: Come on. [WILLIE *shouts and protests as he is led out.*]
KNOX [*on radio*]: Return to base, Eight One, and pick up a new crew member, over.
RADIO: Roger, out.
[JACKIE *and* WILLIE *enter.*]
JACKIE: Prisoner for the cells.
DAVY: Right. [DAVY *exits with* WILLIE.]
JACKIE: Sergeant, you're requested to have Lagan's questioning handled by somebody else. He said try McMinn.
KNOX: Will do.
JACKIE: And we didn't get a copy of the arresting soldier's statement.
KNOX: I thought that was sent through.
JACKIE: We never got it.
KNOX: Yvonne? Yvonne?
YVONNE [*entering*]: Sergeant?
KNOX: What has happened that statement of the arresting soldier, in reference to the Lagan charge?
YVONNE: Sent up five minutes ago, Sergeant.
JACKIE: Thanks. Better late than never. See that McMinn gets it, Sergeant, will you? [*Exits.*]
YVONNE: What's wrong with him?
KNOX: Absolutely nothing. Civility is not included in the training of that lot.
YVONNE [*turning to go*]: Doesn't seem like it. Have you seen that Captain about, Sergeant?
KNOX: Captain?
YVONNE: You know, the arresting soldier?
KNOX: Oh, no, no. That's another one. The less I see of him the better. I'd say he's probably back out on the front line. The

rioters burned a bus a while back. [DAVY *enters*] Was it important?

YVONNE: Nothing that can't wait. [*She looks at* DAVY *and goes out.*]

DAVY: Sergeant, that man's a lunatic. He's ranting on about Bamber Gascoigne going on hunger-strike or something.

KNOX: That poor fella probably doesn't know whether he's coming or going.

DAVY: But he's a geg, isn't he? Always telling jokes. Hear the one he told me? Two Irishmen having a row. One says, 'I'm the biggest liar in the world.' The other one says, 'No, you're not, I am.' The first fella says, 'Prove it.' Your man thinks for a moment and then says, 'I've swam up the Niagara Falls.' The other fella says, 'That's nothing, I saw you doing it.'

[KNOX *and* DAVY *laugh.* DAVY *leans forward on the desk, looks about him, and speaks almost in a whisper.*]

Sergeant. Do you believe that the Special Branch really—

KNOX: CID, Davy. CID is the official term, remember.

DAVY: Well, do they actually beat people up? Like, I mean, is everything you hear about them true?

KNOX: What have you heard?

DAVY: Bits and pieces here and there.

KNOX: Good or bad?

DAVY: Both, really.

KNOX: Let me ask you something, Davy. How long are you out of Enniskillen?

DAVY: Six, 12, 18 months. One year in Dromara and the rest here.

KNOX: About how long have you been doing cell duties?

DAVY: About a month.

KNOX: Come back to me in six months and we'll have a long chat about it, if you want.

DAVY: But if there's so much—

KNOX: Not now.

DAVY: Yes, okay. Oh, ah, Sergeant? You couldn't tell me what duties Yvonne's on next week?

KNOX: I thought you'd packed that in.

DAVY: I was just wondering would we be on the same shift. I'll have to get talking to her.

KNOX: You must have the bug very bad, Davy.

DAVY: I wouldn't go as far as to say that.

[KNOX *checks a ledger.*]

KNOX: As it happens, you should just about bump into each other here and there.

DAVY: Sound, sound.

KNOX: Try and be a wee bit more discreet, Constable McFadden, would you, please? [*A loud yell is heard from Willie's cell.*]

DAVY: What's that?

KNOX: Sounds like your friend.

DAVY: I wonder what the hell's wrong now. [DAVY *hurries to Willie's cell. As he opens the cell door,* WILLIE *falls out on to the floor beside him and lies motionless. When* DAVY *leans over to pick him up,* WILLIE *makes a botched attempt to snatch the keys.* DAVY *quickly gets him to his feet, twisting Willie's arm up his back.* DAVY *speaks angrily*] What in the name of heaven are you playing at?

WILLIE: It always works for George Raft. [*Laughs.*]

[DAVY *locks* WILLIE *back in his cell as* JACKIE *arrives.*]

JACKIE: Prisoner Fogarty, please, Davy?

DAVY: Right. [DAVY *opens Ambrose's cell door.* JACKIE *steps inside*]

JACKIE: On your feet, Fogarty. [AMBROSE *stands up.* JACKIE *waves a chit of paper*] Fingerprints and photographs, Fogarty. [*He moves closer, waving the chit at Ambrose's face*] Specially signed just for you, Mr. Know-all.

[*Black-out.*]

ACT TWO

YVONNE *is busy on the radio. The prisoners are eating.*

YVONNE: If you would go to that location, Two One, and check with the lady in the house, over.
RADIO: It's definitely a B and E?
YVONNE: Yes. Entry was gained through the back door. The meter's been robbed and some items taken from a jewellery box. She only discovered it this morning and apparently she's very upset.
RADIO: We'll go there now, out.
[AMBROSE *is eating in his cell.*]
AMBROSE: I must say, I find nothing wrong with the food. But then again, as my mother used to say when I was a kid [*Mimics*] 'Our Ambrose doesn't eat to live, he lives to eat.' My da put it more bluntly, 'Our Ambrose? He'd eat shite only for the smell of it.' [AMBROSE *is enjoying his food. He feels good and is obviously amused at his current thoughts. He finishes his meal and stands up*] I don't feel too bad, not bad at all. If the next forty-eight hours is like the last twenty four ... [*Sings.*]

Baby—everything's all right, uptight.
Way outta sight, yeah.
Baby ...

What'll I do now? Have to work out something to keep the mind occupied. A pen? A pen would come in handy. Write my life story on these walls. This is Monday, isn't it? I wonder did Christine get Conor to school. Probably didn't. It's at times like these that the wee bugger plays her up. Anytime I'm away. I wonder has she ... I'm sure she's been ringing up about me. A solicitor. I wonder when they're gonna interview me again. What in the name of Jesus could it be? Probably try and bluff me into signing a statement about something or other. Probably go straight for my balls. I'll probably sign. [*Laughs*] Squeal on everybody. [*Mimics*] 'It wasn't me, Mister, it was Billy O'Neill. I only got a lift in the car.' Right. Exercises. I'll have a walt at doing some exercises. Keep me on the go. Press-ups. Try some press-ups. [*He gets down on the floor and starts doing press-up. Sings*]

Jump down, turn around, pick a bale of cottom.
Jump down, turn around, pick a bale of hay.

[*Continues singing. The* CAPTAIN *enters the main reception area.*]
CAPTAIN: Just the girl I'm looking or.
YVONNE: What do you want now?
CAPTAIN: Nothing personal, it's nothing personal. [*He stands to attention and salutes*] My commanding officer requests a copy of the statement by the arresting officer, Captain Levington, in relation to the arrest of the prisoner Lagan—Sir!
YVONNE: There are only two and they're in use at the moment.
CAPTAIN: Would it be too much to ask that the police photocopy one more and have it sent through to Major Higginbottom?
YVONNE: I'll see about it.
CAPTAIN: And while we're on the subject of requests, Yvonne, would you care to join me at the stock-car racing this weekend?
YVONNE: Stock-car racing?
CAPTAIN: Don't think I haven't heard all about you.
YVONNE: Where did you hear that?
CAPTAIN: Now, now, a copper wouldn't ask that.
YVONNE: You don't waste much time.
CAPTAIN: We're only on this earth the once. Well? Are we going to the stock-car racing? Ballymena or some place?
YVONNE: We must have done our homework.
CAPTAIN [*mimics Belfast accent*]: I was talking to a few peelers, like, know what I mean?
YVONNE [*sarcastically*]: Ha, ha.
CAPTAIN: Well?
YVONNE: I'll think about it.
RADIO: Bravo Hotel, Bravo Hotel from One One, over.
YVONNE: Send, over.
RADIO: Returning to base to drop one crew member, over.
YVONNE: Roger on that.
CAPTAIN: Wait a minute! Who is it, who does that voice remind me of? Quick, quick ... yes, got it. Faye Dunaway. If I didn't know, Yvonne, I would swear blind that I was standing here listening to Faye Dunaway.
YVONNE: Do you chat up all the girls like this?

CAPTAIN: Only the ones I fancy. Now, what do you say? Are we going to the stock-car racing or are we not?
YVONNE: I told you. I'll have to think about it.
CAPTAIN: What is there to think about?
YVONNE: I hardly know you for a start.
CAPTAIN: And how are you supposed to get to know me?
YVONNE: I told you, I'll think about it.
[DAVY *enters.*]
CAPTAIN: Oh, here's the RUC's answer to Lieutenant Theo Kojak. How's it going, Theo?
[DAVY *ignores the captain.*]
DAVY: I think the prisoners have finished their lunch, Yvonne.
YVONNE: It'll have to wait a few minutes till Sergeant Knox comes back.
CAPTAIN: Why don't you clear up the dirty plates, Theo? A supercop can do anything. [*Laughs.*]
DAVY: Have I done something on you, Captain?
CAPTAIN: Oh-oh. Kojak's getting annoyed. Better go before I get arrested. See ya, Yvonne! [*The* CAPTAIN *turns to* DAVY] Listen, Crocker, I've only got 24 hours in the day. I want every suspect on the Lower East Side in this building by ten o'clock. [*As he goes*] Who loves ya, baby!
YVONNE: I don't think you like Colin?
DAVY: Oh, we're on first-name terms are we?
YVONNE: I heard it somewhere.
DAVY: And you're right. I don't particularly like him.
YVONNE: Why not? I think he's very attractive. He's funny to talk to.
DAVY: If that's what you're looking for, why don't you go out with Billy Connolly?
YVONNE: Nasty, nasty.
DAVY: Yeah. Did you get the message your father left?
YVONNE: He was here?
DAVY: No, I was with him this morning. He told me to tell you your sister's coming back from Rhodesia in a fortnight's time.
YVONNE: Sandra! That's great. That's really great. Where was Dad?
DAVY: At 'C' Division. He, ah ... he wants me to come to your house at the weekend to finished the trench.
YVONNE: Oh. I thought he'd got somebody else to do that.

DAVY: He couldn't. He said I started it so I may as well finish it. You'll be off at the weekend?

YVONNE: Yeah, I'm going off to the stock-car racing at Ballymena.

DAVY } Who with?
YVONNE [*simultaneously*] } With a friend!

DAVY: You helped me to start the trench.

YVONNE: I won't be helping you to finish it.

[KNOX *enters.*]

Oh, Sergeant. Inspector Wright wants you to phone him and there's a message from Community Relations.

KNOX: Thanks, Yvonne. [*He lifts the telephone receiver*] Have you nothing to do, Mr. McFadden?

[PETER *and* JACKIE *enter the interview room.*]

JACKIE: I've no doubt that, only for m'da, I'd be in the UDA the day.

PETER: He stopped you?

JACKIE: Well, he made me realise that going down to Unity Flats and throwing bricks through people's windows wasn't really a devastating blow to the IRA. I was just counting up the other day. Out of our class at school, there's two dead, fourteen in the UDA, four in the UVF, three UDR and only one peeler. Fuckin' me.

PETER: There's seven of my classmates in the RUC and another two in the UDR. I don't think anybody joined the paramilitaries. There was one fella, Burrows. He robbed my father's shop and claimed the money was for the UVF. Turned out, it was to buy a blue second-hand Toyota to drive his bird about in.

JACKIE: Bangor's a wee bit quieter than the Shankill Road though, isn't it?

PETER: Except when a crowd of soldiers get a lot of firewater in them.

JACKIE: Yeah, going round chasin' all the women. The Brits used to drink on our road a lot but after a foot patrol shot dead a couple of men in a bar, it all stopped. Do you remember that time?

PETER: Vaguely.

JACKIE: Vaguely! Shows you, doesn't it. If you die in ones and twos here now, nobody remembers you. It has to be McGurk's Bar or Warrenpoint before it rings a bell, even six months later.

[STANLEY *enters.*]

STANLEY: How are we getting on, alright?

PETER: Just waiting on you.

STANLEY: Right, the report is that McAlister, who was in the car with Fogarty that day, is definitely across the border, living in Dublin. That'll be a good area to push Fogarty on. Try and shake his confidence. Is he still eating?

PETER: Never leaves a scrap. Rapped the cell door last night and asked for more chips. Wanted another cup of tea this morning.

STANLEY: No loss of appetite. Is he sleeping?

PETER: He has been sleeping well, too.

STANLEY: Well, we'll see what effect the next couple of interviews have on him. What time was that first interview at yesterday.

PETER: Two-thirty p.m.

STANLEY: So it's nearly 24 hours since his last questioning.

PETER: Twenty hours and 16 minutes to be precise.

STANLEY: He'll be dying to talk.

PETER: I've a feeling the volcano'll bubble over today. It's a long time to be on your own.

STANLEY: But it's getting him to say the right things. Get him in, Jackie. [JACKIE *goes to the cells.*]

PETER: It should be interesting to hear his excuse for being in Fruithill Park an hour before the robbery. What do you think?

STANLEY: Cutting some oul' woman's grass or something, I suppose.

PETER: No, I mean, what do you think of Fogarty?

STANLEY: He's a bastard.

PETER: Is he active in military operations?

STANLEY: Of course he is. What the hell do you think I have him in for?

PETER: But, looking at his record, it's a series of contacts and informants saying that they think he's a quartermaster, they heard he was OC, he was seen with such and such. The only thing we can say for sure is that he's active politically. He is seen with men we know are operators, and must know a certain amount about them.

STANLEY: Ambrose Fogarty is in the IRA. He's active militarily, and if you read that report again, you'll see that he was actually seen with a rifle in 1973. All those reports can't be wrong. One or two, yes, but not 17 of them, going back nearly ten years. He is in the IRA. But he's one of the clever sort. Thinks he is anyway. I'm sure he knows plenty about this robbery.

[JACKIE *enters.*]

JACKIE: Want him in?

[STANLEY *nods.* JACKIE *opens the door wide and* AMBROSE *enters.* JACKIE *exits.*]

PETER: Sit down, Ambrose. [AMBROSE *sits*] Been getting enough to eat? [AMBROSE *shrugs.* PETER *refers to a file*] Ambrose Fogarty! Public Enemy Number One. You know why you're here, don't you?

AMBROSE: Nobody's told me anything.

PETER: Where were you Thursday week ago?

AMBROSE: When was that?

PETER: Not last Thursday but the Thursday before, of course.

AMBROSE: Am ... Thursday ... week ago ... I ... a .... I'm not sure ... a ...

PETER: You work, don't you?

AMBROSE: No.

PETER: On the dole?

AMBROSE: Aye.

PETER: And you can't remember the Thursday I'm talking about? Thursday the 6th.

AMBROSE: It's difficult. I'm not sure if ...

STANLEY: Refresh your memory.

PETER: It was the day you were driving about in a white Datsun car with Sean McAlister.

AMBROSE: Yes. Yes, I remember that.

PETER: What were you doing with him?

AMBROSE: I was helping him to do a wee bit of work repairing a pub downtown.

PETER: Which pub?

AMBROSE: A pub in an entry off Ann Street. I don't know the name of it.

PETER: Which entry?

AMBROSE: There's two or three entries off Ann Street. I'm not sure which one it was, honest.

PETER: Okay. So what time did you start work at this pub and what time did you finish?

AMBROSE: Look, what is all this about?

PETER: Just answer the question.
AMBROSE: Am ... started around 11. We worked till about one or so and then we knocked off.
STANLEY: Very convenient.
PETER: What did you do then?
AMBROSE: Went to a pub.
PETER: Which one?
AMBROSE: The White Fort.
PETER: On the Andersonstown Road? What did you go away up there for?
AMBROSE: We had another job to do in the afternoon, so Sean suggested the White Fort 'cause it was near the place we were going to.
STANLEY: What position does Sean McAlister hold in your unit?
AMBROSE: What?
STANLEY: Answer the question.
AMBROSE: I'm not in any unit.
STANLEY: You're a liar.
PETER: Where was this job you had to do?
AMBROSE: Off Fruithill Park ... Glenhill Park, that's it.
PETER: What was the job?
AMBROSE: Repairing a roof.
PETER: What was the number of the house?
AMBROSE: No idea.
STANLEY: Just hold on a minute. What do you think we are? Fools? You don't know the name of the pub. You don't know what entry it was in and now you say you don't know the number of the house that you fixed a roof on?
AMBROSE: I don't remember them sort of details.
STANLEY [*shouting*]: You better start remembering!
AMBROSE: I didn't take any interest in the places. Sean did that. They were his jobs.
PETER: What do you mean?
AMBROSE: The work belonged to Sean and his brother. I was only there one day because his Joe was sick and couldn't weigh in. I'm sure Sean knows all the addresses.
PETER: Do you think we should pull McAlister in then?
AMBROSE: 'S up to you.
STANLEY: What do you mean, 'It's up to you' and you sitting there knowing fine rightly the bastard's across the border!

AMBROSE: Only for two weeks.
STANLEY: What do you mean, 'Only for two weeks'?
AMBROSE: Him and his Joe's away working in Dublin on a job for two weeks. He'll be back up this weekend as far as I know.
PETER: Tell us this, Ambrose. Were you walking along Fruithill Park at any time that day?
AMBROSE: Aye ... we parked the car outside the house we were working at and walked down to the pub.
PETER: Walked?
AMBROSE: Sean said he didn't want to go down in the car. He wanted to walk.
STANLEY: You're lying through your teeth! You mean you had a car and decided to walk instead.

STANLEY [*simultaneously*] You expect us to believe that!
AMBROSE He said he was fed up driving.

STANLEY: Eh?
AMBROSE: Sean said he was fed up driving.

[STANLEY *gets up and move round to shout into Ambrose's face.*]

STANLEY: Fed up nothing! He wasn't fed up when you and him robbed the bank on the Andersonstown Road, was he?
AMBROSE: What?
STANLEY: Yes, sonny. Don't put on your big innocent face in here. Instead of so-called working at the roof, you two reprobates spent the early part of the afternoon planning to commit a crime.
AMBROSE: You must be joking.
STANLEY: Shut up! And only speak when you're spoken to, right? You're not walking out of here this time, Fogarty. The two of you robbed that bank and McAlister's took himself off, leaving you to take the rap! [*He walks around behind* AMBROSE] That's comrades for you! You can be sure he's laughing his head off at oul' stupid Fogarty right now. Pinting it in some pub in Dublin. Now, before we waste any more time, you [*Shoves a pen and paper in front of* AMBROSE] write down there your involvement in this whole thing and let's have less of the oul' nonsense. I've had enough of you!

[*Silence.* AMBROSE *looks down at his hands.*]

PETER: Well, Ambrose?
STANLEY: Start writing.
AMBROSE: I wasn't involved in anything.

STANLEY: I said, start writing! [STANLEY *grabs* AMBROSE *by the shoulder of the coat and shakes him*] Do you not hear or what, sonny? Lift that pen! [*He lifts the pen and places it between Ambrose's fingers*] Start writing, kid! [*Silence.* AMBROSE *lets the pen fall from his hand.* STANLEY *grabs Ambrose's jaw and turns his face round to within an inch of his own*] I'm telling you for the last bloody time. Pick that pen up and write! We know you were there.

[STANLEY *steps back.* AMBROSE *stares down blankly.*]

PETER: Ambrose, what time did you say you finished working on the roof at?

AMBROSE: Around four.

PETER: Around four. And what?

AMBROSE: Went home.

PETER: Didn't go to the pub?

AMBROSE: Straight home.

PETER: With McAlister?

[AMBROSE *nods.*]

STANLEY: Where did you count the money?

AMBROSE: There was no money.

STANLEY: How much did you cop for yourself?

AMBROSE: There was no money.

STANLEY: Liar! You're a liar, Fogarty. And believe you me, we'll cut the lying out of you over the next two days.

PETER: Whereas, if you sign a statement, Ambrose, everything'll be so much easier for you. [*Silence*] Okay. Let me put it this way. Maybe you just drove the car or did the lookout. We've a fair idea it was McAlister and a few others who actually robbed the bank. All we want is for you to write down about McAlister. Tell us the names of the others involved. Right, so you did lookout or some other minor role. We can have a talk with the judge about that. Two-year suspended sentence. No more. Eh?

AMBROSE: I wasn't involved in anything.

[STANLEY *gives* PETER *the nod.* PETER *stands up.*]

PETER: It's up to yourself, Ambrose lad. You can have it the easy way or the hard way. We're only doing a job. We want it the easy way. Think about it, what? C'mon with me.

[AMBROSE *stands up.*]

STANLEY: Let me tell you something, Fogarty. We have three signed statements from three of your mates confirming membership. So, no matter what way it goes, you're getting done. If we do you on the main charge of armed robbery you'll get anything up to 14 years. Taken in possession, intent and so on. Or we could do you with membership. That's anything up to seven years. Maybe even both.

PETER: Or, as I said, you could sign for a minor part in the robbery. The judge can throw all the blame on McAlister, who's across the border, we'll drop the membership thing and you'll walk away with an 18-month suspended under your arm. Couldn't be simpler. Anyway, we'll get you back to your cell so that you can have a nice long rest.

STANLEY: To think everything over carefully.

PETER: Only another two full days to go.

[PETER *opens the door, beckons* AMBROSE *out and leaves with him.* WILLIE *starts banging on his cell door.* DAVY *opens it.*]

DAVY: What's the problem here?

WILLIE: Quick, quick! What time is it? Time?

DAVY: It's wearing round to tea time.

WILLIE: Not long to go, not long to go. Here [*holds out his parcel*], take these farls down to 95 Grosvenor Place and tell my mother I'm sorry, I'll be home late.

DAVY: What?

WILLIE: Quick. They're for my ma's tea. Quick, not long to go, not long to go.

DAVY: I thought they were for the tea yesterday?

WILLIE: Doesn't matter, doesn't matter, she mightn't've noticed. Quick, quick.

DAVY: Catch yourself on, mate. Tell me this. Why do you say everything twice?

WILLIE: Whadaya mean, whadaya mean?

DAVY: You just done it.

WILLIE: What? You trying to make fun outta me, what? I'll smack you, smack you. [*Poses*] I'll drop you like a ton of bricks, ton of bricks. Wanna use the toilet, quick piss, quick piss, know.

DAVY: Oh, c'mon.

[*Just as* WILLIE *leaves his cell,* AMBROSE *arrives, escorted by* PETER.]

PETER: Prisoner for you.

WILLIE: Ambrose! Ambrose! What about you, our kid, alright, alright?

AMBROSE: Hi, Willie.

DAVY: That's enough, back in.

WILLIE: You arrested, arrested?

DAVY: I said back inside. Back inside. [*He pushes* WILLIE *back into his cell and locks the door*] Right. [*To* AMBROSE] In you go.

[AMBROSE *is locked up while* PETER *leaves.* WILLIE *starts banging on his cell door again.* DAVY *opens it.*]

DAVY: All right, I'm coming, I'm coming!

WILLIE: That's twice you said that, twice. [*Laughs*] Go for piss nigh, go nigh?

DAVY: C'mon.

[DAVY *leaves with* WILLIE. KNOX *and* YVONNE *are at the reception desk.*]

KNOX: And you feel under pressure from your father to stay on?

YVONNE: Sort of. Let's put it this way. He doesn't tell me I have to stay on, in fact we don't even talk about it. But I know if I left the force he'd be very, very disappointed.

KNOX: That's a kind of pressure.

YVONNE: But I really want to travel while I'm still young. American, Canada, Egypt, anywhere really. What is there here? This place'll never sort itself out. You'd have more fun living on a desert island with Malcolm Muggeridge than carrying on in this place. At least, not while the IRA's allowed to do what it wants. I want out. Fast.

KNOX: Then get out. I've no doubt your father will understand.

YVONNE: You obviously don't know him well enough. My father just lives for his job. His father before him was an RIC man all his life in County Monaghan. I have no brothers, so it's me that's expected to carry on the tradition.

KNOX: If your heart's not in it ...

YVONNE: I can't just get up and go.

KNOX: Why not? Yvonne, let me give you a word of advice. My mother, God have mercy on her, lived till she was 92 and never saw further than Castlereagh Hills. You're what—22, 23? Get away out of this and have a look around you while you have nothing to tie you down. Go and see how the rest of the world lives. There's over 150 countries and as many languages, religions and traditions. But don't—whatever you do—don't spend the rest of your life regretting that you didn't do it. And don't stay at this game—especially if your heart's not in it.

YVONNE: Is yours?

KNOX: Yeah, strangely enough it is. I'm a bit like your father. I actually like the job.

YVONNE: But do you not get disheartened when you don't see yourself getting anywhere? No end to the troubles? You've been at this station, I don't know how long, and the people outside that front gate still resent you.

KNOX: That's probably the thing that gets me most. I'd love to walk out there one day on my own. Dander up the road a bit and some wee woman come up to me and say 'Good morning, Sergeant Knox', or some such trivial greeting. That would mean a lot to me.

YVONNE: As it is, you're more likely to get your head blown off.

KNOX: Many's a man I knew well. You know, every time word comes in or one of the lads being shot dead or blown up, I experience it all myself. I feel the pain, see the blood and can't help but harbour the bitterness. And I feel the fear. Every single time. The fear that it might be Sergeant Trevor Knox, number 15537, the next time round.

YVONNE: When I get to America, I'll send you an application form for the the New York Police Department.

KNOX: No thanks. I joined long before the troubles started. There's no point in leaving now. I'm a policeman. Belfast, Birmingham or Baltimore. That's it. Just get on with your job. Nothing else for it.

RADIO: Bravo Whisky Nine One to Bravo Hotel. Bravo Whiskey Nine One to Bravo Hotel, over.

YVONNE: Well, you can count me out. [*She moves over and answers the radio*] Nine One, send over.

[KNOX *laughs and returns to some paperwork.*]

RADIO: Permission to contact Alfa Romeo, over.

YVONNE: Go ahead, Nine One, over.

[WILLIE *and* DAVY *enter.*]

WILLIE: Sure that's nothing, they've decided to build a swimming pool round our way. The committee came to my door last week collecting for it.

DAVY: And did you give them anything?

WILLIE: Aye, a bucket of water!

AMBROSE [*walking in a figure-of-eight round his cell*]: '62 winners were Tottenham. Team was Brown, Baker, Henry, Norman ...

No, Brown, Baker, Henry, *Blanchflower*, Norman. McKay, Medwin, White, Greaves—no, Jimmy Greaves wasn't in that team. Smith, Allen, I think, and Cliff Jones. I wonder was Dyson there? '63 winners were Manchester United. Team was Gaskill, Dunne, Brennan—no, I wonder was that the team ... Hold on ... Frig it ... I don't know. I'll come back to that ...

Back to Heavyweights. Where was I ... 1929 ... Jack Dempsey versus Gene Tunney ... [*Sing.*] 'Now he's gonna fight Jack Dempsey/That was brother Silvest ...'

Tunney beat Dempsey, right. That was the famous 'long count' fight. Tunney retired undefeated. Then there was Irishman James J. Braddock ... [*Stops.*] I definitely reckon the last interview went okay. At least nobody got really violent. Maybe your man was right. Maybe I won't be beat up. I'd hate to have the back of my hair pulled. [*He stretches his hand up and tugs at the front of his hair. He then does the same with the hair at the lower back of his head. He immediately winces*] I don't think I could take too much of that. Torture, starvation, brutality, yes, but the leave the back of my hair alone, please. 'Excuse me, you wouldn't start pulling out my finger nails one by one and leave the back of my hair alone?' I'll never forget the Christian Brother. Gibbons his name was. Trailed me out to the front of the class regularly, by the back of the hair. Tears welled in my eyes, but there was no way I was gonna make a sound in front of the rest of the class. [*Laughs*] Not like Dominic O'Reilly. Or Phoenix. Ach, what am I talking abut. I'm still alive. I think it's gonna be all right. I think I can manage. I'm sure it's all in the mind. I think I can afford a lie down. [*He moves down on to the bed*] Now, who took the title off Braddock? Max Baer, yes, Max Baer, around 19 ... 34 ...

[STANLEY *and* PETER *enter the interview room.*]

STANLEY: The next two days are crucial, Peter. I want you to make sure this fella's kept in complete isolation. No cellmates, no newspapers, no news, no conversation whatsoever outside this room. I don't want him to know what time of the day or night it is.

PETER: But those are all standard regulations.

STANLEY: I know that. But I want you to check that they're being carried out to the letter. I want this man. [JACKIE *enters the cell area and collects* AMBROSE] After this interview, I want to check out his story. Find out which bar off Ann Street has had repairs carried out. Get somebody to have a look at every single roof in Glenhill Park, and find out if any work's been done there. And, just on the off-chance, check on the McAlisters. See what the family says about the two brothers going to Dublin. One good break's all we need, and this fella's story will collapse around his ears.

[JACKIE *pushes open the interview room door and enters with* AMBROSE.]

PETER: I'm beginning to agree with you. I think it's one big cock-and-bull story.

STANLEY: You better believe it. Right, I'll leave you two to it. I'll be about. [*Exit.*]

PETER: Ambrose! My oul' son. How's the world treating you, eh? Take a wee seat there. [AMBROSE *sits.* PETER *turns to* JACKIE] Did you hear about Ambrose's last interview?

JACKIE: No, what?

PETER: He sat and spun a load of lies.

JACKIE: Did he?

PETER: I nearly burst out laughing a couple of times, it was that funny.

JACKIE: A bit of a comedian, is he?

PETER: Hysterical.

[JACKIE *takes off his coat and rolls up his sleeves.*]

JACKIE: Well, we'll soon see if he knows any new jokes, 'cause I'm not in form to listen to jokes [*Leans into Ambrose's face*] from anybody! Especially from a no-good bank-robber! A thief!

[JACKIE *stands behind* AMBROSE.]

PETER: Right, Ambrose, from the start. Tell me everything you did on Thursday the 6th.

AMBROSE: Again?

JACKIE: And every time you tell a lie, I'm gonna knock your bollocks in. Have you got that?

[AMBROSE *looks at* JACKIE, *then stares straight in front.*]

PETER: Go ahead, Ambrose. From the moment you got up.

AMBROSE: I've already told yiz.

PETER: We forget. So tell us again.

AMBROSE: I was working that day with Sean McAlister.

JACKIE: Operations Officer in the Lower Falls.

AMBROSE: We did a job in a pub and—

PETER: What time did you start at?
AMBROSE: About eleven o'clock but—
JACKIE: Where was the pub?
AMBROSE: Off Ann Street. I told—
JACKIE: What was the name of it, and if you say you don't know I'm gonna punch you. [*Silence.*]
AMBROSE: I don't know.
[JACKIE *slaps Ambrose's face.*]
PETER: What work did you do in this pub?
AMBROSE [*agitated*]: Plastered the walls in the toilets.
PETER: I didn't know you were a plasterer.
AMBROSE: I'm not. I just laboured to Sean.
PETER: Then what?
AMBROSE: Went to a pub.
PETER: What time did you finish work in the pub?
AMBROSE: About one.
PETER: And you went to another pub round the corner?
AMBROSE: No, on the Andersonstown Road. The White Fort.
JACKIE: What to fuck were you doing up there?
AMBROSE: Having a drink before our next job.
JACKIE: The bank?
AMBROSE: Repairing a roof.
JACKIE: Where?
AMBROSE: Glenhill Park, off Fruithill.
JACKIE: That's the street facing St. Teresa's Chapel?
AMBROSE: Aye. It's—
JACKIE: Which house?
AMBROSE: I'm not sure of the number.
JACKIE: What about the name of the family?
PETER: Are you joking? The way Ambrose has this story worked out, it doesn't allow for names of streets, or pubs, or numbers of houses, and definitely not names of families.
JACKIE: What was the name of the family?
AMBROSE: I don't know.
PETER: Ambrose, do you have a permanently bad memory?
AMBROSE: No, I just remember the things I'm interested in.
PETER: What time did you finish there at?
AMBROSE: I think it was about three.
PETER: Is that right?
AMBROSE: Yeah, about three.

PETER: You're definite about that?
AMBROSE: I couldn't tell you the exact time, but I think it was around three.
JACKIE: That proves it, doesn't it.
AMBROSE: Proves what?
JACKIE: Proves that everything that comes out of your mouth is lies. Because 15 minutes ago you told us you finished work at four o'clock. Now you're saying three. Which is it, lad?
PETER: Was it three or four, Ambrose?
JACKIE: You'd better make up your mind. If you're gonna tell lies, at least stick to the same lie!
AMBROSE: I'm not telling any lies.
JACKIE: What's that then, a slip of the tongue?
AMBROSE: It's nearly two weeks ago. As far as I can remember, we finished about three o'clock.
[PETER *stands up.*]
PETER: Ambrose, stand up. [AMBROSE *looks uncertain*] I said, on your feet. [AMBROSE *stands up.*] Move out to the middle of the room. [AMBROSE *takes a few steps*] Hands down straight by your side. [AMBROSE *responds*] Did you say you were married?
AMBROSE: Yes
PETER: Does your wife enjoy it?
JACKIE [*laughing*]: Enjoy it? That dying-looking bastard couldn't satisfy our budgie.
PETER: Is that right, Ambrose?
AMBROSE: What?
PETER: Can you not satisfy your wife?
JACKIE: Listen, mate, you've just been asked a question, would you like to answer it? [*Silence*]
PETER: He'd probably tell us a pack of lies anyway.
JACKIE: I bet you his willie's not the size of my wee finger.
PETER: Is that right, Ambrose? Is that right? Answer me.
AMBROSE: I'm not answering any personal questions. [*Silence*]
PETER: Take off your clothes. [AMBROSE *looks at him sharply. He stares disbelievingly*] Everything. Take off all your clothes, Ambrose.
JACKIE [*laughing*]: This should be fun. I should've brought my telescope with me.
PETER: Take off his coat for him. [JACKIE *roughly takes Ambrose's coat off him*] Now, Ambrose, I believe in democracy, I'm giving

you the choice of taking your own clothes off, or he takes them off for you.

AMBROSE: You must be joking.

PETER: Do you think so? Take off his shoes. [JACKIE *takes off Ambrose's shoes*] Now, to get to the point. Are you gonna sign a statement about the robbery, or do we strip you naked and leave you standing here for a couple of hours?

AMBROSE: I can't tell you anything about any robbery, 'cause I didn't do anything.

PETER: Membership?

AMBROSE: I'm not a member of anything.

PETER: You *are* going to be stripped naked, Ambrose. Last chance. Membership? [AMBROSE *remains silent*. PETER *nods*. JACKIE *jumps forward and loosens Ambrose's trousers, allowing them to fall to his ankles.*] Now, Ambrose. You do look silly. I'm sure you feel silly. Do you? Which item would you prefer us to take off next, Ambrose?

JACKIE: The lot! Strip the bastard now!

PETER: Ambrose, the ball's in your court. Wanna sign now? [AMBROSE *does not answer*] Very last chance, kid, before we bare you to the elements.

JACKIE: I'll strip everything off ...

PETER: One! Last chance. [*Sings*] 'Ambrose. You're gonna be stripped naked.' I'm gonna do a count-down, Ambrose, and if you haven't responded by zero, I'm afraid it's tough luck. [*To* JACKIE] Ready? [*To* AMBROSE] Ready? Five. Four. Three. Two. One. [*Pause*] Zero!

[JACKIE *dives forward to remove Ambrose's underpants*. AMBROSE *struggles.*]

Ambrose, how far are you gonna carry on this charade?

AMBROSE: I'm not carryin' anything on.

PETER: Are you not? Sit down. [AMBROSE *moves towards the chair*] Not there. Just sit where you were standing. [AMBROSE *hesitates.*]

JACKIE: He said sit down!

[*Pushes* AMBROSE *down by the shoulder, leaving him sitting on the floor.*]

PETER: Alright now? [AMBROSE *looks disgusted*] You don't really look comfortable. Lie back. Come on, make yourself comfortable. [JACKIE *makes for* AMBROSE *but he is already leaning back. He* *lies motionless on the floor*] Is that better? Yes, you look more comfortable now. Any complaints?

AMBROSE: My back's sore.

PETER: His back's sore. No problem. I know an old Indian trick. Turn over on your stomach. [AMBROSE *doesn't move.* PETER *steps forward and prods* AMBROSE *with his foot once or twice*] That's it, roll over. [AMBROSE *rolls over, flat on his stomach*] Right now, back-soothing time. [PETER *steps on to Ambrose's back. He walks back and forward, stopping to prod here and there.* AMBROSE *winces in pain*] Is that any better Ambrose? The pain away yet? [PETER *places one foot on Ambrose's head. He applies some pressure*] Feel like doing a spot of writing yet, Ambrose? A couple of sentences or so?

JACKIE: Trail him up and we'll knock his ramp in now.

[PETER *steps down off* AMBROSE. AMBROSE *immediately rolls over, pulls his trousers up, and gets to his feet.*]

PETER: Who gave you permission to get up? Oh, I see you wanna make a statement. How stupid of me. C'mon, sit down, Ambrose.

[AMBROSE *sits on the chair.* PETER *hands him some paper and a pen.*]

AMBROSE: Can I put on my shoes?

PETER: Why not?

AMBROSE: And you told me there wasn't gonna be any violence.

PETER: You call that violence?

JACKIE: Wait till we really start.

[AMBROSE *puts on his shoes.*]

PETER: Now, what are you going to write for us? [*Silence*] Worked it out yet?

AMBROSE: I've nothing to write about.

PETER: Take the prisoner to his cell.

JACKIE: What? Let me knock his—

PETER: Take him away.

[JACKIE *puts on his coat.*]

JACKIE: Come on, ballocky Bill.

[JACKIE *grabs* AMBROSE *roughly to his feet.*]

PETER: Before you go, I want you to think about something. Ambrose, I have tried, we have all tried, to show you the easy way out of this. Throughout three interviews, you've had every chance to respond. From this moment onwards, it's a weeping and a gnashing of teeth. Somebody's gonna get hurt.

Somebody has to lose. This system tends to produce losers. See ya.

[JACKIE *opens the door. He pushes* AMBROSE *out and throws his coat after him.* PETER *goes.* JACKIE *hands* AMBROSE *over to* DAVY *at the desk.* DAVY *puts* AMBROSE *in his cell and locks it.* YVONNE *enters.*]

YVONNE: I have been asked to ask you to help me shift some files from the back office.

[DAVY *and* YVONNE *go.* AMBROSE *has been standing motionless in the centre of his cell. Suddenly he lashes out and kicks the chair over.*]

AMBROSE: Bastards! Bastards! [*He moves quickly to the bed*] I'm not going through that again! No way! [*He starts pulling the bed out from the wall*] At least not voluntarily anyway. Bastards! They can fight me for it. The next time they come for me they're gonna have to trail me out—unconscious! [*He upends the bed towards the cell door*] Put up with that? Some chance! [*He positions the bed to block the doorway*] I mightn't win but I'm not gonna stand around to be treated like a hunted animal. [*He grips the chair and lifts it off the ground*] I'm gonna cleave the head off the first bastard come through that door. [*Shouts*] The first fucker comes in this cell's getting the head cleaved off him! Man, woman or child! Come on! What's wrong with yiz? Scared? You yellow bastards! Yiz are all right in twos and threes, but there's not one of yiz man enough to stand up on your own!

WILLIE: Who's that, who's that?

AMBROSE: Hey, fat ballocks! You down there! Come you down here and I'll start with you!

WILLIE: What? What'd I do, what'd I do?

[AMBROSE *puts the chair down and moves over to the bed.*]

AMBROSE: Is that you, Willie?

WILLIE: No problem, Ambrose. Me, me, me.

AMBROSE: What are you doing in here?

WILLIE: On holiday. Mini-weekend away from the troubles. [*Laughs*] All meals inclusive. [*Laughs.*]

AMBROSE: But what have they you in for?

WILLIE: Nothin', nothin'. Picked on me for nothin'.

AMBROSE: They picked on me too, Willie, but they've picked on the wrong man this time. I've barricaded my cell. The first peeler comes through the door's getting the head cleaved off him.

The Interrogation of Ambrose Fogarty

WILLIE: Magic, magic. I like, I like. Which hospital do you think they'll take you to? [*Laughs.*]

AMBROSE: I don't care. They're not gonna treat me like an oul' dog and get away with it. Here, Willie. Listen, Willie. If anything does happen to me, you inform my wife as soon as you get out, will you?

WILLIE: No problem, no problem.

AMBROSE: You won't forget now?

WILLIE: No problem. She'll be delighted to hear you stood up to the Branchmen. Bully Ambrose. Magic, magic. I'll tell her, I'll tell her.

[AMBROSE *comes away from the door slowly. A fresh thought has struck him. He looks back round at the makeshift barricade. He jumps back to the door.*]

AMBROSE: Hey! Hey, Willie! Willie Lagan! [*He frantically trails the bed away from the door*] Willie!

WILLIE: Yes, yes.

AMBROSE: Listen, scrub what I just told you. Don't say anything to my wife.

WILLIE: What? [AMBROSE *pulls the bed back towards its original position, up against the wall*] Ambrose, what?

AMBROSE: Willie, don't tell me wife anything. Forget what I just told you.

WILLIE: You drunk, drunk?

AMBROSE: Look, listen. If you do run into Christine, Willie, tell her I'm alright.

WILLIE: What about the barricade, what?

AMBROSE: The barricade's away. Tell her you were talking to me and that I said everything's alright. Will you do that?

WILLIE: Right, right, no problem, our kid. I'll see her. [AMBROSE *tidies up the cell. He stands the chair up, grips it momentarily, then places it against he walls.* WILLIE *shouts*] Ambrose! Ambrose!

AMBROSE: What? [DAVY *enters the cell corridor.*]

WILLIE: Are you, are you allowed to wank in here?

[AMBROSE *falls on the bed laughing.*]

DAVY: Alright, alright, shut it up down there.

[*He strides towards the cells and checks on the prisoners.* STANLEY, PETER *and* JACKIE *enter the interview room.*]

JACKIE: That Fogarty's a cheeky bastard. Asked me to try and get him a pen and newspaper on the quiet.

STANLEY: Peter, is he being kept isolated?
PETER: 'Course he is.
STANLEY: Definitely?
PETER: Definitely. Except ...
STANLEY: Except what?
PETER: Except, when I returned him to his cell earlier on, that stupid idiot, Constable McFadden, allowed him to see another prisoner who knew him. It wasn't my fault.
STANLEY: What?
PETER: Lucky enough, it's only that nut they have in for rioting. Lagan, his name is.
JACKIE: That raker!
STANLEY: Jesus Christ. I left specific instructions. How do they know each other?
PETER: I don't know.
JACKIE: They live beside each other. I was looking at Lagan's statement. He lives in Grosvenor Place and our fella lives around the corner in McDonnell Street.
STANLEY: Get him.
JACKIE: What?
STANLEY: Get the other fella.
JACKIE: The raker, Lagan?
STANLEY: Yes. Get him over here straight away.
JACKIE: Whatever you say. [JACKIE *goes to the cells.*]
PETER: What do you think?
STANLEY: You never know. This fella might know one or two things about Fogarty that could be vital to us. You say he's being held on a riot charge?
PETER: Seems a bit flimsy to me. A load of young lads, you know, the usual mob, were attacking the station yesterday after a protest march and one of the soldiers claims that Lagan was in the thick of it. I mean, no matter how far you stretch it, he hardly fits the bill as an IRA godfather.
STANLEY: Hardly, but we can make it stick if necessary. It'll do nicely as a big stick to beat this fella with, to get some information out of him.
PETER: I'm warning you, he's not the full shilling.
STANLEY: How many of them are?
[STANLEY *exits.* DAVY *opens Willie's cell door.* JACKIE *enters the cell.*]
JACKIE: Right, Slim Whitman, let's have you on your feet.

[WILLIE *jumps to his feet, both hands stabbing the air above him.*]
WILLIE: I like, I like. No problem. [WILLIE *starts dancing round the cell, strumming an invisible guitar. Then he sings*]
 Freedom is a word I rarely use
 Without thinking, without thinking.
JACKIE: Don't be getting excited, Slim. You're only going for another interview.
WILLIE [*immediately forlorn*]: Ah fuck, ah fuck.
JACKIE [*taking* WILLIE *by the arm*]: C'mon, let's go.
WILLIE [*bending down to lift his guitar*]: What about m'guitar?
JACKIE: You can leave that. We're only going round the corner.
 [JACKIE *and* WILLIE *leave the cell.*]
WILLIE: I'm not being released then, no release?
JACKIE: Did you ever hear of Rudolf Hess?
WILLIE: Yes, yes. Nazis. [*Salutes*] Hitler.
JACKIE: Well, you'll be stuck away that long, we're thinking of putting you in along with him.
WILLIE: Ah fuck, ah fuck. [*Sings*] 'Please release me, let me go ...'
JACKIE: Shut up, you idiot, this isn't the Grand Ole Oprey. [*They enter the interview room.* JACKIE *turns to* PETER] Have you got a box of Aspros? You'll be eating them in handfuls before we're finished with this lad.
PETER: Come in, Willie son. Sit down, make yourself at home. Smoke?
WILLIE: Don't smoke, don't smoke, but I'd take a pint of double. [*Starts laughing.*] A pint of double. I like, I like.
PETER: Willie, if I had a pint of double to give you, I'd give you it.
WILLIE: Would you fuck, would you fuck. You're a Branchman, peeler. [*Laughs.*] I'm no mug!
PETER: How do you know Ambrose Fogarty?
WILLIE [*thinks for a second*]: Pass. Pass, by-ball.
 [WILLIE *roars with laughter.* JACKIE *walks around and grabs* WILLIE *by the back of the hair.* WILLIE *lets out a yell.*]
JACKIE: Fun time's over, Willie! Answer the question!
WILLIE: Alright, alright. Watch the head.
PETER: Ambrose Fogarty, Willie?
WILLIE: He lives round our way, McDonnell Street, round the corner.
PETER: What does he do?

WILLIE: Cheats at cards, cards up his sleeve.

PETER: Besides cheating at cards, do you ever see him knocking about?

WILLIE: Yes, yes. He knocks about with a big one from New Barnsley, separated she is, separated.

JACKIE: Listen. Do you realise the seriousness of this situation? You are in a police station and you're being asked questions by police officers. You can be charged with withholding information if you don't start answering questions.

WILLIE: Okay, you win, you win. Ask me another. Fingers on the buzzers. [*Presses his finger on the table and laughs.*]

PETER: Willie, I'm gonna ask you a serious question.

JACKIE: And we want a serious answer.

WILLIE: Completely serious?

JACKIE: Totally serious.

PETER: Is Ambrose Fogarty in a terrorist organisation?

WILLIE: Yes.

JACKIE: That's more like it.

WILLIE: Yes. He's a committee member of the Lower Falls Darts Team.

JACKIE: And they're terrorists?

WILLIE: Well, they have me terrorised anyway! [*Laughs*] I'm barred from their club for life for calling the chairman a no-good, wasting, bastarding parasite! Imagine! Life! I can't throw a dart ever again because I had a dopey row with the chairman, what, what? Life? Isn't it just as well they're not the government in power? They'd hang you for falling behind in your rent!

PETER: I take it you don't like this chairman?

WILLIE: Bastard, bastard. He brought me in front of the committee and sentenced me to life. Said I could appeal in 1990! Nineteen fucking ninety! Wee bastard. I fixed him, I fixed him. [*Laughs.*]

PETER: What did you do?

WILLIE: Well, he owns this prize greyhound bitch, smashing dog, smashing dog, call 'Lightning Strikes', 'Lightning Strikes'. It won its last eight races in a row at Dunmore. Three thousand pound, three thousand pound in prize money. Champion bitch, champion bitch. Well, I climbed over his yard wall in the early hours of the morning and mated his dog with our oul' mongrel, Rocky. [*Roars*] And any other oul' fleabeg there was knocking about too! [*Roars*] I soon made short work of 'Lightning Strikes'. He lets it run about the district now, like an oul' stray. [*Roars.*]

PETER: Did he ever find out who did it?

WILLIE: I suppose he has his suspicions. [*More laughter.*]

PETER: Willie.

WILLIE: That's me, that's me.

PETER: Willie, I like your crack, but we still need one or two questions answered.

WILLIE [*sings*]: There are more questions than answers.
And the more I find out—the less I know.

Good singer me, good singer.

PETER: Willie, I'm gonna put you back in your cell now. But tomorrow the boss will be here and he won't be happy with all your jokes. He's a very tough man. So you'd need to answer any questions he asks you. Is that clear?

WILLIE: Clear, clear.

JACKIE: Or it'll be that there. [*Holds up fist.*]

PETER: All right. You're not worried then?

WILLIE: Worried? [*Gets up, plays an imaginary guitar and sings*]
It takes a worried man to sing a worried song
[*Moves towards the door*]
It takes a worried man to sing a worried song
It takes a worried man to sing a worried song
I'm worried now but I won't be worried long.

[WILLIE *leaves followed by* JACKIE. JACKIE *slaps* WILLIE *on the back of the head.* PETER *gathers his papers and exits.* WILLIE *and* JACKIE *reach the cells, where* DAVY *is waiting.*]

JACKIE: Lock this maniac up, will you. [WILLIE *starts singing the song again as* DAVY *locks him up*] Here, open this door a minute. I want a word with this man. [DAVY *opens Ambrose's cell door.* AMBROSE *is sitting on his bed. His eyes fix on the door at the sound of it opening*] Good news for you, Fogarty, I just thought I'd call in and let you know. We've just interviewed your cell neighbour. Bit of a Country-and-Western singer. In fact, he's a very good singer. He seems to have a lot to say about you. What is it they say in the movies? 'He's singing like a canary.'

[*Black-out.*]

ACT THREE

YVONNE *enters and approaches the interview room door. She has her arms wrapped around a number of folders and papers, clutched to her chest.*
As she reaches to open the door, CAPTAIN LEVINGTON *enters nearby, rather slyly. Just as* YVONNE *enters the room and turns on the light, the* CAPTAIN *sneaks up behind her, knocks the light off and slips his arms round Yvonne's waist.*
YVONNE *is completely taken by surprise and shock.*

CAPTAIN: Hello, Yvonne.
[YVONNE *squeals and jumps forward out of his grasp before looking round to identify the* CAPTAIN.]
YVONNE: Good God, Colin! You frightened the life out of me. Put the light on quickly!
CAPTAIN [*moving towards her*]: Don't be in such a rush, kid.
[*He takes the papers off her and set them down on the table.*]
YVONNE: What are you doing, Colin?
CAPTAIN: Nothing that doesn't come completely natural to me.
[*He puts his arms around her.*]
YVONNE: Please, Colin, someone'll be coming in here any minute for those papers.
CAPTAIN: There's no one here now.
[*By now, the* CAPTAIN *has edged* YVONNE *back against the door. He leans his mouth forward to kiss her.*]
YVONNE: Not now, Colin. [*He kisses her. She responds and they kiss and embrace passionately.* YVONNE *breaks off*] Please, Colin, not now. Someone's bound to catch us on. I'll— [*He kisses her again. She again responds. He then begins to touch and caress her body. She breaks away again*] Oh Colin, please! [*He forces another kiss. Suddenly a loud noise is heard nearby. It sounds like a door slamming*] Someone's coming.
CAPTAIN: Shit!
[YVONNE *immediately breaks away from the* CAPTAIN, *turns the light on and hurries to the other side of the room.*]
YVONNE: It's alright for you. I work here.

CAPTAIN: But there's no one coming. Listen, it's quiet again. Come on, Yvonne.
[*He makes advances again. She moves away.*]
YVONNE: No. No. Not now, Colin. Later on, some other time.
CAPTAIN: Like when?
YVONNE: Later. [*She opens the door.*]
CAPTAIN: Where are you going?
YVONNE: I'm only leaving the door open in case someone comes. They'll see we're only talking. Anyway, you should be able to control yourself until Friday night.
CAPTAIN: Yeah.
YVONNE: You did say you were taking me to the stock-car racing?
CAPTAIN: Yeah, I know what I said. [*He lights up a cigarette.*]
YVONNE: You mean it's off?
CAPTAIN: I didn't say that. When did you say it was?
YVONNE: Friday night.
CAPTAIN: You off?
YVONNE: I can arrange it. Colin?
CAPTAIN: Yeah.
YVONNE: Do you still mean what you said, I mean earlier, when you talked about the summer.
CAPTAIN: Oh crikey. What do you think? Do you think I just go about telling lies?
YVONNE: No, of course not. I'm not saying that. It's just that ... well ... I am very serious about travelling.
CAPTAIN: I told you. There are four hotels. Two in France and two in Spain. My brother's out there now. I mean, I'm only here because my dad insisted on me getting a good grounding in the army before going into the family business. This is my last month. In two weeks I'm off.
YVONNE: You've still to leave me the address.
CAPTAIN: Yeah. Like, if you did decide to come over, you would have to work hard. Dad isn't the type to allow even his own family favours. If anything, he works us harder.
YVONNE: I wouldn't mind hard work.
CAPTAIN: It would probably only be receptionist or something. But at least you would be eating. And seeing a bit of the world.
YVONNE: Not to mention the sun.
CAPTAIN: Not to mention the sun.
YVONNE: This is ridiculous. Absolutely ridiculous.

CAPTAIN: What is?

YVONNE: I bet that if I really did arrive down on top of you in some hotel in France, you'd turn and run the other way.

CAPTAIN: Don't talk rubbish. Look. [*He produces a picture and shows it to her*] If you arrive before the 25th, you'll get me there.

YVONNE: Where's this?

CAPTAIN: A place called Marseilles. It's down south.

YVONNE: I know where Marseilles is.

CAPTAIN: Well anyway, after the 25th I could be anywhere. But I don't think you've any real intentions of leaving this place in the first instance.

YVONNE: Wanna bet?

CAPTAIN: Yvonne, I've met your type a dozen times before. Big ideas. Big plans. And a big mouth. You can't just walk away from this job and you know it. Your old man wouldn't let you for a start.

YVONNE: I make my decisions.

CAPTAIN: You're just a plain, simple, Irish girl who'll never see any further than her nose, never mind the south of France.

YVONNE: I'm not Irish.

CAPTAIN: Well, you're not fucking English.

YVONNE: Don't be so bloody ignorant, Colin.

CAPTAIN: All right, I'm only joking.

YVONNE: I don't see the funny side of it. And I didn't like the way you just came storming in here, pawing over me, I'm not—

CAPTAIN: Alright. I'm sorry, I'm sorry. Don't get your knickers in a twist. Must get back now, duty calls. I'll see you on Friday night then?

YVONNE: You might.

CAPTAIN: Oh my God, I said I was only joking. [YVONNE *remains indignantly silent*] Wait a minute. I know what's wrong with you. Yeah. Not only are you afraid to leave this bloody place but I suspect you're still attached to that carrot-face, Constable McFadden.

YVONNE: Maybe I am. Maybe I am. I don't see how that's any of your business.

[DAVY *enters and walks towards the interview room.*]

CAPTAIN: Poor Yvonne. I can see it all in front of you. You'll marry carrot-face, have a couple of kids and live happily ever after in bleeding, boring Belfast.

YVONNE: I might just do that.

CAPTAIN: Yes, Yvonne, love, you just do that. [DAVY *enters the room. The* CAPTAIN *turns, walks into* DAVY *and smiles broadly*] Hello, Davy!

[*The* CAPTAIN *exits.* DAVY *stares at* YVONNE *for a moment. He sees the two undone buttons of her shirt.*]

DAVY: Sorry I missed the party.

[YVONNE *hurriedly does up the buttons.*]

YVONNE: Oh Davy, I was ... I was just in here leaving in some papers when the Captain—

DAVY: Yeah, it looks just like that.

YVONNE: Don't be stupid, Davy, the Captain— [DAVY *turns sharply and exits*] But Davy ... Davy!

[*She stops in the room for a few seconds, looks perplexed, then hurries off stage.* SERGEANT KNOX *is at reception, using the radio.*]

KNOX: Bravo Hotel, Bravo Hotel to Five One, over. Bravo Hotel, Bravo Hotel to Five One, over.

RADIO: Hotel, send, over.

KNOX: Five One, would you go to the owner of the chip shop referred to earlier and inform him that his car has been located in Alpha Quebec's patch, over. You might also inform him that we were unable to recover the box of pasties he was going on about.

RADIO: Will do, roger out.

[DAVY *enters.*]

KNOX: Davy, take over here for a while, till I go and find Yvonne, will you?

DAVY: Check the soldiers' sleeping quarters.

KNOX: And what sort of remark is that to make?

DAVY: I've just ... Do you know what I've just ... Ach, it doesn't matter. She'll get her come-uppance with that character.

KNOX: I take it you're talking about the captain?

DAVY: Who else?

KNOX: I agree with you about him, but I think you're being very unfair to Yvonne.

DAVY: I don't.

KNOX: I suppose that tone of voice suggests you haven't managed to get her to out with you again?

DAVY: It's not for the want of trying. I've asked her dozens of times. I've went out of my way to coax her, but she won't wear it.

KNOX: Maybe that's your problem.

DAVY: What?

KNOX: Trying to hard. Maybe it's time to ease off a wee bit and then she might begin to wonder.

DAVY: I don't know now if I even want to see her again.

KNOX: Ach, I wouldn't let it get me down. Your best bet is to let Yvonne run on for a while. I guarantee you she'll not be long catching herself on.

DAVY: She's gone past that stage.

KNOX: Look, didn't she say she was going to the stock-car racing on Friday night? Your move is to turn up there with big Veronica out of Drugs, and act like you're having a great time.

DAVY: Big Veronica out of the Drugs Division?

KNOX: The very one.

DAVY: Oh, I couldn't do that. That would cause problems.

KNOX: How?

DAVY: I like a wee smoke of marijuana myself, now and again.

[*Both men laugh.* KNOX *goes.* PETER *and* JACKIE *enter from the street.* JACKIE *looks at the incident books while* PETER *lifts a file from a table.*]

JACKIE: To tell you the truth, I was glad to see her going in. She had me up half the night, every night for a month. Hiya, Davy.

PETER: I know the feeling.

JACKIE: How many have you now?

PETER: One boy and one girl and it's more than enough.

JACKIE: That's my fourth.

PETER: Jesus Christ.

JACKIE: Feeding time in our house is like a religious ceremony. They eat as if it was the Last Supper. Now you know why I volunteer for all the overtime I can get.

PETER: Better than Sirocco, eh?

JACKIE: Don't talk about that place. I only stuck it eight weeks, after my da speaking for me and all. There was blue murder in the house over it.

PETER: Your father worked in Sirocco too?

JACKIE: Thirty-one years. [*Imitates voice*] 'You have to go out and earn a living wherever you can get it,' he kept saying.

PETER: What did he say when you put on the uniform?

JACKIE: Shocked. A bit shocked, but as pleased as punch in the end. Although my mother has done nothing but worry from the day and hour I signed up. The wife takes it a bit more philosophically. She reckons I'm so thick-skinned, a bullet would bounce off me.

[PETER and JACKIE go. In his cell, AMBROSE jumps up from the bed and paces the floor.]

AMBROSE: What the hell's keeping them? My third day and no interrogation yet? It must be the early hours of the morning now. Something's up. What about Willie? 'Singing like a canary'? I wonder is he still there. [He goes over to the cell door.] Willie! Willie Lagan!

WILLIE: That you, Ambrose?

AMBROSE: Willie. Did they mention my name in your last interview?

WILLIE: Not once, no.

AMBROSE: Are you sure, Willie?

WILLIE: Definitely, definitely, not once, no.

AMBROSE: So what do you think they're gonna do with you?

WILLIE: Don't know, don't know. What about you, what about you, what's happening?

AMBROSE: Ah, they're trying to pin a dopey oul' charge on me.

WILLIE: What, did you kill somebody Ambrose, what?

AMBROSE [*chuckles*]: You know me better than that, Willie. I couldn't kill anybody if it was to save me life.

WILLIE: Ambrose.

AMBROSE: What?

WILLIE: 'Member the time you broke your leg running away from the soldiers in Albert Street? [*Laughs*] Great crack, great crack. Like it? Crack, crack?

AMBROSE: I can assure, Willie, it wasn't funny at the time.

[*Loud laugh from* WILLIE.]

WILLIE: Na, no joke, no joke.

[DAVY *enters the cells area.*]

AMBROSE: Willie, you won't forget to see Christine when you—

DAVY: Alright, alright, wrap it up. That's the last time you two's being warned!

WILLIE: Why, what are you gonna do, Quaseemoto, lock us up? [*Laughs.*]

AMBROSE: Maybe they're gonna execute us, Willie!

DAVY: I said that's enough!

[PETER and JACKIE *enter the interview room.*]

JACKIE: Have you ever shot anybody, Peter?

PETER: You tell me, then I'll tell you.
JACKIE: No. No, I haven't. Closest incident was in Cromac Street two years ago. We got a call to the post office. We arrived just in time to see the guys turning the corner into Eliza Street. I fired one shot and, just as the two guys disappeared, an elderly woman stepped out on to Cromac Street. Bullet went straight through her shopping bag. Two fuckers got away.
PETER: Close enough.
JACKIE: Too close. And you?
PETER: Yeah, I've shot somebody.
JACKIE: Badly wounded?
PETER: Dead.
JACKIE: Dead!
PETER: Oh, it was a long time ago. I was only 21 at the time. A guy was climbing over a wall after planting a bomb in a factory. There was a bit of a gun battle and I shot him. Once in the head and once in the chest. Not bad for a nine-millimetre Browning at 45 yards.
JACKIE: It must have been rough for you.
PETER: Not really. It's all part of the job. Same as joiner uses a saw, I use a gun. Can't do the job without it, in fact.
JACKIE: Not in this country anyway.
PETER: Don't kid yourself. It's the same all over now. There's a violent crime every six minutes in New York. Los Angeles City Morgue is that overcrowded they've had to build racks up the walls to accommodate all the murder victims. Violence is now a way of life. Look at John Lennon, Reagan, the Pope. The world's going mad. A cop can't do his job without a gun anymore. The only place they're not robbing and shooting each other on the streets is fucking Russia!

[STANLEY *enters.*]

STANLEY: Right, Jackie. Fetch Willie Lagan for us.

[JACKIE *moves towards the door.*]

PETER: Bring a gun with you. You never know what's liable to happen.
JACKIE: I think I'll manage. [*He goes.*]
STANLEY: What are you talking about?
PETER: I'm just pulling his leg.
STANLEY: Well, I want you to pull Willie Lagan's leg. Right out of its socket if necessary.

PETER: Oh, exciting.
STANLEY: We've only 24 hours left. Fogarty must be made to talk. So what we need from Lagan is a signed statement implicating Fogarty in IRA activities. When we hit him with that, he'll be ours for the taking.
PETER: No holds barred?
STANLEY: No holds barred. I'll join the proceedings if necessary.
PETER: No problem, Stanley. It's as good as done.
 [STANLEY *goes.* DAVY *opens Willie's door and* JACKIE *enters.* WILLIE *is prancing about the cell, imitating a monkey, grunting and shrieking.*]
JACKIE: What in the name of Christ! [WILLIE *grunts and shrieks. He jumps on to the bed*] Come Willie, it's interview time. [*He moves forward and takes* WILLIE *off the bed by the arm*] What are you playing at?
WILLIE: Monkey, monkey. If I'm gonna to be caged up, I might as well act like a monkey!
 [*He jumps about under Jackie's restraint.*]
JACKIE: Well, come on round to the interview room and we'll see if we can get you some bananas.
WILLIE: Guitar, guitar. Take my guitar with me?
WILLIE [*singing as he leaves the cell*]:
 And as they marched him to the scaffold
 His head he proudly held up high.
 Brave Willie Lagan, we salute you
 And we never ...
 [JACKIE *and* WILLIE *enter the interview room.*]
WILLIE: You still here, still here? Have they not got you a break since yesterday? That's cat, bad, bad.
PETER: Don't you worry about me. It's yourself you need to be worried about. Have you decided what you're going to tell us?
WILLIE: Yes. A joke, a good joke. Tell you a good joke, not long, not long.
 Man says to me, 'Willie, my wife's an angel.' I says, 'You're lucky, mine's still living.' [*Laughs*] One more, one more. Doctor's surgery, Doctor's surgery. Packed, crowded. I walks in and lets off a big fart, a big fart. Man says to me, 'Willie, how dare you fart in front of my wife.' I says, 'Sorry, I didn't know it was her turn.' [*Laughs*] I like, I like, I like! 'I didn't know it was her turn.' [*He forces a handshake on* PETER *and* JACKIE]

Magic, magic. Every one a gem. [*Another fit of laughter*] 'I didn't know it was her turn!'

PETER: Willie. At nine o'clock tomorrow morning you will be taken to Townhall Street and formally charged with drunk, disorderly and riotous behaviour, as a result of which you will spend six full months in Crumlin Road prison.

WILLIE [*stops abruptly, then bursts out laughing again*]: I like, I like. Good joke, good joke. Know any more?

JACKIE: Think this is fun, do you?

[*He moves towards* WILLIE *aggressively.*]

PETER: Just let him get the giddiness out of his system for a moment or two. [*Pause*] Are you finished yet, Willie?

WILLIE: Yes, yes, finito.

PETER: Ready to answer a few questions?

WILLIE: Yes, yes. Fire away. Hold on, hold on. What's the star prize? A car, a car? No. No. A year's supply of dummy-tits. [*Laughs*] Right. Fingers on the buzzers. [JACKIE *bangs Willie's fingers*] Sore, sore.

JACKIE: I said, the fun's over!

PETER: If you remember, Willie, we were talking about Ambrose Fogarty, a neighbour of yours. Remember?

WILLIE: Yes, yes.

PETER: Now, Willie, I want you to tell me everything you know about him.

WILLIE: Like what, like what?

PETER: Well, everybody knows he's in the IRA. Have you ever seen him with a gun?

WILLIE [*jeers*]: Ah! Have I ever seen him with a gun? I know what you're at. You want me to become a Brussel!

PETER: A Brussel?

WILLIE: Brussel sprout—tout!

PETER: Look at it this way, Willie. Are you working at the moment?

WILLIE: Yes, yes.

PETER: What are you doing?

WILLIE: Good job, good job. I'm a hod carrier in a marshmallow factory. [*Roars.*]

PETER: Seriously, Willie, are you working?

WILLIE: No work, no work. Paid off.

PETER: On the Buroo?

WILLIE: That's right, that's right.
PETER: That couldn't be very much each week.
WILLIE: Bad, bad.
PETER: I can offer you a substantial sum each week just to give us little snippets here and there on people like Ambrose Fogarty. Now there's no need to worry. Nobody has to know except us. We'll pay the money to you any way you want. Anywhere you want.

[WILLIE *thinks it over.*]

WILLIE: Nobody'll know?
PETER: Not a sinner.
WILLIE: Every week?
PETER: Without fail.
WILLIE: How much, how much?
PETER: How much would you want?
WILLIE: Am, a ... a ... hundred pounds a week, tax-free and four weeks holiday a year.
PETER: I'm serious, Willie. We could send you a cheque for £20 every week.
WILLIE: Twenty pounds a week? I'm serious too. That's way below the union rate, too low, too low.
JACKIE: Union rate?
WILLIE: If I brought that to the Regional Secretary of the Northern Ireland Touts' and Informants' Union, they'd laugh at me. No way, £20 a week! Touts' Union wouldn't wear that, wouldn't wear it.

[PETER *takes out £20 in £5 notes and counts them on the table.*]

PETER: Now, Willie. There's £20 on the table and there's the door. If you tell me of just one incident involving Ambrose Fogarty, that twenty pound'll be in you pocket and you'll be out through that door in five minutes. What about it?
WILLIE: Can't do it, can't do it. Don't know nothing, nought.
JACKIE: I don't think he needs the money at all. If he's signing the Buroo and he says he plays the guitar and sings in the clubs, then he's all right for a few bob. In other words, he's breaking the law.
PETER: That's right, two sources of income.
JACKIE: Illegally claiming benefits.
PETER: Worth a year in jail, eh Willie? [WILLIE *remains silent*] Got you this time, have we?

JACKIE: If you don't come across with some talking inside two minutes, the boss is going to be here and you'll be in serious trouble.

WILLIE: Can I say something, what?

PETER: Go ahead.

WILLIE: All right, I won't play the clubs anymore.

PETER: That's very good of you.

JACKIE: Too right, you won't.

[*Suddenly the door bursts open and* STANLEY *enters.*]

STANLEY: Has he told you anything yet?

[*He throws his coat off, rolls up his sleeves and sets his watch on the table.*]

PETER: Not a thing.

JACKIE: Only jokes.

STANLEY: Is that right? Stand up!

[STANLEY *trails* WILLIE *up.*]

WILLIE: Watch the coat, watch the coat.

[STANLEY *strikes* WILLIE *with a fierce punch to the stomach.* WILLIE *bends over and* JACKIE *pushes him to the ground.* STANLEY *and* JACKIE *trail* WILLIE *back on to the chair.* WILLIE *is in considerable pain.*]

STANLEY: Know any jokes now, do you? [*He punches* WILLIE *again*] Prepared to talk yet? We'll soon see. What is it this man has in his cell with him?

JACKIE: A guitar and a parcel of bread.

STANLEY [*To* PETER]: Away and smash up the guitar.

[PETER *goes to the cells to fetch the guitar.*]

WILLIE: Listen, listen. Don't touch my guitar, please, please.

JACKIE: Well, are you gonna start talking?

STANLEY: Is Ambrose Fogarty in the IRA?

WILLIE: Yes, yes, he probably is.

STANLEY: Never mind probably. Is he or is he not?

WILLIE: I'm not sure, I don't know. [JACKIE *punches* WILLIE] Yes, yes, he is!

STANLEY: I'm sure you've seen him doing something at some time or another?

WILLIE: Don't think so, don't think so. [JACKIE *punches him*]

STANLEY: Ever see him with Sean McAlister? [WILLIE *shakes his head.* JACKIE *strikes him*]

WILLIE: Yes, yes. I did.

STANLEY: When?

The Interrogation of Ambrose Fogarty 149

WILLIE: All the time.
STANLEY: When? This week, last week, the week before, when?
WILLIE: I can't remember exactly. [JACKIE *hits him*] Two weeks ago, aye, it was two weeks ago.
STANLEY: What were they doing?
WILLIE: Nothing, nothing. [JACKIE *strikes him.*]
JACKIE: What to fuck were they doing, Lagan?
WILLIE: Nothing, I swear.
STANLEY: You're a liar! They must've been doing something. Walking, talking, in a club, in a car, what were they doing?
WILLIE: Nothing.
JACKIE: Answer the question!
STANLEY: Eh?
WILLIE: In a car, in a car.
STANLEY: Where?
WILLIE: Bottom of our street.
STANLEY: Doing what?
WILLIE: Nothing. They just got out of a car at the bottom of our street.

[PETER *returns with Willie's guitar.*]

STANLEY: Right, sonny, if you don't start talking within five seconds, I'm smashing this thing into smithereens.
WILLIE: Please, please, don't hurt my guitar, please.
STANLEY: What did they do when they got out of the car?
WILLIE: Nothing, I swear, nothing.

[STANLEY *holds the guitar up and throws it to* PETER *at the other side of the room.* WILLIE *attempts to move but is restrained by* JACKIE. PETER *thows it back but* STANLEY *lets it fall to the ground.*]

WILLIE: Ah fuck, ah fuck.

[STANLEY *walks over and raises his foot above the guitar.*]

STANLEY: Are you going to answer the question?
WILLIE: They fired a rifle, but it was just in the air, just test-firing I think, know, trying it out.
STANLEY: And they just got back into the car and drove away?
WILLIE: That's right, that's right.
PETER: How did you know it was a rifle, Willie?
WILLIE: I don't know. All's I know, it banged like fuck.
PETER: Did it fire one shot at a time or a whole lot quickly together?
WILLIE: Yes, yes, there was a right lot.

PETER: Like a machine gun?
WILLIE: Yes, yes, like a machine gun. Frightened the balls off me.
PETER [*To* STANLEY]: There's your machine gun.
STANLEY: Yeah.
WILLIE: Do you mean they were using yours? Cheeky bastards!
STANLEY: I don't suppose you're prepared to appear in court, Lagan, to testify to what you've just told us?
JACKIE: Or sign a statement?
WILLIE: Ah fuck, I'm still young yet. Too young to die. Too young.
STANLEY: We could drop all the charges against you.
WILLIE: Let me think about it, what. Think, think.
STANLEY: Take him back to his cell.
WILLIE: Am I being released now, what? Now like, I've told you all about Fogarty, the lot, I must be up for release.
STANLEY: We'll wait and see how we go with Fogarty.
WILLIE: I might be released?
STANLEY: You might.
WILLIE: Magic, magic. Shake, shake. [*He offers to shake hands.*]
STANLEY [*To* JACKIE]: Take him away.

[WILLIE *jumps up and grabs his guitar.* JACKIE *opens the door.*]

STANLEY: Do you play that thing at all?
WILLIE: No, I don't!

[JACKIE *pushes* WILLIE *out and both men go to the cells.*]

STANLEY: That could be the break we are looking for. A stupid oul' fool from round the corner has nearly wrecked Ambrose's wee shop.

[STANLEY *and* PETER *leave the stage.* JACKIE *hands over* WILLIE *to* DAVY *and leaves the stage.* DAVY *locks* WILLIE *up and goes.* WILLIE *starts banging on his cell door.* AMBROSE *hurries to his own cell door.*]

WILLIE: I want out! I want out! I want—
AMBROSE: Willie! Willie!
WILLIE: Yes, Ambrose.
AMBROSE: You alright.
WILLIE: I'm alright, but they beat up my guitar, smashed it.
AMBROSE: Why did they not release you?
WILLIE: Why is the earth round—how the fuck do I know why they didn't release me?
AMBROSE: Willie! Willie, did they mention me this time?
WILLIE: Mention you? Who do you think you are, Yasser Arafat, what?

AMBROSE: Are you sure?
WILLIE: Calling me a liar, what, what? I'm in jail too, you know. Got the works, the lot, filled in.
AMBROSE: You were beat up?
WILLIE: Ambrose, there's one of them a madman, mad he is. Why, why do they do it, Branchmen, eh?
AMBROSE: Now you've asked a question, Willie. Why are Branchmen Branchmen? It's all to do with the system, Willie. Do you know what the system is, Willie?
WILLIE: Yes, yes. I'm constipated myself at the minute, bad, bad.
[STANLEY *and* PETER *arrive at reception.* STANLEY *checks out something on the incident book.*]
STANLEY: He's bound to cave in when we throw this stuff at him.
PETER: I can't wait to see his face.
STANLEY: I can't wait to smash his face.
PETER: Stange, but I couldn't help feeling a wee bit sorry for your man Willie Lagan there.
STANLEY: What do you mean?
PETER: Ach, nothing really. Just a wee bit sort of sorry to see him getting knocked about.
STANLEY: Well don't. He won't feel sorry for you or your wife and children if you get a bullet in the back from one of his cowardly neighbours. Like Ambrose Fogarty.
PETER: Now, there's a man I have no sympathy for. This is effectively our last chance to see him put away.
STANLEY: That's if you don't break down feeling sorry for him in the middle of it.
PETER: Not with this fella.
STANLEY: Well, we can't do it without getting him to make a statement and putting pen to paper. You know what half of these judges are like. By the way, what was the report on those things you were checking out?
PETER: Not terribly beneficial, I'm afraid. There was a pub off Ann Street that had its toilets replastered but the owners only knew one of the workers as Sean. We couldn't ascertain one way or the other whether any roofing repairs were carried out in Glenhill Park and when we visted the McAlister house the parents were very hostile. Just said the sons weren't in and, if we wanted them, why didn't we go looking for them.
STANLEY: Good enough. Get Jackie and let's get under way.

[YVONNE *enters the cells area pushing a trolley. She stops beside Ambrose's cell.*]

YVONNE: Could I have this cell opened, please?

DAVY: It's opened.

[*She enters the cells and lifts the plate and cup, watched closely by* DAVY. *Embarrassed, she pushes the trolley on to Willie's cell.*]

YVONNE: It's got very warm in here today, hasn't it?

DAVY: I'm alright. [DAVY *unlocks Willie's door*] Your dishes?

WILLIE: No problem, no problem. [*He hands them over*] Is that my girl? It is, good, good, good. Coming in for a lumber? What? A nice big lumber, me and you? A couple of smacks of the rubbers, what?

DAVY: Alright, back inside.

WILLIE: Toilet, toilet, I wanna use the toilet.

DAVY: In a minute, in a minute.

WILLIE: That's two minutes. Said it twice, twice.

DAVY: Very funny. Just hold on a minute till we get sorted out and I'll come back and let you go to the toilet.

WILLIE: No problem, no problem.

[DAVY *locks the cell door.*]

YVONNE: That's the lot, isn't it?

DAVY: That's it.

[*She turns the trolley and moves off.*]

YVONNE: I'll see you later then.

DAVY: See you.

[*She stops near the exit.*]

YVONNE: By the way, in case you're still thinking what you're thinking, you've got it all wrong.

DAVY: I'm not thinking anything.

YVONNE: You accept that nothing went on between me and the captain in that room?

DAVY: Huh!

YVONNE: Do you, Davy? This is important to my job. I don't want anybody running around this station talking about me.

DAVY: Yvonne, I don't *care* what went on.

YVONNE: And another thing. I have to work with you, so there's no point in me and you continually fighting the peace out, is there? I want us to be friends.

DAVY: Friends? We were supposed to be engaged in a fortnight's time.

YVONNE: Okay, so it's not as formal as that anymore, but that shouldn't stop us being good friends. Maybe we could even go out for a drink to the Sports Club sometime.
DAVY [*sarcastically*]: How does this Friday night suit you?
YVONNE: Davy. Listen, Davy—
DAVY: No, you listen to me for a change. I had feelings for you. Strong feelings. But you decided, in your usual arrogant way, to tramp all over them. Not only did you tramp on them but you jumped on them, danced on them and kicked them. Now, strong and all as my feelings were, I'll never feel the same again for you after what I've seen of your behaviour over these last few days. Yvonne, I mightn't have the social status you're looking for, but I've got principle. You? You're a ... you're no better than a whore. [*She immediately slaps him on the face*] A sign of guilt if ever I saw one.
YVONNE: Don't you ever accuse me of anything, Davy McFadden! When I want lectured on morality and men you're the last person I'll go to. You walked into that room and immediately thought the worst. I can't help it if your twisted little mind is sex in the brain. But I'm not in the habit of having it off with men in police stations or anywhere else. And I'm certainly not a whore. If that's what you're looking for, you'll find plenty of them around Dee Street.

[*She turns to leave.*]

DAVY: Yvonne? [*She stops*] Fuck off.

[*She goes.* WILLIE *bangs on his cell door, realises it is open and steps out of his cell.* DAVY *swings round and sees him.*]

WILLIE: You never locked the cells door, never locked it.
DAVY: How the bloody hell!

[*He rushes down to* WILLIE *and ushers him back into the cell.*]

WILLIE: Toilet, toilet? Go now, go now?
DAVY: No, you bloody well can't!

[*He slams the cell door shut and locks it.*]

WILLIE [*sings*]:   Please release me, let me go,
        For I can't hold it in anymore ...

[STANLEY *enters the interview room.* JACKIE *arrives at the cells to fetch* AMBROSE *while* PETER *hands in a document to* SERGEANT KNOX *at reception.*]

KNOX: Oh, there you are. I was wanting to inform you that there have been several enquiries about Mr. Fogarty. In fact his wife hasn't been off the phone. And his solicitor wants in to see him as soon as possible. You know what Jones is like. [PETER *shrugs his shoulders*] It is my duty to report those facts to you.

PETER: You've reported them. [*He turns to move on.*]

KNOX: But what'll I tell his wife or anybody else that rings?

PETER: What everybody else is told. He's still helping police with enquiries.

[PETER *walks on to the interview room.* JACKIE *arrives with* AMBROSE, *leaves him in the interview room and immediately goes.*]

PETER: Sit down, Fogarty.

STANLEY: Stand up!

PETER: Do you know how long you've been in here now? [AMBROSE *shrugs his shoulders*] Over sixty hours. Know how many people have enquired about you?

STANLEY: Not one. Not a ruddy sinner.

PETER: Your wife hasn't been seen, nor heard of, since your arrrest. Your so-called comrades haven't bothered their backsides either.

STANLEY: No statements in the paper, no protests. They haven't even bothered to get you a solicitor.

PETER: Do you get it, Abmrose? Nobody gives a fiddler's. Not one person.

STANLEY: What do you do all this for? The cause? You joined to further the cause. You worked hard, you did your duty, you did everything that was asked of you. You gave up a lot of your own time. No doubt about it. Ambrose Fogarty has been an excellent volunteer. A 24 hours-a-day man.

PETER: Risked his life and freedom many's a time. The last time of course, being only a fortnight ago on the Andersonstown Road.

STANLEY: And what for? To be forgotten about inside three days. You're sitting here facing 15 years while your 'idealistic' comrades are bevvying away in one of their many drinking clubs.

PETER: Yes, but his leaders stand by him.

STANLEY: Oh, aye. The leaders! The leaders haven't even got the guts to live in Belfast. They just make the odd sortie up north to make a few fiery speeches, urging all the young lads on the Buroo from the Falls Road to attack the Brits.

PETER: And then they fuck off to the safety of Dublin.

STANLEY: And it's left to fools like Fogarty to do the dirty work.
PETER: And end up in jail.
STANLEY: Or dead. Answer me a question, Fogarty. How many of your Dublin GHQ staff have ended up dead while attacking the enemy on the streets of Belfast? Come on. Name me one? Just one?
PETER: And there haven't been any frantic phone calls from Dublin enquiring about him.
STANLEY: Not at all.
PETER: It's about time you wised up, Ambrose. Once you step inside this police station, you're on your own. Your family, friends and comrades don't care. 'Did you hear Ambrose Fogarty got 15 years? God, that's terrible. Make that four pints of Harp and two vodkas, Harry!' [*Laughs*] It's a joke, isn't it.
STANLEY: If it wasn't so damn serious. When you're not working for McAlister, what else do you do?
AMBROSE: Sign on.
STANLEY: Wouldn't you know.
PETER: That was a foregone conclusion.
STANLEY: Here's a man who opposes Britain tooth and nail, wants Brits out and all the rest, yet he's over to the social security office as quick as the next to claim British money.
AMBROSE: There are no jobs.
STANLEY: Only bank jobs, eh? Why don't some of you go out and get jobs and earn an honest, decent living?
AMBROSE: I told you, there are no jobs. There's over 50 per cent unemployment round our way.
STANLEY: And why's that? Because people like you have been doing their best to wreck the economy since 1969.
AMBROSE: The figures were nearly as bad before 1969.
STANLEY: Don't talk nonsense.
AMBROSE: Who's talking nonsense? Northern Ireland has traditionally been an unemployment blackspot. Heightened by the fact that unemployment has been concentrated in Catholic areas. Ballymurphy, 60 per cent, Ballymena, two point nine per cent. Where's the nonsense there? That's the facts.
PETER: A right old politician we have here.
STANLEY: Did you not know? Fogarty is a failed student. Two years at Queen's University was too much for him.
AMBROSE: I didn't like university. I left to get married.

PETER: You plumped for a career in terrorism instead.
AMBROSE: I'm not a terrorist.
STANLEY: You're not a Franciscan monk either.
PETER: Are you interested in politics?
AMBROSE: Suppose I am.
PETER: Well, what do you believe in?
AMBROSE: Am I being charged because of my political views?
PETER: No.
AMBROSE: Then, I'd prefer not to discuss my politics.
STANLEY: Listen, sonny, don't try and be clever in here. You know rightly you're not in here because of your political views. You're in here because of your decision to use violence and robbery to further those views.
AMBROSE: I disagree with using violence for anything.
STANLEY: Huh! Who do you think you're talking to—a foreign press reporter? That line doesn't wear in here. We know a bit more about the likes of you than the world's press does.
AMBROSE: I have nothing to hide from anyone.
PETER: You're hiding your politics.
AMBROSE: I'm not.
PETER: Then tell us what you believe in. Are you a republican, a socialist, a unionist, a conservative, or what?
AMBROSE: Do you know what you are?
PETER: Yeah, of course.
AMBROSE: I'm sure I don't have to ask what your politics are.
PETER: No, I'll tell you. I vote middle of the road.
AMBROSE: Middle of fuck.
PETER: I'm telling you I do. He doesn't.
STANLEY: No, I vote for the Big Man. And I don't only vote for him, I keep him informed on certain matters—goings on, inside the police.
AMBROSE: Bit of a mole.
STANLEY: I regard it as doing my duty. For God and country. It's only my duty.
PETER: What do you think of the Big Man, Ambrose?
AMBROSE: I think that if this was a normal country inhabited by rational human beings, far from being a leading politician, he would be a traffic attendant on the Lagan towpath. Only allowed to open his mouth when he got hungry.
[STANLEY *immediately stands up.*]

STANLEY: Do you know that in his personal life, he is a warm, friendly man. I've never met a man with more compassion and understanding. He is a man of strong principles, is impeccably honest and insists on the same from all those around him.

AMBROSE: So is the Ayatollah Khomeini.

[STANLEY *sits down.*]

PETER: Who's your hero then? Chairman Mao?

AMBROSE: I don't indulge in heroes. Life's not made up of heroes. It's made up of ordinary, unsung people trying to search out a living.

PETER: And you're on the side of the ordinary-downtrodden-man-in-the-street.

AMBROSE: You're learning.

STANLEY: What were the unfortunate victims that died in La Mon?

AMBROSE: I told you before. I detest the use of violence. But since you mentioned it, the victims of La Mon were exactly the same as the victims on Derry's Bloody Sunday. Ordinary, innocent, decent people.

PETER: Are you suggesting two wrongs make a right?

AMBROSE: Not in the slightest. I'm just reminding you of things it seems you prefer to forget. Selective retention, I think the sociologists call it.

STANLEY: Nobody can blame the police for La Mon or Bloody Sunday.

AMBROSE: No, but you can be blamed for the death of young Michael McCartain on the Ormeau Road recently. Not to mention Devenny and Rooney in '69.

PETER: 1969 was a long time ago.

AMBROSE: Yes, but the men who did the damage are still in the RUC.

STANLEY: Who the hell do you think you are! Sitting there pontificating about the country's police force. And you a bloody bank robber! A person who steals off other people!

AMBROSE: That's untrue.

STANLEY: What's untrue about it? Are you still going to sit there and tell me that you didn't collaborate with Sean McAlister to organise and carry out the robbing of a bank on the Andersonstown Road on Thursday the 6th?

AMBROSE: You know rightly I didn't.
STANLEY: We know rightly you did. And better still you know we know. And there you are sitting as if butter wouldn't melt in your mouth.
PETER: Where were you on Thursday the 6th?
AMBROSE: Again?
STANLEY: Just do what you're told. You got up at what time?
AMBROSE: Well ... I started work around 12 or so and worked till ... I think it was well after two.
PETER: And?
STANLEY: Speed up these answers, we haven't got all day.
AMBROSE: We had lunch then in the White Fort Inn on the Andersonstown Road.
STANLEY: How far away is that from the bank?
AMBROSE: Which bank?
STANLEY: Answer the question!
PETER: The one nearest the pub!
AMBROSE: I'm not sure.
STANLEY: You're a liar!
PETER: You're at it again, Ambrose.
AMBROSE: I'm telling you the God's honest truth.
PETER: You're not. Inside 24 hours you've changed your story about your movements. You said the last time you started at eleven and finished at one. Now it's started at twelve and finished at two. That's the third time you've told a different story.
AMBROSE: It's hard to remember exact times.
STANLEY: I suppose then you wouldn't remember what you did the night before Thursday the 6th?
AMBROSE: The night before—
STANLEY: With our friend McAlister.
PETER: At the bottom of Grosvenor Place?
AMBROSE: I can't really remem—
STANLEY: Answer the bloody question! [*He bangs the table with both hands and gets to his feet*] I've had just about enough of this.
PETER: We know you test-fired a sub-machine-gun that night.
STANLEY: We have witnesses.
PETER: You can't deny this one.
STANLEY: Did you or didn't you?
AMBROSE: Of course not, I was—

STANLEY: You did! We know you did. Now, I want you to write down on that piece of paper everything that happened over those 24 hours. [*He shoves a pen and paper in front of* AMBROSE] I don't care if you say you only drove the car or did look-out or whatever, but you better sign for something. You're not walking out of here m'boy. No way.

PETER: You're better facing up to that now. If you sign, you could get off lightly. If you don't sign, we'll hold you personally responsible for planning and organising the entire operation. As I said before—anything up to 15 to 20 years.

STANLEY: This is the last time I'm going to do this. [*He places the pen in Ambrose's hand*] If you don't start writing this time, I'll not be responsible for what happens to you.

[*The room door opens slightly.*]

JACKIE [*behind door*]: Has he not signed yet?

[PETER *jumps up from the table and moves to the door.*]

PETER: It's all right, leave it for another few minutes. He's going to sign now. [PETER *closes the door.*]

STANLEY: Well, Fogarty?

[AMBROSE *moves his hand slowly to the top of the page. He stops, drops the pen on the table and sits back.*]

STANLEY: What the hell are you doing?

PETER: You're asking for trouble.

STANLEY: Are you going to sign, Fogarty? [*He moves over to* AMBROSE *and starts shaking him by the shoulder*] Sign it, sign it, sign it! [*The door suddenly bursts open.* JACKIE *enters, throwing off his coat and rolling up his sleeves.*]

JACKIE: Where is the bastard? I'll soon knock the nonsense out of you mate! Get on your feet! Get on your feet, I said! [*He trails* AMBROSE *to his feet*] You won't sign, eh! [*He punches* AMBROSE *fiercely in the stomach*] We'll soon see about that. [STANLEY *grabs Ambrose's arms from behind.* JACKIE *repeatedly punches him and yells abuse*] Bastard! Cunt! Cunt! Bastard! [AMBROSE *finally falls to the floor, taking blows from both* JACKIE *and* STANLEY. PETER *sits calmly at the table*] Get up you cowardly bastard! [JACKIE *and* STANLEY *trail* AMBROSE *to his feet.* STANLEY *stands ready.* JACKIE *walks round and round* AMBROSE] You're a cunt. What are you? A cunt! Cunt, cunt, cunt! [*He grabs Ambrose's arm and twists it, forcing Ambrose's head to the floor*] Who robbed the bank? Answer me! Answer me, cunt! Admit you took part in robbing the bank. Tell me! Tell me! [JACKIE *is almost hysterical*] You're a thieving cunt, what are you? Cunt, I asked you a question. What are you? What to fuck are you? Answer me! Answer me! Don't you think you're getting away this time, mate. You've another 12 hours to go and I'm just going to beat the ballocks off you for 12 solid hours. Got that? Have you got that? Do you not hear me talking to you, cunt? Are you deaf as well as stupid? Do you fancy this for 12 hours? And let me tell you this. [*Reaches down with his free hand, grips* AMBROSE *by a lock of hair and marches him down to the end of the room*] If you don't admit and sign before those 12 hours are up, we'll just walk you outside this station and rearrest you all over again. Just like that. Only this time, it'll be a seven-day detention order, eh? Fancy that, cunt? Do you fancy that? Fancy that, fancy that, fancy that? [*Grips Ambrose's hair in two hands, holding him on his tiptoes*] By fuck, I'll bring you down to size before I'm finished. Isn't that right, cunt? Cunt, cunt, cunt, cunt, cunt, cunt, cunt! Isn't that right? Now [*trails* AMBROSE *by the back of the hair on to a chair by the table*], we are going over to sign a confession. You, mate, lift that pen and write down in detail what we all know happened. Lift it! Lift the pen. [*He shakes Ambrose's head*] I said [*Bends Ambrose's head right down to the table and bangs his face against the paper on the table three times*] lift that pen! [*Holds Ambrose's face crushed against the table*] You've got five seconds to lift that pen, cunt. Five seconds. [*He shakes Ambrose's head. After a few seconds,* AMBROSE *brings his right hand up on to the table and searches for the pen. He finds it, pauses and then throws it across the room*] Bastard! [JACKIE *and* STANLEY *both set upon* AMBROSE, *eventually leaving him in a heap in a corner of the room.*]

STANLEY [*To* PETER]: Take him back to his cell. [PETER *moves over and supports* AMBROSE *to his feet. He walks him to the door*] Fogarty! [PETER *and* AMBROSE *stop*] I'm arranging immediately for a seven-day detention order for you. [PETER *and* AMBROSE *go out.* SERGEANT KNOX *is at the desk. The telephone rings. He lifts the receiver.*]

KNOX: Yes, Bill ... probably around three o'clock ... right ... 'bye. [*He puts the receiver down.* AMBROSE *and* PETER *arrive.*]

PETER: Take this prisoner back, Sergeant, please.

KNOX: Right. [*Shouts back*] Yvonne, keep your eye on the desk!

YVONNE [*off-stage*]: Okey dokey!

[PETER *goes to the interview room.* KNOX *escorts* AMBROSE *to his cell.*]

KNOX: Lock this man up.

DAVY: Right Sergeant. [*To* AMBROSE] In you go.

[AMBROSE *turns to* KNOX.]

AMBROSE: I want to make a complaint, Sergeant.

KNOX: What about?

AMBROSE: I've just been beaten up.

KNOX: Get some paper, Davy. Let's go inside. [DAVY *fetches some paper from his table.* AMBROSE *and* KNOX *enter the cell.*]

KNOX: You want this to be a formal complaint?

AMBROSE: As formal as you can make it.

[DAVY *hands in the paper.*]

KNOX: Thanks, Davy. Right, what happened?

[KNOX *sits down.*]

AMBROSE: Two members of the RUC have just systematically beaten me up.

KNOX: How do you mean beaten?

AMBROSE: How do I mean? Sergeant, why do they do it?

[STANLEY, PETER *and* JACKIE *are in the interview room.* STANLEY *paces up and down.*]

JACKIE: I wouldn't mind being a disc jockey.

PETER [*laughs*]: Catch yourself on.

STANLEY: I wouldn't do anything else. I know I'm doing something worthwhile. Not only is it the right thing, but so many people are depending on us doing a good job. When an old-age pensioner gets mugged, who is it investigates? Us. When people get their cars stolen, who is it treks round for hours looking for them? Us. What happens when people use violence to gain political objectives? We've to search out the culprits and get them in front of the courts. Us! It's left to the police.

[*The dialogue is intercut between Ambrose's cell and the interview room.*]

KNOX: I suppose somebody has to do it.

AMBROSE: Sergeant, what sensible, level-headed person would work at a job which entailed punching other human beings on a daily basis? 'I had a hard day at work today love, is the tea ready? I punched the fuck out of ten people today.' Who would do it?

PETER: And a fat lot of thanks we get too.

STANLEY: Of course, it's not the money. I would earn more working on the nightshift in Michelin's. But it makes you wonder why mavericks like Fogarty actually do what they do for no money.

KNOX: I don't know, son, but there's a lot of bad boyos comes in here. I'm not saying you're one, but they must have you in for something.

AMBROSE: That's right. I've come this far because I believe in something. Christ, it's a sick society that can throw up police stations where people are beaten up systematically. And a sick police force that carries it out.

PETER: But is there no other legal way of geting convictions against the wild men?

STANLEY: Quite simply, no. Most of them are hardened operators who come in here knowing the whole set-up inside out. While we can't get witnesses to stand up in court, these jokers know it's only a matter of sitting the three days out. Peter, what's a few slaps around the face if it keeps the likes of the Shankill Butchers safe from the community, behind bars?

AMBROSE: How many innocent people have been beaten up in here through mistake or suspicion?

KNOX: That's impossible to tell. I just look after my end of things by filling in any complaints that are made and sending them on.

AMBROSE: Sending them on to who?

KNOX: All complaints are investigated by senior police officers.

AMBROSE: What? Do you mean to tell me that my complaint against the police is going to be investigated by the police themselves. What would have happened if Watergate had been investigated by Richard Nixon?

STANLEY: It's a contribution to peace. Putting all the gunmen behind bars is the final result. Everyone's sick of violence. The community wants peace.

AMBROSE: Huh, peace! Outside the word 'love', 'peace' must be the most abused word in the English language. There's no such thing as a pacifist. Who was it threatened an eye for an eye?

STANLEY: And love thy neighbour.

AMBROSE: Unless he's of a different religion.

STANLEY: Do unto others as you would have them do unto you.

AMBROSE: Only do it first. Forget about the complaint, Sergeant.

STANLEY: Jackie, go and instruct Sergeant Knox to release Fogarty.
JACKIE: Looks like he's slipped through our fingers.
STANLEY: I'm afraid so.
JACKIE: Think we'll ever get another chance?
STANLEY: Ambrose Fogarty? His sort always come back.
JACKIE: What about the other fella, Lagan?
STANLEY: You don't have to ask me that.
JACKIE: Right.
   [JACKIE *goes.* WILLIE *starts singing as the next series of events takes place.* JACKIE *arrives at the desk.* PETER *and* STANLEY *leave the interview room.* KNOX *leaves* AMBROSE *to be locked up and goes to the desk, where* JACKIE *tells him Stanley's decision.* KNOX *turns to the cells, takes* AMBROSE *out, gives him his personal effects and shows him to the front exit. On his way back,* KNOX *comes across the* CAPTAIN, *who is in civvies and carrying a grip.*]
KNOX: Where are you off to?
CAPTAIN: A place called England. Bermondsey, to be exact.
KNOX: But aren't you ... I thought you and Yvonne were going out this Friday night.
CAPTAIN: Yvonne? Sergeant, I hope to be getting drunk down my local this Friday night. [*He moves towards the exit*] And every other Friday night, if I can help it. Six years is a long time in the army. See ya.
KNOX: But don't you want to go in and say cheerio to her?
CAPTAIN: You do that for me, Sergeant, would you?
   [*He smiles broadly and exits.* KNOX *moves off stage.* DAVY *opens Willie's cell door.*]
DAVY: Right, Willie, you're leaving here now, let's go.

WILLIE: Magic, magic. I like it, I like it.

[*He grabs his things and makes for the door.*]

DAVY: Not so fast, not so fast.

[DAVY *and* WILLIE *move towards reception.*]

WILLIE: Magic, magic. Hear the one about the man who was collecting down our street? Holds out a collection box and says to me, 'Dr. Barnardo's Home'. I says, 'I didn't know he was away!' [*Roars with laughter*] 'I didn't know he was away!' I like, I like.

DAVY: I don't know what you're laughing at. There's a vehicle waiting at the front gate to take you to Townhall Street. You're being kept in custody to face three separate charges in Court on Monday morning.

WILLIE: Ah fuck, ah fuck.

[WILLIE *drops his parcel of bread, spilling the pieces of soda farl out on to the stage.*]

[*Lights.*]

PICTURES OF TOMORROW
(1994)

Pictures of Tomorrow was first performed at the Lyric Players Theatre, Belfast on 14th April 1994. It was directed by Andy Hinds. The cast was as follows:

Ray	Alan Bennion
Len	Ted Valentine
Hugo	James Green
Young Len	Peter Ballance
Young Hugo	Connor Grimes
Young Ray	John Paul Connolly
Kate/Josephina	Amanda Maguire

The plays is set in contemporary north London and Spain during the Spainish Civil War.

ACT ONE

The stage is an open playing area. At centre stage, there is a light armchair, two hard-backed chairs and a coffee table. At stage right is a bay window and, beside it, an entrance leading to the hallway and a London street. Upstage, we get a sense of Spain. Golden, yellow, hot, sunny and bright. The entrance to a farm out-building is at stage left. We see olive trees. The full stage at any time can be the playing area for a London flat or Spain or both. Downstage, an elderly man enters.

RAY OLIVER *is 81 years of age. He is not in the best of health. He 'carries' his left arm and walks slowly. His appearance is dishevelled. He carries a jotter and a transistor radio which he places on the floor beside the armchair where he sits. He turns the radio on.*

Upstage, at exactly the same time as RAY OLIVER *enters,* YOUNG RAY OLIVER *enters. He is 25 years of age. He is stripped to the waist and is shaving. He looks into a small mirror on the out-building wall. A young woman,* JOSEPHINA, *enters from the out-building, carrying a heavy box of ammunition and couple of rifles strung over her shoulder. She places them beside* YOUNG RAY *and exits.* YOUNG RAY *watches her admiringly. Presently, loud contemporary rock music is heard from the London street.*

RAY: Bloody noise.
  [*He hurries over and closes a window. We hear an announcement on the radio.*]
RADIO: And now over to the BBC Weather Centre.
WEATHER PERSON: The outlook for today is mainly bright and sunny. There may be some showers in the south east, but these should pass quickly, while tonight will be cool and dry. [RAY *is writing furiously.*] Tomorrow, rain is expected in all parts and should continue through into the early part of next week. So really, you should enjoy the sun today while it lasts. More weather at six.
RAY: More bollocks at six. [*At this, Ray's granddaughter,* KATE, *enters from the street. She is 26 and wearing a grey tracksuit, runners and a woolly sweater. As* KATE *enters downstage,* YOUNG RAY *exits upstage.*]

KATE: Who's getting it now?
RAY: Bloody BBC weathermen. Wouldn't know the difference between a hurricane, sugar cane or Michael Caine.
KATE: Oh, you and your weather charts. [KATE *puts her bags down and begins tidying the flat.*]
RAY: That's all very well, but I wouldn't have to keep them, if the BBC was even half accurate.
KATE: You don't have to keep them.
RAY: And who's gonna keep the BBC in check? Two years of charts I have there, and as soon as I get a chance to collate them, the whole lot's going to my MP.
KATE: What's the weather got to do with you? You never go out.
RAY: They're being paid public money. Look, just take this week. [*He flicks through the pad.*] Monday, they said it would rain. The sun split the trees. Tuesday, they said more rain. It was practically a bloody heatwave. Then they said the rest of the week would be sunny. And what happens? It's pissed all week—
KATE [*interrupting*]: I see the Festival parade's about to begin.
RAY: Festival?
KATE: I passed the park gates just as a brilliant steel band started to play.
RAY: That's another thing. They call it a community festival. Was I consulted? Was Mrs. Bradford across the hall? Or little Paddy from downstairs? No. We're just a bunch of geriatric old bastards. We're meant to go into our beds and lie down and die for the entire weekend. Community festival, my arse. More like an excuse for terrorising the decent people of the district.
KATE: It's only young people enjoying themselves.
[*She opens a window. We hear Pogues-type Irish music and someone shouting over a microphone.*]
RAY: Enjoying themselves? People who run so-called 'community festivals' usually have a political agenda at the back of it all.
KATE: Look, we've had enough ranting and raving for one morning. Time to get ready, please.
RAY: Ready?
KATE: You know what day it is.
RAY: Yes, it's Saturday lunch-time and it's no different from any other Saturday lunch-time.

KATE: Oh yes, it is.
RAY: You're right, it is. But not in the way you think so.
KATE: Look, grandad. Both you and I have spent a long time sorting this out. We've put it off twice already. You've met the people. You said yourself they were nice.
RAY: Because they're nice doesn't mean I want to live with them. Mrs. Bradford across the hall carries my chair down to the back garden on sunny days, but I don't want to lick cream off her backside.
KATE: Grandad!
RAY: I'm not moving anywhere. All I want is some peace.
KATE: You'll need some new things. A housecoat and pyjamas. I'll get them in town for you.
RAY: I never wore pyjamas in my puff and I'm not going to start now.
KATE: You'll need to. There'll be a lot of people about, including females. All there to give you their undivided attention. You met Miss McVeigh, you saw your room and you said yourself the gardens were beautiful.
RAY [*quietly*]: I'm not moving.
KATE: They're holding a reception especially for you this afternoon. All the other residents will—
RAY [*shouting*]: I'm not moving to no old peoples' home! [*Pause.*] That's it. Final. Kaputt.
[*He turns the radio on. She turns it off.*]
KATE: We agreed.
RAY: Who agreed? You?
KATE: The family.
RAY: The family? Your mother? You actually found her?
KATE: You know we rang Peter.
RAY: Peter? What's he got to do with me?
KATE: I thought he was your son.
RAY: A waster, if ever there was one. A good day's work would frighten the life out of him. And you rang him?
KATE: He's working now. On an ACE scheme.
RAY: He's 40-bloody-7.
KATE: My mum thought he should be consulted.
RAY: Why doesn't your mum come over here and consult me?
KATE: You know you always lay into her.
RAY: I've every right to lay into her.

KATE: She cries for you.
RAY: A bit late in the day.
KATE: She tries her best.
RAY: So did your grandmother.
KATE: Look, this isn't getting us very far.
RAY: Snap. And if it's okay with you, I'm expecting visitors.
[KATE *is stunned.*]
KATE: What?
RAY: You heard me.
KATE: You have visitors? You haven't had a visitor in this flat in years.
RAY: I have now.
KATE: Who?
RAY: Friends of mine.
KATE: You don't have any friends.
RAY: You'd be surprised.
KATE: Grandad. This is beginning to get on my nerves. You've lived on your own since granny died, you seldom leave the flat—
RAY: Mrs. Bradford takes—
KATE: The back garden is not 'out'. You see no one from one week's end to the next, apart from me. You've had a stroke, you now have Alzheimer's, you're in need of constant professional care. You agreed you need it and I've gone to a lot of trouble to arrange it. Now, what the hell is going on?
RAY: I haven't got Alzheimer's. The doctor thinks I might have it.
KATE: Either way, there's plenty wrong with you. So what in heaven's name are you doing inviting people round here on the very day you are to move house?
RAY: What a euphemism! You call bolting me away in a geriatric hen-hole moving house?
KATE: No, but I could have you shot! [KATE *exits.* RAY *sits resolute for a moment. Then he struggles up and goes over to the suitcases. He stares at them. He angrily lifts the suitcases and empties the contents on the floor.* KATE *enters with more clothes and stops. She begins tidying the clothes in silence for a moment.*] Who are these visitors?
RAY: Old friends.
KATE: From?
RAY: The old days.

KATE: Who are they?

RAY [*getting irritated*]: Old friends. Comrades from the Spanish Civil War. Can I not see my old friends before I ... before I kick the bucket?

KATE: Of course, you can. But why today?

RAY: Len should have been here. The Cardiff train was due half an hour ago.

KATE: He's travelling all the way from Wales?

RAY: Why shouldn't he?

KATE: Where else are they descending from?

RAY: There only is another one. He's from Belfast.

KATE: My God! You're dragging an elderly man all the way from Belfast?

RAY: Not quite. He's lived in Hammersmith since 1939.

KATE: Well, at least clean yourself up before they arrive.

RAY: Mind your own business.

KATE: You won't get away with not washing in your new home.

RAY: I'm not going to any new home. And no one tells me when to wash, except me.

KATE: Your friends will smell you.

RAY: Don't talk to me about smells. They've seen me take my trousers down and shit right in front of them. And I've seen them do exactly the same. I know Len and Hugo better than their own families do. In Spain, smelling each other's smells was like reading each other's letters. A confirmation of comradeship.

KATE: You planned for this to happen today.

RAY: I didn't. Len's been writing to me for years, wanting the three of us to get together. Hugo's always on to me, 'Ray, let's get together for a drink. Let's have a reunion, sing a few of the old songs and talk about Spain. C'mon, Ray, old mate, let's get together with Len one last time?' I've always refused up to now.

KATE: So why change your mind now? What's so life-and-death about now?

RAY: There's nothing life-and-death about it. It's just that ... the world has changed in the last few years. I just feel it's time for us to talk things over.

KATE: But what am I going to tell these people at the home?

RAY: Tell them ... tell them I snuffed it in the middle of the night.

KATE: Alright. You meet your mates this afternoon. I'll ring the home and tell them to expect you early this evening.
RAY: You'll do no such thing.
KATE: I'm taking you in my car.
RAY: Crap.
KATE: I'm going to ring the doctor.
RAY: You can ring the Royal College of Surgeons for all I care.
KATE: It's for your own good.
RAY: Bollocks.
KATE: I'm going out now to buy you some pyjamas. I'll be back here at exactly six o'clock. You be ready and waiting. [KATE *exits.* YOUNG RAY *enters. He lifts the box of ammunition and places it in front of the coffee table. He does the same with the rifles. He exits for a cloth and returns.* JOSEPHINA *enters with some food and coffee for him. He proceeds to eat while she cleans the rifles. At this* YOUNG LEN BUSSELL *enters, wearing a good suit and carrying a grip-bag. He coughs.* YOUNG RAY *and* JOSEPHINA *turn round sharply.*]
YOUNG RAY [*going towards him, but still eating*]: Who are you?
YOUNG LEN: Len Bussell.
YOUNG RAY: From?
YOUNG LEN: Wales. Garw Valley, South Wales.
[YOUNG RAY *holds out his hand.* YOUNG LEN *can't take his eyes off Young Ray's plate of food.*]
YOUNG RAY: Ray Oliver, London. Pleased to meet you. [YOUNG LEN *shakes, but stares at the food.*] You hungry?
YOUNG LEN: Starving.
[YOUNG RAY *holds out a piece of bread in his hand and looks at it.* YOUNG LEN *thinks it's for him.*]
YOUNG RAY: Yeah, so am I. This is our first food for 36 hours.
[YOUNG RAY *proceeds to eat it. He nods to* JOSEPHINA *to get* YOUNG LEN *some food. She exits.*]
YOUNG LEN: I've been told to report to you.
YOUNG RAY: Good. Ready for war?
YOUNG LEN [*hesitant*]: I a … I think I'll need some training.
YOUNG RAY: You mean you haven't gone through our six-month officer training course at Sandhurst?
YOUNG LEN: I'm afraid not.
YOUNG RAY: Oh, then I'll have to put you in charge of peeling spuds and cleaning out the shitehouse. [YOUNG RAY *proceeds to open the box of ammunition.*]

YOUNG LEN: Excuse me … sir.
YOUNG RAY: Ray. [JOSEPHINA *returns with some bread and gives it to* YOUNG LEN. *Exits.*]
YOUNG LEN: Excuse me, Ray. I know I'm not a trained soldier and all that, but I did come here to fight Franco. I wonder if you could find me some duties more directly connected to the war?
YOUNG RAY: I was only joking. As soon as we sort you out with gear, I'll book you a seat at the frontline, where you'll be close enough to pick Franco's nose.
YOUNG LEN: I didn't come here to joke.
YOUNG RAY: You didn't?
YOUNG LEN: No.
YOUNG RAY: Well, let me tell you something, Taffy. After you've spent a couple of weeks lying in the muck and shit of the trenches, with international fascism doing its level best to separate your balls from your bollocks, you'll pay good money for someone to make you laugh. [JOSEPHINA *returns with some military clothing for* YOUNG LEN. *Exits.*]
YOUNG LEN [*apologetic*]: I thought you were trying to make fun of me.
YOUNG RAY: I was. It's called the art of survival. It's not just your skin you have to save here, you know. You've got to fight like mad to stop yourself going round the twist.
YOUNG LEN: Do I get any training?
YOUNG RAY: A week, maybe two, in Albacete. After which, we'll expect you to kill ten fascists a day. [*Quickly.*] That's another joke.
YOUNG LEN: Just point me in the right direction.
YOUNG RAY: How was your journey?
YOUNG LEN: Bloody long and hard. I left home eight days ago. Told my mother and father I was going to Colwyn Bay for the weekend. I sent a letter from London telling them the truth.
YOUNG RAY: I'm sure they'll understand.
YOUNG LEN: My mother will be heartbroken. I'm her eldest son. I joined my father down the mine two years ago, but now my father's in very bad health and I'm the breadwinner.
YOUNG RAY: *Was* the breadwinner.
YOUNG LEN: I don't know how they'll manage. I feel desperately guilty.

YOUNG RAY: Well, as you and I know, Len, the fight for the Spanish Republic is more important than being a miner or a breadwinner. Fascism must be stopped here, or it will sweep the world.

YOUNG LEN: That's what Nye Bevan said.

YOUNG RAY: Nye Bevan? I wouldn't listen to too much he said. Bloody Labour Party.

YOUNG LEN: I'm in the Labour Party.

YOUNG RAY: Oh.

YOUNG LEN: That's where I heard Nye Bevan speaking. At a Labour rally in Cardiff in defence of Spain. Boy, can he speak. I never heard a man who can make you want to cry, cheer and fight all at the same time. Absolutely spellbinding. I went up to him after the meeting. I waited till most people had gone. I called him to one side and said, 'Excuse me, Mr. Bevan, but I'd like to go to Spain to fight for democracy'. He gave me the most curious look. 'This is a war, you know. It's not people shouting round corners,' he said. I said, 'I know that, but I was wondering if you knew how I could get to Spain'. He warned me against it. He told me one in three volunteers were dying in Spain and that I should go away home and think very carefully about it. I said, 'I'm sorry, Mr. Bevan, but I've given it all the thought I need. I want to go to Spain'. A week later, I was on my way.

YOUNG RAY: To Colwyn Bay?

YOUNG LEN: God forgive me.

YOUNG RAY: This bloody ammunition! Three quarters of each box is useless.

YOUNG LEN: How did you get to Spain?

YOUNG RAY: Very simple. I was working as a compositor in Fleet Street when the party put out the call for volunteers. I applied immediately.

YOUNG LEN: The Communist Party?

YOUNG RAY: Of course. Joined when I was 16. The week after the General Strike 1926. After I watched my father sit down and cry because he couldn't feed his family.

YOUNG LEN: How did your people take it?

YOUNG RAY: Oh, great. They're both in the party now. They've been great. My biggest problem was tearing myself away from Rachel Prescott, the most beautiful girl in the whole of

London. Think she's quite upset that I'm here. [*He instantly pulls out a photograph of a girl and shows it to* YOUNG LEN.]

YOUNG LEN: She's very nice, very nice indeed.

YOUNG RAY: She's beautiful. Thinks I'm totally batty. Doesn't know what Spain's got to do with me. But, I haven't told anyone, we got engaged the day before I left.

YOUNG LEN: Congratulations. It must be love.

YOUNG RAY: She writes to me twice a week. Even sent me a hat she made, with my initials embroidered on it. [YOUNG RAY *shows* YOUNG LEN *the hat.*] She says if I wear it into battle, I'll never be shot. [YOUNG LEN *has selected his clothes.*] Get what you need?

YOUNG LEN: I think so.

YOUNG RAY: Right, over to your billet. I'm putting you beside an Irishman. Eamon Downey, the poet. He's a fine young fellow, but he never shuts up. And when he should be fighting, he's writing bloody poetry.

[*They are about to move off, when* YOUNG LEN *accidentally drops his helmet. He picks it up and looks at it, a little nervously.*]

YOUNG LEN: Is it true? That one in three volunteers are dying?

[YOUNG RAY *looks at* YOUNG LEN, *looks away and back at him.* YOUNG RAY *smiles.*]

YOUNG RAY: Who's counting? [*He goes over to* YOUNG LEN.] At this very moment, the biggest battle since the Great War is raging at Jarama, just outside Madrid. Franco has publicly declared he wants the capital urgently. He's getting very close. He's hit the bar a few times. He's got German planes, German pilots, Italian soldiers, Moroccan soldiers, Portuguese, Spanish, all running at the Madrid defence. But they haven't scored yet. All the British and Irish boys have been in the thick of it. Some have died. Some of us have survived. But nobody's counting.

[YOUNG RAY *exits.* YOUNG LEN *stares after him. We hear loud music as* LEN BUSSELL *enters from the street. He stops beside* YOUNG LEN.]

LEN: Heavens, that music's loud. [YOUNG LEN *exits.*]

RAY: No, it's not. It's great fun. The festival committee says it's great fun. [RAY *closes the door behind him, fading the music.*] No problem finding the place?

LEN: No. Taximan knew the district well.

[LEN *is 78 years of age, An ex-full time trade union official, he is still a fit, sprightly man. He is dressed very neatly with an overcoat, suit, shirt and tie, brylcreem on his hair, etc.*]

RAY: Take your coat off. Sit down. Hugo will be here very soon, so I'll leave the tea till he comes, okay?
LEN: Fine with me. But will Hugo want tea?
RAY: Hey, it's good to see you, Len. It's incredible, but you've hardly changed since I last saw you.
LEN: You must be joking. I'm 78 and I feel a hundred and eight.
RAY: You're talking? I was two hundred on my last birthday.
[LEN *takes out a pipe.*]
LEN: Mind if I smoke?
RAY: Len, you were a devout Methodist, didn't smoke or drink.
LEN: I started this after we lost the last miners' strike.
RAY: You said something in your letter about meeting your daughter in London?
LEN: Yes. I thought, since I was coming up to see you and Hugo, I'd take the opportunity to visit my daughter.
RAY: I'm sure you're looking forward to it.
LEN: Can't wait. It's really silly. It's been a long time and I've two grandchildren I've only seen pictures of.
RAY: You'll enjoy that.
LEN: They're meeting me at Putney Bridge tube station at eight o'clock and I'm staying the night with them. They're making a big thing about my visit.
RAY: Well, it is good to see you, Len. It really is.
LEN: And how have you been? I can't say you haven't changed. 1968? Almost 30 years ago.
RAY: You made a pretty good trade union leader. I've seen you on TV a few times.
LEN: With my face washed, I hope.
RAY: I haven't always been in the best of health, Len. I had a stroke a couple of years ago and, only a fortnight ago, my doctor confirmed I'm at the early stages of Alzheimer's Disease.
LEN: Christ, I'm sorry to hear that, Ray.
RAY: My granddaughter, Kate, looks after me.
LEN: Your granddaughter.
RAY: Well, she's more like a daughter, really. Marion and I have raised her since she was ten.
LEN: You've had your hands full.
RAY: She's been away at university, but she's back working in London now. Last month, she had to come and collect me

from Fulham football ground. I was found sitting at the players' entrance with an autograph book. I don't remember a thing about it.

LEN: I really am very sorry to hear that, Ray. But why do you keep going back to see Fulham? They hadn't won anything when you were in Spain and they still haven't.

[RAY *smiles.*]

RAY: At least we have football teams in London. What have you got in Wales, only rugby teams and male voice choirs?

LEN: Don't you start Hugo about the Welsh.

RAY: What's the chances that the first thing he shouts when he comes through that door is 'manos arriba!'

LEN: Yeah, manos flaming arriba. [*Mimics.*] 'I was the only man never heard them words. I wasn't captured.' [*The men are laughing.*] Hugo was the biggest liar I ever came across.

RAY: He loved trouble, didn't he?

LEN: Loved it.

RAY: In fairness, he hated Franco. I never came across a braver man in Spain. Hugo was my Alan Ball.

LEN: *Alan Ball?*

RAY: In every great football team, you need certain types of players. A great goalkeeper, a midfield ballplayer, a goalscorer. But you also need a worker. Somebody who'll run and run, cover every blade of grass and win balls. The type of job Alan Ball did for England in the 1966 World Cup. Hugo was my Alan Ball. Volunteered for everything.

LEN: Do you remember the time General Lister visited us at the front?

RAY: Didn't Hugo shake hands with him or something?

LEN: Shake hands? He volunteered a plan he had for killing Franco. He wanted permission to surprise Franco while he was having Holy Communion and slit his throat.

RAY: Pity it never came off.

LEN: It still annoys me to think that Franco, the man that started it all, lived into his old age and died peacefully in his bed.

RAY: Unlike many of the young men who went out with us.

LEN: Like Eamon Downey. Do you remember his beautiful poems?

RAY: Of course, I do.

LEN [*reciting*]: 'As my spirit spirals forward seeking strength, I

catch myself painting pictures of tomorrow.' Downey-the-poet the boys used to call him.
RAY: Yeah, yeah, Downey-the-poet.
LEN: He was such a smashing fellow. Wasn't he, Raymond?
RAY: Eamon was my midfield artist. My Bobby Charlton. Always brimming with ideas. Always in the thick of things, prodding and poking the opposition, but never losing his composure.
LEN: And who was I in your great Spanish football team?
RAY: You? Nobby Stiles.
LEN: Nobby Stiles? I wasn't anything like Nobby Stiles.
RAY: He was the heart of the '66 team. The hard man. Quiet off the field, but a tiger on it.
LEN: I was shit scared most of the time in Spain.
RAY: When you arrived, yes. You were the shy little naive village boy from the Welsh valleys. But we all soon found out what a tough, stubborn little bastard you could be.
LEN: I have a great memory of you in Spain, Ray.
RAY: Always complaining about the coffee.
LEN: My one great memory of you, and this is leaving aside all the great, very brave things you did as our commanding officer, I will always remember you singing 'Mack the Knife'.
RAY: What a ridiculous thing to remember.
LEN: I'd love to hear you singing it again, Ray.
RAY: I can hardly breathe now, never mind sing.
LEN: How long is it since you've seen Hugo?
RAY: A year ago. At a Communist Party function. He's always on the 'phone. But I haven't been able to get about much since the stroke. Look at my bloody arm. [*He holds up his arm. It shakes.*]
LEN: So, you're still a committed party member after all these years? [RAY *shakes his head slowly.*]
RAY: No.
LEN: You never mentioned any of this when I wrote to you.
RAY: I didn't see the point.
LEN: This is quite a shock. I expected you to be one of the die-hards, Ray. In fact, I was talking to Hugo just last year and he assured me you were a fully paid-up party member.
RAY: I still am. Unbroken membership since 1926.
LEN: So what are you talking about?
RAY: I'm paid-up. But my heart hasn't been in it in recent years.

The Berlin Wall coming down was like one of those slow-motion dreams you have, where you're falling from a high building and you're powerless to do anything about it. When the Soviet Union collapsed, I hit the ground and was able to watch my skull splinter into a thousand little pieces. All in slow motion. I've given up, Len.

LEN: I never thought I'd hear you say that.

RAY: Listen. I stuck it out, right through Hungary, 1956. I remember feeling uneasy about Czechoslovakia in 1968, but I believed it had to be done. The doubts were shoved well to the back of my head. But now, now even the Russian people have rejected it. It's all come to a very, very sad and confusing end.

LEN: You've told the party?

RAY: No, I haven't. And I'm not going to.

LEN: You must have been to some meetings?

RAY: No. I've been able to use this [*Holds out his shaking arm.*] as an excuse.

LEN: This is ... this is quite incredible, Ray. If you've stopped believing, you have to tell them.

RAY [*sharply*]: No. No, I can't.

LEN: For your own sake.

RAY: I can't walk away after all these years. It's been my whole life. Every day for 60 years, I woke up, I thought 'Party'. Every friend I had was in the party. I even married a Communist. There's been nothing else. I had no life whatsoever outside the Communist Party. I was on the national executive. I was a hero of the Spanish Civil War. I'm looked up to by thousands of party members. I don't want to let all those good people down. I don't want to betray anyone. I haven't got the courage to walk away.

LEN: Does Hugo know this?

RAY: No.

LEN: Are you going to tell him today?

RAY: You mustn't say a word, Len.

LEN: You haven't even discussed it with him?

RAY: Are you mad?

LEN: Surely, even he'll understand.

RAY: Len, Hugo loves me. And I think the world of him. But he's a dyed-in-the-wool old Stalinist. He's as active now as he was when he joined. It's a bit like watching Alan Ball still trying to cover every blade of grass at Wembley 30 years after the event.

LEN: Always trying to recapture his youth.

RAY: Sometimes I'd give anything to be 19 again. To get all the old certainties back.

LEN: In your younger days there are no contradictions. When I first discovered socialism, I wanted to pass it on to every man, woman and child.

RAY: When I first read Marx, it warmed my heart. It was beautiful to read. It took a little German Jew to make me first understand who I was, who my people were. He explained why there was the haves and the have-nots. He even told us who was to blame.

LEN: All we had to do was work out how best to change things.

RAY: That's when it got tricky.

LEN: I joined the Labour Party.

RAY: I definitely didn't join the Labour Party.

LEN: But we agreed on Spain.

RAY: Everybody agreed on Spain. That's why men and women from all over the world came to join the International Brigade.

LEN: They came from 53 different countries. The most unusual army ever assembled in the history of the world.

RAY: But I don't want this to sound sentimental or stupid, Len, but ... I have always been proud to know you.

LEN: And me you.

RAY: No, I mean this. Me, you and Hugo, we went through so much together.

LEN: So why did you never agree to us getting together before this? [*The front doorbell rings.*]

RAY: That must be Hugo now.

LEN: I'll get it, Ray. [LEN *exits. Upstage, it is night-time. The silence is broken by the distant sound of* YOUNG HUGO *singing* 'The Internationale'. *It gets louder.*]

YOUNG HUGO [*off-stage*]:
So comrades come rally
And the last fight let us face
The Internationale
Unites the human race

[*He enters on-stage, gesticulating, bottle of wine in hand, shouting.*]
Viva la Republic Espanya! Viva la Communist Party! Where

the hell is Eamon Downey? Viva la Pasionaria! [*He shouts, punching the air.*] Viva la Republic Espanya ! Viva la Communist Party ! Viva la Pasionaria! [*He looks around.*] Where the hell is Eamon Downey?

[*At this,* JOSEPHINA *enters. She furiously remonstrates with* YOUNG HUGO *in Spanish.*]

JOSEPHINA: Callarte tu boca, estas haciendo demasiado ruido, callarte.

YOUNG HUGO: What?

JOSEPHINA: Que estrepito tranquilo hombre!

YOUNG HUGO: Listen, love. I got expelled from Slate Street School when I was nine. I can hardly speak English, never mind Spanish.

JOSEPHINA: Por favor, no cantar, los militarios estan intentado de dormir. [*The girl grips* YOUNG HUGO *and tries to take the wine off him. He, in turn, grabs her and tries to dance with her. She fights him off.*]

YOUNG HUGO: Viva Irlande! Viva the Falls Road! Viva Leeson Street! Downey, come out wherever you are!

JOSEPHINA: Por favor, un fochito de silencio ya estas!

YOUNG HUGO:
So comrades come rally
And the last fight let us face …
[*The girl slaps* YOUNG HUGO *hard on the face, just as* YOUNG RAY *and* YOUNG LEN *emerge half-dressed from an out-building.*]

YOUNG HUGO: What the … ? [*He grabs the girl and begins shaking her.*] Who the hell do you think—

YOUNG RAY: Right, right, right, that's enough.

YOUNG LEN: Easy on, easy on. [*They separate the fight.*]

YOUNG HUGO: Did you see what she did to me?

JOSEPHINA: Estas imborracio, demasadio ruido.

YOUNG HUGO: She slapped me on the face, the bitch.

YOUNG RAY: I take it you're Boyd, from Belfast?

YOUNG HUGO: It doesn't matter who I am, but who does this bitch think she is?

JOSEPHINA: Tienes que este en la cama, hay una guerra sabes.

YOUNG HUGO: Yeah, and up your arse, too.

YOUNG RAY [*firmly*]: Okay, Boyd, that's enough. Over there, and I'll talk to Josephina.

YOUNG HUGO: Over where? Who do you think you are?

YOUNG LEN: Listen, mate. This is Ray Oliver, your commanding officer.

YOUNG HUGO: Ah, Christ, no. You're Ray Oliver? Ah, Jesus, I'm sorry, mate. Sorry, sorry about all this. I was supposed to be here earlier. I'm Eamon Downey's mate from Belfast.

YOUNG RAY: Okay, move off.

YOUNG HUGO: Right, right. [YOUNG LEN *guides* YOUNG HUGO *across stage.*] Who is that witch anyway?

YOUNG LEN: That's Josephina. She cooks for us. It is okay, I'll deal with him.

YOUNG HUGO: I'm not eating anything she cooks.

YOUNG RAY: Gracias. Muchas gracias.

YOUNG LEN: You'll eat every bite she puts in your mouth and be glad of it.

JOSEPHINA: Make sure he goes to sleep.

YOUNG RAY: It's okay. [JOSEPHINA *turns to go.*] Buenas noches.

JOSEPHINA: Buenas noches. [*She exits.* YOUNG RAY *joins the others.*]

YOUNG RAY [*To* YOUNG HUGO]: You need coffee.

YOUNG LEN: I'll make some.

[YOUNG LEN *exits.*]

YOUNG HUGO: I am very sorry, Mr. Oliver. I didn't mean to waken everybody up.

YOUNG RAY: I'm Ray.

YOUNG HUGO: I'm Hugo. Hugo Boyd, Falls Road, Belfast.

YOUNG RAY [*pointing to* YOUNG LEN]: He's Len. So, why did you not arrive along with the rest of the recruits?

YOUNG HUGO: It wasn't my fault, I swear to God. In Barcelona, our train was delayed and when it come, it was jam-packed with refugees running from the fascists. I mean, absolutely jam-packed. There was no way I could get on it. Honest to God, I tried.

YOUNG RAY: How come the other 44 recruits were able to get on it?

YOUNG HUGO: I'm reporting that crowd. Who do you make a complaint to around here?

YOUNG RAY: About what?

YOUNG HUGO: Them other recruits. They trailed women and children off that train to get on it. I saw women hurt and crying.

YOUNG RAY: So what did you do?

YOUNG HUGO: What could I do? The bloody train went without me.

YOUNG RAY: You were left on your own?

YOUNG HUGO: Completely and absolutely on my Jack Sloan.

YOUNG RAY: You contacted the International Brigade headquarters?

YOUNG HUGO: Not straight away.

YOUNG RAY: Why not?

YOUNG HUGO: Well there was an anarchist office beside the train station, but I wasn't going in there, right? Next door to that, there was a ... let me find a polite way of saying this ... a whore house. But as a principled communist, I couldn't let myself darken its doorway, right? [YOUNG LEN *arrives with the coffee.*]

YOUNG LEN: Why not?

YOUNG HUGO: It was bloody well closed. Then, next to that was a pub.

YOUNG RAY: A pub?

YOUNG HUGO: Now, you have to consider the situation. I had been travelling since I left Belfast 14 days ago, with strict orders not to draw attention to myself in England or France, in case the authorities stopped me coming here. No talking to strangers, no socialising, no drinking. I hadn't a drink in 14 tucking days. That's the predicament I found myself in.

YOUNG RAY: So you succumbed?

YOUNG HUGO: No, I did not. Not immediately. But as I entered that pub I heard music. Flamingo music.

YOUNG LEN: Flamenco.

YOUNG HUGO: Flamenco, whatever it is. As soon as I walked in the door, there was two of the ... ooh, the finest looking women I ever saw, doing Flamingo dancing.

YOUNG LEN: Flamenco.

YOUNG HUGO: By God, it's stirring stuff, isn't it? The two of them came straight over and started dancing with me!

YOUNG LEN: You enjoyed yourself then?

YOUNG HUGO: Enjoyed myself? One of them didn't want to let me go. Senorita, she said her name was. She wanted to take me back to her house and stay the weekend. I says, 'Senorita, nothing would give me greater pleasure, but I'm a Belfast communist on my way to beat the bollocks out of Franco and mere matters of the flesh will have to take a back seat'.

YOUNG RAY: You left, then?
YOUNG HUGO: Not at that exact moment.
YOUNG LEN: Why not?
YOUNG HUGO: She took me upstairs.
YOUNG RAY: What about fighting Franco?
YOUNG HUGO: Fuck Franco. A man in need will temporarily shed the greatest cause at the sight of a good pair of tits.
YOUNG RAY: Well, the cause is still very much here. And you need some sleep to prepare for it. [*They get up to go.*]
YOUNG LEN: Six o'clock start in the morning.
YOUNG RAY: That's four hours away.
YOUNG HUGO: Why, what's happening?
YOUNG RAY: We're going on the offensive at Brunete.
YOUNG LEN: Franco will not be amused.
YOUNG HUGO: Franco? Will he be there? In person, like?
YOUNG RAY: Could well be.
YOUNG HUGO: Good, good, good. Tell the Vatican to prepare for Franco's funeral. What sort of weapon will I be getting? Put me in charge of a tank so that, when I aim, I won't miss his big, fat, ugly, stinking, fascist, Catholic, Nazi, pea-brained, baldy, Spanish nut.
YOUNG LEN: Well, I don't think you left anything out.
YOUNG HUGO: I did. He's a big-nosed glipe as well.
YOUNG RAY: Hugo. Sleep. [*At exit.*]
YOUNG HUGO: Right, right. Sleep. By the way, where's that reprobate Downey?
YOUNG RAY: Leading the advance party, the Yanks and the Canadians.
YOUNG LEN: By the time we rise, Downey'll be in the thick of it.
YOUNG HUGO: Did I not tell you about the time me and him went—
YOUNG RAY: Sleep, Hugo!
YOUNG HUGO: Yes, yes, right, kip. Some shuteye.
[YOUNG LEN *and* YOUNG HUGO *exit, while* YOUNG RAY *finishes off his coffee. Off-stage, we hear a commotion as* YOUNG HUGO *discovers his sleeping quarters.*]
YOUNG HUGO: What? I'm supposed to sleep in that?
YOUNG LEN: It's fine. You'll get used to it.
YOUNG HUGO: Used to it? It's a friggin' barn. Kane's Rag Store wouldn't be in it. I'm going back to the Flamingo dancers in

Barcelona. Who could teach me how to dance Flamingo?
[LEN *and* HUGO *are in the hall out of view. There has been a dispute and the men are shouting. They enter.*] Where's the nearest pub to here?
YOUNG LEN: Will you shut up, Hugo?
HUGO: It wasn't my fault!
LEN: Hugo, will you shut up!
[YOUNG RAY *exits.*]
HUGO: I'm not letting him away with that.
LEN: Shut up, Hugo.
[HUGO *is 78 years of age. He is carrying a crash-helmet under one arm and a haversack on his back. He wears a dark brown suit, shiny and worn, a white shirt open at the neck and a black beret on his head. He is extremely agitated.*]
HUGO: That bastard punched me.
LEN: You hit him first.
HUGO: He deserved it. He nearly knocked me off my bike.
LEN: It was an accident. Wipe that blood from your mouth.
HUGO: Blood? Right, I'll show the bastard—
LEN: C'mon, sit bloody well down.
HUGO: It's alright for you, Len, you weren't punched by a six-foot lorry driver.
LEN: Forget it, Hugo.
HUGO: I'll remember his face.
RAY: This is typical.
HUGO: What is?
[*The others sit down while* HUGO *remains standing. He generally prefers to stand or pace about than sit.*]
RAY: Always in trouble of some sort.
HUGO: I didn't start it.
RAY: You're an old man now, Hugo.
HUGO: What do you mean?
RAY: I mean, the next time you attend a funeral, you'll be exempt from carrying the coffin.
HUGO: Who? I'm as fit today as I was when I arrived in Spain in 1937. How are you, Ray, old mate?
RAY: Fine, Hugo. [*They shake hands.*]
HUGO: Good to see you, Len.
LEN: And you too, Hugo. [*They shake.*]
HUGO: I walk five miles every day, drive the moped to Brighton

once a week and I'm available any time the wife feels up to it. Which isn't very often. Here, that was a nice wee woman I saw on the stairs there.

RAY: Mrs. Bradford.

HUGO: Nice pair of legs.

RAY: That's my neighbour you're talking about.

HUGO: Well, invite her up.

RAY: She's too young for you. She's only 68.

HUGO: Good, an unwanted pregnancy won't be an issue then.

RAY [*attempting to get up*]: Right. Lunch-time, gentlemen. I'll put the kettle on.

LEN: Sit where you are, Ray. I'll put the kettle on.

RAY: Thanks, Len. First on the left.

HUGO: Kettle? I thought this was a reunion of old comrades. Where's the drink?

RAY: Tea first.

LEN [*moving to exit*]: Don't tell me you're still a boozer, Hugo?

HUGO: No, I gave it up. I only drink now at weddings, funerals, christenings, Holy Days of Obligation, all public and bank holidays, Christmas, New Year, Easter, Valentine's Day, Father's Day, Mother's Day, St. Patrick's Day and every Tuesday and Saturday. No, I gave up drink as a bad job years ago. [*He laughs.* LEN *exits to the kitchen.*]

RAY: Still the same old Hugo.

HUGO: Still the same old Hugo. Only younger.

RAY: Fag?

HUGO: I'll have one of my own roll-ups, if that's okay. [RAY *lights a cigarette.* HUGO *lights his.*]

RAY: Thanks for coming.

HUGO: Don't mention it. But this is the last day of the British Open. I could be watching it with the lads in the pub. [*Takes an swing with an imaginary golf club.*]

RAY: By the way, I'll get you a drink soon, but let's take it easy. You know what the vicar's like.

HUGO: I'm alright with the fags, Ray. I really don't care much for drink these days.

RAY: Well, Jesus, I do. Don't leave me on my own. I just don't want to chase him away.

HUGO: Remember the time we spiked his drink in Gandesa?

RAY: Shshush.

HUGO: He walked up the village main street in his underpants.
[RAY *and* HUGO *try to suppress their laughter.*]
RAY: Then he tried to kiss Josephina, the cook. [*More laughing.*]
HUGO: Oh, right, before I forget. [HUGO *takes a long brown envelope out of his pocket and hands it to* RAY.] This is for you.
RAY: What is it?
HUGO: The conference in Birmingham.
RAY: Hugo, you know I'm not fit.
HUGO: I'll arrange for a car to pick us two up.
RAY: I can't afford to go.
HUGO: What do you think that is? The party sent it. Your expenses and something extra for the bevvies.
RAY: Hugo.
HUGO: The party needs you in Birmingham, Ray. It's going to be a crucial conference.
RAY: I can't take this.
HUGO: Instructions. No argument. Bert wants you there.
RAY: How is Bert?
HUGO: Same as ever. A cantankerous wee shite.
RAY: What's that smell?
HUGO: Len's burnt the toast.
RAY [*sniffing*]: No, it's not … toast. It's a strange smell.
[HUGO *holds out his cigarette.*]
HUGO: It's a … it's probably this.
RAY: What is it?
HUGO: It's only a wee bit of Bob Hope
RAY: Drugs? Jesus Christ. Hugo, you're the only man I know who immatures with age.
HUGO: When I was 21, my da said to me, 'Hugo, son, life is short. Try everything at least once, except religion and sheep-shagging'. Unfortunately, I only discovered dope ten years ago.
RAY: Say nothing to Len.
HUGO: Ach, he should a been a bishop instead of a trade union leader. Doesn't drink, doesn't use bad language, doesn't look at dirty books and believes the Labour Party is socialist. Huh.
RAY: I'll give you this, Hugo, your mouth shows no sign of slowing down.
HUGO: I told you, there's no part of me slowing down. I'm like the Royal Family. I'll keep going till I'm found out.

RAY: Your health's been good, then?
HUGO: Haven't been to a doctor since I got married. 1942.
RAY: What about the wife?
HUGO: It's a lovely sunny day, isn't it?
RAY: Yes, but—
HUGO: We're expecting to have a nice, pleasant day today, right?
RAY: Of course, but—
HUGO: So why do you have to mention my wife?
RAY: But you're still together?
HUGO: In much the same way as China and America sit on the same United Nations Security Council.
RAY: I thought she might have left you by now.
HUGO: Who? A river can't leave the mountain. How is it you start off a marriage with all these things in common. Live side by side for fifty years and end up the only thing you have in common is the fact that you're married to each other. I suppose it might have been different if she could've had children.
RAY: Marion's been dead three years.
HUGO: You always were lucky.
RAY: Hugo, my wife was an alcoholic. She made my life hell.
HUGO: I always told you, shoulda married that girl you went with before Spain. Rachel somebody.
RAY: She married a solicitor.
HUGO: She deserved that. No. I wouldn't wish that on any wee girl.
RAY: My life might have been so different with Rachel Prescott. No, I know it would have been different.
HUGO: You've only wasted fifty years of your life. It coulda been worse. Just imagine if you had had a great life, everything you wanted, happy and contented. Would you want to go? Would you be ready to pop off without complaint? Not at all. This way, with a messed-up life, you'll be happy to get it over with. [*Mimics, holding his hands on his chest.*] 'What's this, pains in my chest? Great, take me, take me!'
RAY: Are you ready to go?
HUGO: Not until I've slept with a black woman. [*Laughs.*] What about you?
RAY: Strangely enough, no.
HUGO: Probably because you think you'd bump into your

alcoholic wife.

RAY: I thought that ... when I reached the ... the ridiculous age of 80, there'd be no problem. I'd go whistling, cheerfully. But that's not the case at all. I don't want to go. I do not want to go. Okay, I'm 81, I don't have an 18 year-old body, but I'm okay. I feel fine. Who says I have to go?

HUGO: You're yapping. Waffling. Give it a rest and pour yourself a drink.

RAY: My granddaughter wants to put me in an old peoples' home.

HUGO: Oh.

RAY: Old peoples' homes are for old people.

HUGO: Do you know what we need? We need a drink.

RAY: Yeah, you're right. [LEN *enters.*]

LEN: Here we are, nothing like a good cup of tea.

RAY: Oh, fantastic.

LEN: What's all the shouting been about?

HUGO: It's him. He doesn't like old people.

RAY: I didn't say that. I just don't want to live with them 24 hours of every day.

LEN: Who says you should?

HUGO: His granddaughter. She wants to put him in an old peoples' home.

LEN: When's all this supposed to happen?

RAY: Today.

LEN: Today?

RAY: She has it all arranged. She called here earlier to pack my bags and take me in her car.

LEN: And?

RAY: I threw her out.

LEN: Good for you.

HUGO: I thought as much. It's not like you to let anybody jump all over you, like, is it? That's not the Ray Oliver I knew.

RAY: She's coming back.

HUGO: When?

RAY: Six o'clock this evening.

LEN: What for?

RAY: To take me to the home.

HUGO: So. Throw her out again.

RAY: I agreed last week that I'd go.

HUGO: So? You changed your mind.

LEN: You've told your granddaughter that you don't want to go? [RAY *nods.*]

HUGO: Right, that's it. We'll be here when she comes and, between the three of us, we'll 'repel the attack', right, lads?

LEN: I'm sure she'll listen to reason and understand.

RAY: Unfortunately, she's a bit like myself. Headstrong.

HUGO: Well, we kept Franco's army out of Madrid, we can beat off Ray's granddaughter. Let's have a drink and draw up the battle plans. [*He takes a bottle of whiskey from his haversack.*] Just for you, Ray, old mate.

LEN: Isn't it a bit too early in the day for drinking, Hugo?

HUGO: Well, when Jesus was turning the water into wine, it was only the ones who turned up early were able to get drunk. Who wants a Black Bush?

LEN: You're a terrible case, Hugo.

HUGO: Any glasses?

RAY [*pointing*]: In the kitchen.

LEN [*exiting*]: For God's sake.

HUGO: Here, I forgot to tell you. I've been invited to Barcelona.

RAY: What for?

HUGO: Ach, just one of my old girlfriends wants me to meet my grandchildren. [LEN *returns. The men laugh.* HUGO *pours drinks for himself and* RAY.] Len?

LEN: No. I'd take a beer, if there was a beer.

RAY: In the fridge.

HUGO: One-beer Len. Watch you don't get drunk.

LEN: No danger. [LEN *exits again.*]

RAY: He's meeting his daughter at Putney Bridge tube station at eight o'clock. He can't turn up smelling of beer.

HUGO [*shouting*]: That's what's wrong with the Welsh. Dylan Thomas died of drink and he's a national disgrace. We made Brendan Behan a national hero before he was cold in his grave. All the same, it must be sad for the Welsh. They produce one good writer, one good writer, and he drinks himself to death. The Irish could afford ten Brendan Behans.

RAY: Who's produced more writers than England?

HUGO: England? Apart from Shakespeare, who I admit was a good minor playwright, the only writers to come out of England were Spike Milligan and the guy who writes *Only Fools*

And Horses for the BBC. Both of Irish extraction, I might add.
RAY: I grant you, the Irish do produce good writers.
HUGO: More writers per square inch than any country in the world.
RAY: Because you had nothing else to do. [LEN *enters.*]
LEN: The English were too busy building an empire.
HUGO: Well, I'd rather sit in a house writing a poem than go around raping and plundering half the world.
LEN: Ireland's a place where half the population sits around writing self: pitying ballads and the other half travels the world singing them.
HUGO: Oh, you two are ganging up on me now?
RAY: You started it.
LEN: We're only retaliating.
HUGO: Well, I never heard the words 'manos arriba'.
RAY AND LEN: Here we go.
HUGO: In two years in Spain, I never came close to holding my hands up.
RAY: We didn't give ourselves up.
LEN: We were captured. [HUGO *'covers' them with an imaginary rifle, prowling around them.*]
HUGO: Manos arriba! Manos arriba! Hands up! You dirty, commie International Brigaders! Manos arriba! Que hace usted aqui?
RAY: We weren't fast enough to avoid capture. Every time there was the smell of danger, you were away like the clappers.
LEN: Jessie Owens the second.
HUGO: In war, two things determine a great soldier. The ability to hold on to your smokes and the resolute determination never, *never,* to be a hero.
LEN: You were wounded more times than us.
HUGO: Yes, but if you check my medical records, you'll see all my injuries were inflicted from the back. Back of my left arm, back of my left heel, back of my thigh … I was running away every time!
LEN: While we stayed and fought.
HUGO: That's why you ended up in Burgos Prison and I didn't.
RAY: Cut the codology, Hugo. You were a bloody good soldier. You were my Alan Ball.
HUGO: Alan Ball was a tube.
RAY: He was not.

HUGO: He was like a headless chicken running up and down the pitch. All legs and no brain.//
RAY: You were Alan Ball.//
LEN: I was his Nobby Stiles.//
HUGO: If I was anybody out of that team, I was Bobby Charlton, the midfield general.//
RAY: Rubbish.//
HUGO: Okay, at least ... at least ... I was Bobby Moore.//
RAY: I was your commanding officer. I was Bobby Moore.//
HUGO: What about the goalscorer, Geoff Hurst?//
RAY: No.//
HUGO: Martin Peters?//
RAY: Alan Ball! You were Alan Ball, and you should be proud of it.//
HUGO: Well, at least Alan Ball was a better player than Nobby Stiles.//
RAY [*winking at* HUGO]: Shut up and pour yourself another drink.//
HUGO [*feigning*]: Ah, no. I couldn't ... well, only if you join me.//
RAY: You wouldn't get us some water, Len, please?//
LEN [*standing*]: I am not going to stay here while you two get drunk.//
HUGO: We're heroes of Spain. We deserve the odd drink. The man's not all that long out of Burgos Prison.//
LEN: Who? He was only there a weekend. I was two years in Burgos. [LEN *exits.*]//
RAY: In 13 months, I killed seventeen thousand, five hundred and sixty-six lice in Burgos.//
[HUGO *pours more whiskey, including a large portion into Len's beer.*]//
HUGO [*The two men laugh.*]: We'll give him a Gandesa. It must have been terrible. You two lying tucked up in your beds, while I was fighting the last losing battle of the Ebro.//
RAY: Yes. You did cover yourself in glory.//
HUGO: I was a good soldier.//
LEN [*returning*]: We were all good soldiers.//
RAY: Do you remember the first time the three of us fought together?//
LEN: The battle of Brunete.//
HUGO: July the 6th, 1937.//
RAY: They had us up at six o'clock in the morning.//

[YOUNG LEN *enters, buttoning up his jacket.* YOUNG HUGO *enters. He is irritated and still only half-way through dressing and snatching bites from some bread.*]

YOUNG HUGO: Frigging disgrace, getting men up at this hour.

YOUNG LEN: Raring to go, Hugo?

YOUNG HUGO: It's sleep I need. Why can't they organise the war so that you get a good sleep and a good lie-in in the morning? That way, we'd be in a better state to fight.

YOUNG LEN: Why don't you go back to bed?

YOUNG HUGO: Who? I'm looking forward to this.

HUGO [*looking at* YOUNG HUGO]: I was like hell. Standing there that morning, I don't think I've ever been so terrified in my life. I'll always remember the sun that morning, shining deep, hard into my eyes, like it was telling me 'Right, Boyd, waken up, this isn't the Falls Road, this is the real thing. This is Spain. All your joking and drinking and flamingo dancing is over. Pick up your rifle'.

[YOUNG HUGO *picks up his rifle. He looks at* YOUNG LEN.]

YOUNG HUGO: How are you feeling yourself?

YOUNG LEN: Perfect. At last, the Republic's going on the offensive. We can now start pushing them back. I'm excited.

LEN: Excited? I was so scared, I couldn't sleep a wink all night, couldn't eat any breakfast. I hated the waiting, the hanging around. It gave you time to imagine what your brains would look like splattered across some field.

HUGO: At that very moment, I couldn't think of anything else but Belfast. In my mind's eye, I was walking down the Falls Road, waving to people I knew in Royal Avenue. I was watching the people of Belfast on their own streets. The dockers, the shipyard men, the poor millworkers, the unemployed, the wretched. It was them I was there for. At that moment, I would have given anything to be among them.

LEN: As I stared out over the straight rows of olive trees, all I could think of was the Brecon mountain in South Wales. When I was 15, that was the first mountain I climbed with my mother and father, on a Labour Party ramble, 1931. And I remember looking across at the lorry waiting to take us to Brunete, and all I could see was my mother and father, sitting on the lorry, kissing and cuddling. Then my mother started handing out sandwiches to some French volunteers. I remember her face was so beautiful. So sad. I had betrayed my mother, and even in the biggest battles, her face was always there. Like it was tattooed ten feet in front of my eyes.

[YOUNG RAY *has entered. He is reading a letter.*]

YOUNG LEN [*smirking*]: Another letter from Rachel.

YOUNG HUGO: 'Dear Raymond, Piss Off. I've found a tall, dark, handsome, obscenely-rich lover.'

YOUNG RAY [*embarrassed*]: A letter from the party in London, actually. More recruits on the way.

YOUNG HUGO: Uh ah. [YOUNG LEN *laughs.*]

YOUNG RAY: Are you men ready?

RAY: You didn't know it, Hugo, but it *was* another letter from Rachel. A month before, Eamon Downey and I had got locked into an argument about commitment. I had confided in him how much I was missing Rachel. He was appalled. He said if I was a true communist, if I was serious about defeating Franco, I should break off my engagement to Rachel. He said the revolution doesn't need any girlfriends. You knew Eamon, he was so fanatical, so brilliant with words. I wrote to Rachel and broke it off. The letter you saw me reading that morning had me close to tears. Rachel was distraught. I really wanted to cry. But all around me was ... was this war. Men with guns, tanks loaded with shells, the smell of war was everywhere, and then, in front of me, were you lot. And I was your commanding officer. It was bizarre. Of course, I hated Franco. It was just that I loved Rachel Prescott more. I thought about saying a few words to the men, but ... but all I could do was sing.

[YOUNG RAY *begins to sing* 'Avanti Popolo'.]

Avanti popolo, a la roscosa
Bandeira rosa, bandeira rosa
Avanti popolo, a la roscosa
Bandeira rosa, triumphera.

[YOUNG RAY *continues to sing, softly.*]

LEN: It was the right thing to do at the right time. Your singing sent shivers running down my back. God, I might have been scared but I was proud to be there.

HUGO: When the singing started, my adrenaline started pumping. I was ready for anything.

LEN: I remember the exhilaration as I watched the other men board the trucks, Germans, Dutchmen, Chinese...

HUGO: Russians! An absolute babble of languages!
LEN: All fighting together for the dignity of man!
HUGO: For an end to poverty!
LEN: Democracy !
HUGO: People all over the world declared their support for the Spanish Republic.
LEN: Hemingway visited!
HUGO: Orwell fought! [YOUNG LEN *and* YOUNG HUGO *join in the singing.* HUGO *and* LEN *are now almost shouting.*]
HUGO: Pablo Neruda spoke out!
LEN: Paul Robeson came to the front and sang!
HUGO: Brecht demonstrated!
LEN: Sean O'Casey supported us all the way!
HUGO: The workers of the world were, at last, truly united!
LEN: Fascism would be routed!
HUGO: Franco defeated!
LEN: Kill the bastard!
LEN AND HUGO: Salud! No pasaran!

[*At this, the young men start another verse of* 'Avanti Popolo', *this time louder. With rifles raised, they march on-the-spot, stamping their feet to the rhythm of the song. At the same time,* LEN *and* HUGO, *with fists raised, march up and down past each other, singing along with the young men in a rousing, climactic celebration.* RAY *remains in his chair. As* HUGO *gets carried away, he jumps up on a chair near the exit, punching the air with his fist. The song ends sharply, as* KATE *enters and looks up at* HUGO.]

KATE: I thought the Spanish Civil War ended years ago.

[Black-out.]

ACT TWO

Ray's flat. KATE *is standing with her coat on and her arms folded. She is doing her best to contain herself.* RAY *is seated and drinking.* LEN *is seated and puffing on his pipe. All eyes are on* HUGO, *who is in the middle of the floor, physically demonstrating a theory of his.*

HUGO: What I'm saying is, anyone who comes near you, anybody you see in the street, each of us in this room, we're surrounded by containers.
LEN: Containers?
RAY: You're definitely going off your head.
LEN [*looking around*]: There's no containers around me.
HUGO: Invisible containers. They're not meant to be seen.
RAY: But you can see them?
HUGO: Anyone can see them. If you look, if you really get to know someone.
LEN: What do you mean by containers?
HUGO: They could be anything. Wine bottles, black plastic bags, china tea cups, milk churns, plastic cups, anything.
RAY: And what's in them?
LEN: Is there supposed to be anything in them?
HUGO: Yes, yes, of course. That's what it's all about. They contain everything that we keep private about us. I call them our Horseshit Containers.
RAY: Thank God old age hasn't affected me like you, Hugo.
HUGO: I'll give you an example. See me? Look at me. Look closely. Just above my left shoulder, here, there's a little tube of toothpaste, right. This small tube—actually, it's family-sized—this tube holds all my hatred for my da.
RAY: Your dad's not still alive?
HUGO: He died in 1959.
RAY: So, what the hell?
HUGO: You tell me. I've tried. I've worked hard to forget, but he hurt me at a most important stage of my life and I can't get that out of my head.

LEN: Was there a big falling out?
HUGO: Yes.
RAY: When?
HUGO: 1935.
LEN: Boy, you hold a grudge.
RAY: And you never made up?
HUGO: Sort of, yes. We were 'okay' when he died, that's why it's only a tube of toothpaste and not a beer keg. [*Moving swiftly on to* RAY] Now, take Ray Oliver, 81-year-old Spanish Civil War veteran, anybody, anybody with eyes in their head can [*Physically demonstrates*] see this sitting directly on top of his head. [*To* RAY] Your hair needs washed.
LEN: What is it?
HUGO: It's a beautiful little Chinese Ming vase. Beautifully patterned, little delicate handles on each side and a nice little lift-off lid.
RAY: What do you think's in it, Hugo?
HUGO: Rachel Prescott.
RAY: Rachel Prescott?
HUGO: And your other women.
RAY: My other women? [RAY *laughs out loud. He takes a good laugh.*]
HUGO: Watch, Len, don't lean over too much to your left. You'll knock over that lemonade bottle beside your shoulder.
RAY: Fifty years of Welsh mistresses!
LEN: I've only had two! [RAY *and* LEN *laugh.*]
HUGO: It's pound coins, actually.
LEN: Ohhh!
RAY: I always thought you were a repressed capitalist.
HUGO: I don't think you ever got over Rachel Prescott, Ray.
RAY: A lemonade bottle full of pound coins.
HUGO: You've always said you messed up with her.
RAY: Shut up, Hugo.
KATE: Grandad? [RAY *looks at her.*] Can we talk?
RAY [*sharply*]: No.
LEN [*getting up*]: Come on, Hugo, I think we should head off ...
RAY: No. You're my guests. I want you to stay.
LEN: We'll go outside for a bit of fresh air. See what's happening in the street.
HUGO: The gassing of the old age pensioners doesn't start till eight.

RAY: Nobody's going anywhere. This is my flat, my party. Stay where you are. Hugo, pour out the whiskey there. Len, take a drink?

LEN: The beer's fine with me.

RAY: Good, good. All we need now is for my granddaughter to take herself off home and let us get on with our drink. Right, lads?

KATE: Right lads nothing. The three of you are pathetic.
[*Silence.*]

RAY: Get out! Get out. Kate, I don't have to put up with this.

KATE: What is going on here? I mean, what is going on here? I don't know you two men, but I really don't know why three elderly men are sitting round getting drunk when one of you is practically an invalid and is meant this weekend to be sorting out the rest of his life.

RAY: Without your help, thanks.

HUGO: If only I was drunk.

LEN: If you don't mind me saying, dear, and I know it's turned out a very awkward time, but I haven't seen your grandfather in nearly thirty years. We were only enjoying a little get-together.

HUGO: We came through a lot together, before you were even born. You might not be aware of it, but your grandfather was a great man. A hero of the Spanish Civil War. You need to show him a wee bit more respect.

KATE: I love him because he's my grandfather—

RAY: You've a funny way of showing it.

KATE: —not because he fought in some war. I don't even know when the Spanish Civil War was. The 1920s, 1930s? Who cares?

HUGO: We care.

KATE: Good for you. I care for the here and now and what's going to happen to him.

LEN: What do you work at, Kate?

HUGO: Are you blind, Len? She's a Grade A yuppie. 'The here and now'. 'I'm alright, Jack'. This is one of Thatcher's children, Len. They don't give a toss for man nor beast. Probably spends her week with her feet up at a computer, when she's not swanning in and out of fancy wine bars.

KATE: I'm a social worker, if you really want to know. And if spending eight hours a day, every day, on the worst council estates London has to offer is some sort of qualification for yuppiedom, I'm the Duchess of York.

LEN: You do care, then?

KATE: About my work, yes.

LEN: But you don't run a business.

KATE: I like my work.

LEN: What do you believe in?

KATE: I believe no one should be hungry, abused or homeless.

HUGO: You're talking socialism.

KATE: No, I'm not. I'm talking Africa, the Third World.

LEN: So why should you work in London?

KATE: Because there is hunger, abuse and homelessness in London. But if you want to argue over politics, what you should argue over is black starving Africa.

HUGO: And I suppose you're a Green freak as well.

KATE: I've talked it over with Miss McVeigh at the home and we think we have a solution. Just give me five minutes?

LEN [*stands up*]: C'mon, Hugo. Let's go down and get that fresh air.

HUGO: Right. I haven't had a good dance since Nelson Mandela got out of jail. [*They move to exit.* HUGO *passes near* KATE] Watch that heavy black bag doesn't fall down on top of you. [*She doesn't reply.* HUGO *gets to the door.*] All that sexual repression. [*The two men exit. We hear loud Waterboys music as the men exit.*]

RAY: Your grandmother fucked me up. Your mother disgraced me. What are you trying to do?

KATE: And you're nothing more than a poor put-upon victim.

RAY: I didn't deserve what I got.

KATE: Didn't you?

RAY: You have no idea.

KATE: Don't I?

RAY: You're not much more than a child.

KATE: I have heard stories.

RAY: What? The incoherent ramblings of stupid women?

KATE: They call it their side of the story.

RAY: Kate, listen to me. You have no idea. You have no idea what it's like to come home at four o'clock in the afternoon, after a hard day's work, and find your wife sitting in the kitchen half-drunk. To find a glass of vodka hidden under the sink and empty beer tins in the bin. Do you know how devastating that is?

KATE: Why did she drink?

RAY: Jesus Christ! Why is there salt in the sea? Alcoholics don't need excuses.

KATE: I'm not talking about excuses. I'm talking about reasons.

RAY: There's no such thing.

KATE: I'm not so sure.

RAY: What are you talking about?

KATE: I know about your other women.

RAY: What? You're not listening to that fool Hugo? That was just a joke.

KATE: No. I was listening to my grandmother.

RAY: Drunk, no doubt.

KATE: Maybe. I used to think that probably it was the ramblings of a confused, embittered woman. Hugo's Ming vase just makes me wonder.

RAY: That Ming vase stuff was nonsense.

KATE: Grandmother told me about the women in your office.

RAY: Huh, that again.

KATE: Bernie Mooney, the Irish girl. [*Pause*] The Blackpool lady.

RAY: These are figments of your grandmother's imagination.

KATE: You didn't have to flaunt your indiscretions by bringing them to your local pub, taking them on holiday.

RAY: Kate, your grandmother was paranoiac. Any woman I ever spoke to—

KATE: Do you know what it's like to sit at home, night after night, not knowing where your husband is? Who he's with?

RAY: You don't know. You just do not know. You're like the cop who arrives at the scene of a fight and arrests the person who is retaliating. You don't know all the facts.

KATE: My mother told me she used to come down the stairs at night to find gran sitting crying her eyes out.

RAY: Oh, so you're invoking your mother now. The woman who abandoned you when you were ten years old.

KATE: She's still my mother.

RAY: Someone should have told her that.

KATE: Who is Rachel Prescott?

RAY: That was way before I even knew your gran.

KATE: Who is she?

RAY: Does it matter now?
KATE: Hugo seems to think it does.
RAY: That's his opinion.
KATE: What's yours?
RAY: Look, if you want to know about Rachel Prescott, I'll tell you. She was my first girlfriend before I went to Spain. We finished while I was out there. I came home and met your gran and that was that. End of story.
KATE: Did you love Rachel?
RAY: No ... not really. Maybe, at the time, but ... it didn't last long.
KATE: It doesn't sound like that to me.
RAY: I've had enough of this.
KATE: Hugo says you messed up.
RAY: Could I be left alone please?
KATE: Well, just don't some crying to me, ever, ever again.
RAY: You don't know half the bloody story. Now, go home.
KATE: I'll tell you what I'll do now. I don't ever want to hear you talking about gran's drinking again. Not until you've put your hand on your heart and asked how much you contributed.
RAY: Alcoholics are born, not made.
KATE: Well, maybe if gran hadn't had to go through her life trying to be Rachel Prescott, she wouldn't have needed drink.
RAY: Nobody needs drink.
KATE: Nobody needs hypocrites.
RAY: Out!
KATE: All the women in your life ever wanted was some love and you couldn't give it to them because you married the wrong woman. Honestly, I feel so sorry for you.
RAY: Out!
KATE: I'm going. I did come here to try and persuade you, again, to move to where you can be looked after. And as from now, I don't give a fig whether you stay here or emigrate to the mountains of Andalucia! [*Exits and slams the door behind her.*]
RAY [*shouting*]: Come back when you know the whole story! [RAY *leans back against the wall, tired and reflective*] I wish to hell I was back in Spain!

[YOUNG RAY *enters. He has a piece of paper in his hand.* YOUNG HUGO *and* YOUNG LEN *enter. Grim-faced, they meet, shake hands and embrace.* YOUNG HUGO *is particularly distressed.* YOUNG RAY *addresses the men.*]

YOUNG RAY: The front is being threatened in three or four different places and this unit has been ordered back into the line. I know this is a particularly difficult time for all of us. Eamon Downey's been sharing our lives for over a year now. He was more than just a comrade. He was a dear friend. A young man just 22 years of age, an earnest young man, a man of great intellect despite his young years. And a poet, a poet of enormous potential. We all remember his insatiable appetite for debate, his constant striving to define what we mean by communism and socialism. He often talked about his native Belfast. About the poverty of the people he grew up among. And their children. That's what drove him on. His vision of the future, the next day, tomorrow. We lost other good men we all knew and fought with. Their deaths only serve to strengthen our resolve. Fascism will not win. We have the responsibility of the entire workers of Europe, to make sure it doesn't win. No pasaran!

I took this off the field kitchen wall. It's a poem written by Eamon after his first day's fighting at Jarama. [*He reads*]

> The morning dawns on straight rows of twisted olive trees
> As taut, silent men assemble.
> Idyllic waters from afar pour over me
> Quenching thirst, feeding fear.
> Wild berserk thoughts warm up, bend, then break
> 								and float away.
> As my spirit spirals forward, seeking strength,
> I catch myself painting pictures of tomorrow.

YOUNG HUGO: Again. Again, read it again!

YOUNG RAY:
> The morning dawns on straight rows of twisted olive trees
> As taut, silent men assemble.
> Idyllic waters from afar pour over me
> Quenching thirst, feeding fear.

[*The three men shouting.*]

> Wild berserk thoughts warm up, bend, then break
> 								and float away.
> As my spirit spirals forward, seeking strength,
> I catch myself painting pictures of tomorrow.

[*Bombs go off. The young men throw themselves on the ground and take up firing positions.*

Ray's living room. Elvis Presley singing 'Surrender' *blares loudly. The room is untidy now, with coats, beer-cans, glasses of drink, ashtrays, cups etc, strewn around.* LEN, *with his shirtsleeves rolled up and tie removed, enters dancing across the room with an imaginary partner. He sings along with Elvis. The music ends.* LEN *heads for his drink.* RAY *looks at his watch.*]

RAY: Listen, Nobby. It's now twenty past eight. Aren't you even going to phone your daughter?

LEN [*empties his glass*]: Screw my daughter.

RAY: You're leaving her standing at Putney Bridge tube station.

LEN [*pouring himself another drink*]: She left me. I didn't leave her.

RAY: This is most unlike you, Len.

LEN: I have my pride.

RAY: At least slow down on the booze.

LEN: You're sounding like my wife.

RAY: You're behaving like my wife. I love to see you enjoying yourself, but I don't like the idea of your daughter standing at a tube station waiting on you. The girl will be worried.

LEN: Worried? That page is missing from her dictionary. She wasn't worried when she ran off to London seven years ago and never contacted us for six weeks. Six weeks, Ray? We thought she was dead.

RAY: Why did she run off?

LEN: You tell me. I always provided a good home for her. She wanted for nothing. Two weeks before she was due to start Welsh Studies at Cardiff University, she disappeared.

RAY: Without a word?

LEN: Not a peep. I have another son. He's a lecturer in the local tech. He did everything we ever asked of him. But this girl? I don't know ... and to cap it all, she married an Englishman. It's like she's doing everything she can think of to defy me.

RAY: Do you have to take it so personal? Maybe she just wanted to live in London?

LEN: It's funny how, when it comes to my daughter, I'm only imagining things. You've just been rowing with your own family.

RAY: That's right. I have a daughter I hardly ever see.

LEN: Who was it said daughters always love their fathers?

RAY: My daughter Helen had Kate when she was 16. The father didn't want to know. Then she had two more children to two

different men. Now she lives with a bastard who beats her. Poor Kate's always been torn between her mother and us.
LEN: But at least you still see your daughter.
RAY: Only to row.
LEN: At least you have that.
RAY: Well, get on the phone and you can row with yours.
LEN: I can't.
RAY: Why not?
LEN: I don't speak to her.
RAY: I thought you arranged to meet her?
LEN: I didn't arrange anything. My wife did it all.
RAY: Well, for heaven's sake, Len, lift the phone.
LEN: I'm her father. Why doesn't she ring me?
RAY: Len, the world knows your children are not your children. They came from us, but they don't belong to us. We can give them our love, but not our thoughts. All we are is bows, to be bent back as far as needed, so that the arrows can fly off. In their own direction.

[HUGO *enters, singing. He is wearing a party hat, streamers etc.*]

HUGO: When you're in love with a beautiful woman
    You watch your friends
    You watch your—
RAY: Where have you been?
HUGO: Seeing your granddaughter safely to her car, where do you think?
RAY: You left half an hour ago.
HUGO: She was upset.
RAY: I bet you've been to a pub.
HUGO: No, I was down at the festival trying to score. But they only laughed at me. Then I went over to the group that was playing and asked them if they knew any flamingo music. But they were from the Dutch Ivory Coast or somewhere.
RAY: I haven't heard flamenco in years.
HUGO: I still do it in the Spanish Club on the first Friday of every month. Sex to music, it is, what? Oh, and I was talking to Mrs. Bradford on the stairs.
RAY: What about?
HUGO: Nothing much. But she invited me in.
RAY: She did not.
HUGO: She did.

RAY: What for?
HUGO: I suppose the woman's lonely.
RAY: Rubbish.
HUGO: She is.
RAY: And what happened?
HUGO: I gave her one.
RAY: You what?
HUGO: You heard me.
RAY: That's a lie.
HUGO: Really, it was at her insistence.
RAY: You're an awful liar, Hugo.
HUGO: I don't know why I like women. They're one great big walking lie from head to toe, aren't they?
RAY: How do you make that out?
HUGO: Their appearance. What you see isn't what you get. Start with the hair. They dye it, bleach it, rinse it, perm it, curl it, even wear wigs. Then there's all that powder and paint on their faces, earrings, necklaces. Then you have shoulder pads, stuffed bras, push-up bras, girdles, tights, high heels. High heels, the biggest con of them all. What elegance a pair of high heels gives to the female form. It's a bit like what the Eiffel Tower does for an ordinary city like Paris. Still, Mrs. Bradford does have a nice pair of legs.
RAY: Hugo, you have as much chance of pulling Mrs. Bradford as Fulham have of winning the European Cup.
HUGO: Who? She's mad about me. [*At this,* LEN, *who has been preoccupied, turns to the others. He has been crying.*]
LEN: I haven't seen my beautiful daughter in seven years. [*The others are silent, embarrassed*] I've two little granddchildren, my own flesh and blood, I've never set eyes on. You know, you rear your children to the best of your ability. I had no idea how she felt. I really had no idea. She wrote a letter to her mother, saying how she hated me. How I gave her no childhood. I was always away, always out on trade union business, politics, never there when she needed me. I spent my life saving the workers and losing my own daughter. I have to get to Putney Bridge station. Is there a phone, Ray?
RAY: In the hall.
HUGO: Sit down. Sit down and have a last drink before you go.
LEN: I'll have to phone.

HUGO: Here, Len. Have a drink and we'll have a last yarn. Then we'll all go home. [HUGO *pours* LEN *and drink and sits him down*] What about it, eh?

LEN: I've never drank so much in all my life.

HUGO: Since the day you walked up the middle of Gandesa in your underpants! And tried to kiss Josephina, the cook.

LEN: I did not.

HUGO: You did.

RAY [*preoccupied*]: How was Kate, Hugo?

HUGO: What?

RAY: When you took her to the car? What did she say?

HUGO: Well, she did mention something about going to buy an AK47 automatic assault rifle.

RAY: What did she say?

HUGO: She's annoyed, to put it mildly.

RAY: Tough.

HUGO [*pointing*]: You were OTT.

RAY: Who?

HUGO: I think your granddaughter is genuinely trying to help you. She told me about your Alzheimer's. You have to watch it, Ray.

RAY: Hold on a minute. A couple of hours ago, you two were on my side.

LEN: That's before we heard her side of the story.

RAY: What about mine?

HUGO: She's adamant, Ray. She told me to tell you, if you don't ring her within 24 hours, she's never coming back.

RAY: I will not be dictated to.

LEN: Heavens, you know, the older you get, the more your family problems accumulate.

HUGO: Speak for yourself. I have no offsprings. Except for the childer in Barcelona. But that's another story.

LEN: We three, we've a lot in common. We've given a hell of a lot of our lives to politics, to public life. I suppose something has to suffer.

HUGO: I worked at the building game all my life and I've lost count how many times I was shown my cards simply because I was a communist. I was a good spark, too. Wired the BBC Television Centre in six weeks.

LEN: Sometimes, you wonder why men do it?

HUGO: Well, when you're in a real political party, like me and Ray, you know why you do it. Right, Ray?

RAY: Maybe it's all just to do with ego.

HUGO: Ego?

RAY: The need to go into public life, to do good, to have our names mentioned, to be praised, to be loved. All ego.

HUGO: So I went to Spain and risked my shagging life just so somebody would say nice things about me?

RAY: No. But there may have been other reasons.

HUGO: Like what?

RAY: Personal reasons. Things we might have pushed to the back of our heads at the time.

HUGO: Well, I went to Spain to fight fascism. What did you go for?

[*The young men jump to their feet.*]

YOUNG LEN: The sun!

YOUNG HUGO: Women!

YOUNG RAY: The food!

YOUNG HUGO: Sex!

[*The young men dart forward, taking up covering positions in and around the old men.*]

YOUNG LEN [*suddenly itchy*]: And the dreaded lice! I now hate the lice more than I hate Franco. I propose that the war should be brought to a temporary halt so that both sides can come together to declare war on the lice.

YOUNG RAY: Give over, Bussell. We've just crossed the River Ebro on another offensive. Franco'll be finished in six months.

YOUNG LEN: Another six months of this? Bombs, bullets, trenches, starvation, unbearable heat during the day and freezing cold at night.

YOUNG RAY: Well, we all knew what we signed up for.

[*The young men change positions again.*]

YOUNG HUGO: Strange you should say that. When we were lying in reserve yesterday, Josephina's brother started talking to me.

YOUNG RAY: Edmondo?

YOUNG HUGO: He asked me what I was doing here.

[*Laughter.*]

YOUNG LEN: He what?

YOUNG RAY: Did you not tell him you're here to look for Lope de Vegas' 2,000 long-lost plays?

YOUNG LEN: What did you say?

YOUNG HUGO: I told him I was fighting Franco, and he said 'Yes, but what else are you doing here?'

YOUNG RAY: Was Edmondo drunk?

YOUNG HUGO: I don't know, but he insisted there had to be another reason. He said there had to be a more personal reason.

YOUNG RAY: I'm guilty! I want to take it out on Franco for making me miss all Fulham's home games this season.

YOUNG LEN: Well, there's nothing personal in it for me. I came all the way from Blaengarw for one thing and one thing only. To defend the democratically-elected government of Spain.

YOUNG RAY: What did you tell Edmondo?

YOUNG HUGO: Nothing. But when he wasn't looking I pissed in his coffee.

[*More shelling. The men cover their heads.*]

YOUNG RAY: Len?

YOUNG LEN: Over here.

YOUNG RAY: Hugo! [*Silence*] Hugo! [*Longer silence.*]

YOUNG HUGO: What?

YOUNG RAY: You bugger.

HUGO: That Edmondo. He used to do my head in, insisting we must have had other reasons for going to Spain. He was a right moonbeam.

RAY: I went to fight fascism. But, if I'm really honest, a lot of it had to do with Rachel Precott.

HUGO: Rachel Prescott?

RAY: Part of me actually went to Spain to try and make her jealous. To make her love me more.

HUGO: You can't be serious.

LEN: I was in absolutely no doubt about my eagerness to fight Franco. But sometimes sitting in the warm Spanish sun made me realise how much I hated working down the pit. Going to Spain stopped me from dying of boredom. Unfortunately, it also drove my mother to an early grave. She took my going very badly. Then, when she heard I was in Burgos prison, she took a mild stroke.

YOUNG LEN: When I get home, I'm taking my mother on a full week's holiday to Colwyn Bay and I'll wait on her hand and foot.

LEN: Then she was told I'd been sentenced to death and executed. She refused to believe it and wrote letters to MPs and newspapers.

YOUNG LEN: She loves the cinema. I'll take her to the cinema every day.

LEN: I was in Burgos for two years. And 19 days before I was released my mother died.

RAY: When did you find out she had died?

LEN: I arrived off the train at Victoria Station to be met by a welcoming party of hundreds of people. MPs, friends, well-wishers, reporters. People were singing and clapping me on the back and my brother called me aside and told me ... my mother was dead. Two minutes later, I had to make a speech to the crowd.

RAY: That must have been dreadful, Len.

HUGO: The day I joined the Communist Party—the 8th of January, 1935—my da stopped speaking to me. He used to pass me on the stairs in silence. He was a ferocious Catholic. A member of the Clonard Confraternity, which is kinda like ... being a priest but you're still allowed to have sex. He built an altar to Our Lady above my bed. The morning I left to go to Spain, my mother hugged me and cried. But my father pushed past me and hurried on to work.

YOUNG HUGO: I'm going back to Belfast, and I'm gonna walk into our house and tell my da to catch himself on.

HUGO: I walked into our house at exactly a quarter past eight on a Saturday morning and held my hand out for my da to shake it. This is after being away for two years. And he got up, put his coat on and walked past me out into the street.

YOUNG HUGO: Then I'm going on to become general secretary of the Communist Party of Ireland.

HUGO: Six months later, I had a major row with the party in Belfast and took off for London.

YOUNG RAY: I'm going to make a big pot of real English tea, buy a season ticket for Fulham, then I'm going to find a nice girl from the party to accompany me for walks over Clapham Common.

RAY: I made a beeline straight for Rachel's house, but she'd gone to the Channel Islands to marry that solicitor of hers. I literally didn't eat for three days. Because of my profile in Spain, I

couldn't get a job back in Fleet Street. That's when I hired my first lorry and started buying and selling scrap metal.
YOUNG RAY: Well, in the meantime, folks, we've still got the Ebro in front of us. Two days leave, then it's back out for the second half. With the wind against us.
YOUNG HUGO: But we are a couple of goals up. We are in front.
YOUNG LEN: If only I were playing a leisurely game of football on Blaengarw village green.
YOUNG RAY: I'd give up a week's smokes to be standing on the terraces cheering on Fulham.
YOUNG HUGO: I'd give up a year's smokes to get into Josephina's knickers.
YOUNG LEN: Your language is atrocious, Hugo.
YOUNG RAY: I'm going to tell Edmondo how you've been talking about his skin and blister.
YOUNG HUGO: No, Ray, don't be doing that. What with me going out with Josephina at the moment.
YOUNG RAY AND YOUNG LEN: You what?
YOUNG HUGO: Josephina. Me and her's going kinda steady at the minute.
YOUNG RAY: You are mad, Hugo.
YOUNG LEN: Josephina's boyfriend is a political commissar at the front and she never looks at other men.
YOUNG HUGO: Is that so?
YOUNG RAY: I've known her nearly a year now and I can't get her to smile.
YOUNG LEN: I wrote her a poem and she tore it up in front of my face.
YOUNG RAY: She has absolutely no interest in men.
YOUNG HUGO: That's strange, because I've been seeing her for six weeks now. We've been to Madrid together, I've met her family in Alcaniz. She's terrific in bed. You two are way behind the times.
YOUNG RAY: You're a liar.
YOUNG LEN: It's impossible.
YOUNG HUGO: Want me to prove it?
YOUNG RAY: Yeah.
YOUNG LEN: Yeah. Prove it.
YOUNG HUGO: Okay.

[JOSEPHINA *enters.* YOUNG HUGO *smartens himself up. He looks*

across at JOSEPHINA.]
YOUNG HUGO [*To others*]: You wouldn't do me a favour?
YOUNG RAY: What?
YOUNG HUGO: Well, because we are members of the same unit, she has insisted that we only meet secretly. If you would ... [*Beckons them away.*]
YOUNG RAY: Oh yes, right.
YOUNG LEN: Yes, but how are you going to prove anything?
YOUNG HUGO [*hesitatingly*]: You'll, a ... you'll see me kissing her.
YOUNG RAY: You're on.
[YOUNG RAY *and* YOUNG LEN *hide behind the outhouse door, ready to listen and look.* YOUNG HUGO *approaches* JOSEPHINA.]
YOUNG HUGO: Buenos dias, Josephina.
JOSEPHINA: Buenos dias.
YOUNG HUGO [*haltingly*]: A que hora sirven el almuerzo?
JOSEPHINA [*loudly*]: No entiendo, no entiendo!
YOUNG HUGO: Shushhh. Y'don't have to shout. Okay, since you've been getting lessons from the Americans, we'll try the English. [*Quietly, careful for the others not to hear*] Josephina ... why do you ignore me?
JOSEPHINA [*loudly*]: I don't ignore you.
YOUNG HUGO: Shushhh! I've asked you to go out with me, walk with me, talk with me, even let me help you cook, but ... but you stare at me as if I wasn't there. I love you, Josephina.
JOSEPHINA: You're nuts. There is a battle on, a fight on. Go and fight fascists.
YOUNG HUGO: You don't realise, Josephina, a word from you, a kind word from you, for me, would be like winning a village from the fascists.
JOSEPHINA: You're bananas.
YOUNG HUGO: A kiss from you would be like us retaking San Sebastian. Making love to you would be as beautiful as chasing Franco out of Spain.
JOSEPHINA: You Irishman, you crazy. [*She turns to go.*]
YOUNG HUGO: Espere un momento? [*She stops*] I thought I should let you know tonight is the last meal you will be cooking for me.
JOSEPHINA: Good. You go home.
YOUNG HUGO: No.
[*Over behind the outhouse door.*]

YOUNG LEN: What's he saying?
YOUNG RAY: I can't hear.
YOUNG LEN: He doesn't seem to be getting very far. [*They laugh.*]
YOUNG HUGO: No, I'm not going home. I'm going to die. I have been selected by the great General Lister to go on a special mission to kill Franco.
JOSEPHINA [*suddenly interested*]: You? General Lister?
YOUNG HUGO: Yes. He wanted one man to give up his life to get close enough to Franco to kill him and I have been selected. I will be dead in ... 24 hours.
JOSEPHINA: Ohhh.
YOUNG HUGO: But I will die proudly, for the freedom of Spain. When victory comes to democratic Spain, I know my sacrifice will not have been in vain.
[JOSEPHINA *is deeply moved and rushes to embrace and kiss* YOUNG HUGO. *The others are amazed.*]
YOUNG RAY: They're kissing.
YOUNG LEN: He was telling the truth.
YOUNG RAY: Lucky bugger.
YOUNG LEN: For once, he was telling the truth.
JOSEPHINA: Oh, poor Hugo.
YOUNG HUGO [*loudly*]: Will you do something for me, Josephina?
JOSEPHINA: I will do anything for you.
YOUNG HUGO [*loudly*]: Before we go to bed tonight, will you teach me to dance flamingo?
JOSEPHINA: I shall dance with you until the stars leave the sky.
[*She kisses him and exits.*]
YOUNG RAY: You lucky bugger.
YOUNG LEN: How did you manage it?
YOUNG HUGO: Ach, she's just another woman. This oul Spain is turning out not all that bad after all, is it? How long did you say, Ray, it would take us to defeat Franco?
YOUNG RAY: About six months.
YOUNG HUGO: Surely we could make it last a bit longer than that.
[HUGO *is sitting on a chair. He takes out a few marijuana cigarettes. He lights one up for himself and calls* LEN.]
HUGO: Here, Len. Have another one of these magic Woodbines.
[LEN *comes across and kneels down in front of* HUGO, *who places a cigarette in his mouth and lights it*] There you go. [LEN *inhales deeply, then lies down on the floor beside* HUGO. *At this,* JOSEPHINA

enters. She is carrying a bottle of wine and a glass. She approaches YOUNG HUGO.]

JOSEPHINA: Hugo, Hugo, you must come. [*She hands him the glass and pours him some wine*] My brother, Edmondo, and my other sisters. We have a party for you. You must come. [*She holds out her hand to* YOUNG HUGO. *The three men are stunned.*]

YOUNG HUGO: A party for me?

JOSEPHINA: This is your last night on this world and we want to make you happy. Please, you must come now.

[YOUNG HUGO *takes her hand and stands up. She leads him off, smiling at him.* YOUNG RAY *and* YOUNG LEN *look at each other, puzzled, then jump to their feet.*]

YOUNG RAY: Hey, wait for us!

YOUNG LEN: Don't start the party without us!

YOUNG RAY: Did you hear her say 'sisters'?

[*They rush off.* HUGO *is on the chair.* LEN, *flat on his back, is singing* 'The Deeply Dippy Song' *by Right Said Fred.* HUGO *is urging him on and joining in the chorus.*]

LEN [*singing*]: Oh my love, I can't make head nor tail of passion
        Oh my love, let's sail on seas of passion now

[*The song ends and both men laugh.*]

HUGO: You're full of surprises, Len. How the hell do you know that song? [*They both lift their cigarettes.*]

LEN: I babysit my little granddaughter and she plays it non-bloody-stop. She can sing it in Welsh, you know. The question is how do you know it?

HUGO: I never miss *Top of the Pops*.

[*More laughter.*]

LEN: God, these cigarettes are great.

HUGO: You like it?

LEN: I love it. God, if I'd been on these during my trade union days, there wouldn't have been any bloody strikes.

HUGO: That's how I discovered it. Remember the Wapping dispute? After two weeks on the picket line, a very nice *Sunday Times* journalist initiated me. After that, I couldn't get enough of it. Can you imagine what I looked like? A 72-year-old pensioner tramping in and out of the pubs in Hammersmith trying to score a ten-deal. After a while, I said 'Bugger this for a game of monopoly'. Now, I grow my own.

LEN: You do not!

HUGO: Bloody right I do. The wife waters it every day. She thinks it's an umbrella plant. [*At this, loud Spaniush flamenco music is heard from the street.*]

HUGO: Ah! Flamingo!

LEN: Flamenco!

[HUGO *takes to the floor in flamenco pose. The music gets louder.* HUGO *dances. He is joined by* LEN. HUGO *doesn't fancy* LEN *for a partner.*]

HUGO: I think I'll get Mrs. Bradford.

LEN: Yeah.

RAY [*struggling up*]: Never mind Mrs. Bradford. I'll dance with you.

[*The three men dance at downstage right. Upstage, the three young men and* JOSEPHINA *enter with bottles of wine and a flurry of light and music.* JOSEPHINA *and* YOUNG HUGO *take centre stage and dance.* YOUNG RAY *is upstage and* YOUNG LEN *is downstage left. As* JOSEPHINA *continues to dance, the three old men link up with their three younger selves, the Rays upstage, the Hugos downstage and the Lens downstage right. As the music ends abruptly, the old men stare at their younger selves in a moment of recognition.*]

HUGO: I'm away to see Mrs. Bradford.

[HUGO *exits.* RAY *and* LEN *return to their seats.*]

JOSEPHINA: Now, I must go. Edmondo will be waiting. [*She kisses* YOUNG HUGO *quickly on the lips.*]

YOUNG HUGO: You can't go now.

JOSEPHINA: I must. Edmondo is waiting to drive me to Madrid. I have been elected a delagate to the party congress.

YOUNG HUGO: But what about me?

JOSEPHINA [*running off*]: Buenos noches!

YOUNG HUGO: I'll buenos noches you!

[YOUNG RAY *and* YOUNG HUGO *are drinking from bottles of wine.* YOUNG RAY *is very drunk.*]

YOUNG LEN: What do we do now?

YOUNG RAY: Let's go and get Franco!

YOUNG HUGO: I don't know about you, but I think I'll sneak off to Maria's house.

YOUNG LEN: Josephina's sister?

YOUNG HUGO: Yeah. When Josephina was on two days leave last week, I did it with her sister.

YOUNG LEN: Maria?

YOUNG HUGO: She's only 19. Loves it, she does.
YOUNG RAY: Right. Who wants to see a bottle of pissy Spanish vino disappearing right before your eyes?
[YOUNG RAY *puts the wine bottle to his mouth and makes a good attempt at finishing it in one go.*]
YOUNG LEN: Raymond Oliver. I've never seen you drunk before.
YOUNG RAY: That's because I've never been drunk before.
YOUNG LEN: That Spanish plonk is stronger than you think.
YOUNG HUGO: It's also my Spanish plonk. [*Snapping it back.*]
YOUNG LEN: Too much of that stuff will do your heads in.
YOUNG RAY: At this very moment, there's more than wine doing my head in. Anybody fancy going home?
YOUNG LEN: And Rockerfella will give his money away to the downtrodden.
YOUNG RAY: I'm serious. I think it's time to go home.
YOUNG HUGO: Soda farls and a big plate of champ, with a big dab of margarine in the middle.
YOUNG RAY: The war's as good as over, lads. We're losing.
YOUNG LEN: No, it's not. Granted, it's not going our way at the moment. But I've a feeling things will turn our way very soon.
YOUNG HUGO: I got a new rifle yesterday.
YOUNG RAY: It's over. Are you blind? Hitler and Mussolini have stood by Franco, while we've been deserted by everyone except what little the Russians get through to us. The great fight for democratic Spain is over. [*Moving downstage*] Hugo, I want a share of your next girl or I'm placing you on a charge.
YOUNG HUGO: That's not fair.
[YOUNG RAY *lies down drunk.*]
YOUNG RAY: At least let me watch? [*He sleeps.*]
YOUNG LEN: When he gets into that state, there must be something wrong.
YOUNG HUGO: A month ago, we charged over the Ebro. Now, we're back on this side of the river. Franco's a bastard. Ray's right. Fascism is winning.
YOUNG LEN: I look forward to the day when Chamberlain and Roosevelt are staring up the nose of fascism.
YOUNG HUGO: When I left Belfast to come here, I can honestly say I had no idea it would be this bad. If it wasn't for him, I wouldn't be here.
YOUNG LEN: Same here. I arrived here the same day as a young

fella called Charlie Donnelly from Tyrone. We were thrown straight into the battle at Jarama. On our first day, we were both deeply shocked by the ferocity of the fighting. We took an unmerciful pounding from Franco's artillery, hours before we even saw a fascist. Men were falling all over the place. A young English chap was hit and fell over me. His guts spilled out on to the ground. He says, 'I'm hit', and started to stuff his guts back into his belly with his hand. It was heart breaking. Soon, I found myself dug in below an olive tree with Charlie. The roar of guns all around us was unbearable. Every time a shell fell near me, my guts contracted and the blood sucked right out of my body. Above us, some olives had been burst and were dripping down on us. Charlie puts his hand up and squeezed a bunch. 'Look,' he said, 'even the olives are bleeding.' Two days later, our line broke and we retreated back to the sunken road. The men were shattered, demoralised, our commanders had been killed. Then Ray appeared from nowhere. He began to bark orders. He went over to one man, physically stood him up, dusted him down and put his rifle back in his hand. He went along the road cajoling, urging, pleading, until hundreds of men were stood up and ready to go back into the line. Ray and Jock Cunningham then marched at the head of us. Ray got someone to start singing 'The Internationale' and, before we knew it, we'd taken back our positions. Sounds corny, but that's exactly how it happened. I saw it with my own eyes.

YOUNG HUGO: After my first day at Brunete, I found myself lying in a shell hole, shivering and shocked out of my life. Ray came up, found a blanket, put it over me, told me everything would be alright. And it was.

YOUNG LEN: He's a natural leader of men.

YOUNG HUGO: He and Eamon Downey were a good combination.

YOUNG LEN: Eamon put it in words.

YOUNG HUGO: And Ray made it happen. It's hard to accept that Eamon is dead.

YOUNG LEN: Two days his body lay in no-man's-land. No one knowing if he was alive or dead. [YOUNG RAY, *lying prone on the ground, stirs.*] Well, what are we going to do about him?

YOUNG HUGO: There's only one thing for it. [*They lift* YOUNG RAY *up.*]

YOUNG LEN: What's that?

YOUNG HUGO: I'll have to get him a girl somewhere or I'm in big trouble. [*Moving off*] I could put a word in with Dolores from the field hospital. But she wants to marry me.

YOUNG RAY [*singing*]: Oh the shark has sharpened teeth now ...
[*The others join in the singing as they exit. Ray's living room.* RAY *and* LEN *are in earnest discussion.*]

RAY: Hugo's been a good friend to me. I mean it. A good friend.

LEN: Yes, and all the more reason why he should know about your decision.

RAY: What good would it do? I'm 81 and I probably don't have long to live.

LEN: You have to be true to yourself.

RAY: Hugo's always been so straight with me.

LEN: But he never told you how Eamon Downey died.

RAY: I don't know what you mean.

LEN: Hugo was there. He was there when Eamon died.

RAY: No, he wasn't.

LEN: Ray. Hugo was there. I know. After I was released from Burgos, I met a man from Liverpool. He told me he ended up in the next hospital bed to Hugo after the battle of Brunete. He said Hugo was in a terrible state and told him everything that happened.

[YOUNG HUGO *hurries on, agitated, stands in a spot.*]

YOUNG HUGO: I was beside Eamon. Not right beside him, but close. When we got the orders, we charged forward, but they were waiting. Jesus Christ, it was open slaughter. Men fell all around me. There was nothing we could do but turn back. I saw Eamon falling. He shouted 'I'm hit, I'm hit'. The rest of us just ran like hell. It was every man for himself. When we got back to our lines, I realised I was wounded in the leg. It was a small flesh wound. Then I heard Eamon. He started calling my name again. He pleaded. I didn't know what to do. The fascists had us pinned down. I couldn't do anything. We listened to Eamon moaning all night, right through the night. Death sounds. It was awful, bloody awful. Jesus Christ, it was awful ...

RAY: Hugo never told me that.

LEN: So you don't owe Hugo anything.

RAY: What are you saying? Are you trying to say he did something wrong?

LEN: I'm merely pointing out that all this allegiance you have to Hugo ... it wasn't always returned. He wasn't always straight with you.

[*The door opens and* HUGO *enters, solemn-faced. He stops beside* YOUNG HUGO.]

HUGO: I have a confession to make. [*Silence*] I never got an erection the whole time I was in Spain.

LEN: You what?

HUGO: A hardner. I never got one in two years. The stresses of war.

LEN: What about all the women? Didn't you sleep with Josephina?

HUGO: That's another confession. I didn't. She fancied you.

LEN: Me?

HUGO: I never got within a snooker cue of her.

LEN: So why didn't she approach me?

HUGO: 'Cause I told her you had VD. [YOUNG HUGO *rushes off.*]

LEN: You dirty ... [*The men laugh.* HUGO *pours some drinks*] How did you get on with Mrs. Bradford?

HUGO: Fine. We had a drink. Now she's dancing with a wee Pakistani man. Here, she was talking about you, Ray. She said you two get together regularly for wee drinks. I think you two are a number, Ray? What's the story?

RAY: I think you need psychiatric help.

LEN: I would agree there.

HUGO: Here, and she told me a smasher, Ray. She said you and her got drunk together the night the Berlin Wall came down. Now, is that true or is it not true?

LEN: I think he did.

HUGO: She says, she says you helped her to write a letter to that bastard Gorbachev thanking him for letting the wall come down. That's when I realised she was definitely off her trolley. [HUGO *roars laughing.*]

LEN: I watched the Berlin Wall coming down with my wife and we both got so excited we cried. It was the most wonderful occasion.

HUGO: It was betrayal.

LEN: For heaven's sake, Hugo, are you never going to change?

HUGO: Am I going to betray the working class? No. Never.

LEN: You can't continue with exactly the same set of politics after such monumental changes have taken place. You can't be thinking straight.

HUGO: In your book, if a man sticks to the same basic principles that first inspired him, he's not thinking straight. In my book, it's called guts. Having the bottle to stick by your beliefs, even when they become unpopular.

LEN: Hugo. Stalinism was wrong in the 1930s and it's even more wrong in the 1990s. Thank God Mikhail Gorbachev came along.

HUGO: Typical Labour Party twaddle. 'Communism's wrong. Capitalism's flawed, but we think we can make it work.' Capitalism is immoral and evil and I'll never stop believing that.

LEN: I agree.

HUGO: No, you don't. You only pretend to agree. You accept capitalism.

LEN: Until we have something better in its place.

HUGO: So, in the meantime, we live with poverty and exploitation?

LEN: Whatever. But we can't have any more Berlin Walls.

HUGO: Ray? Ray, do you hear this tripe?

RAY: I hear it.

HUGO: Tell Mr. Half-a Loaf, here, what we fought for. Tell him what we went to Spain for.

LEN: Hugo. I went to Spain, too.

HUGO: What for? A sun tan?

LEN: For very similar reasons to you. But I didn't go to bring Stalinism to Spain.

HUGO: Ray, will you talk to this man? He seems to forget the great achievements of communism this century. Remind him that the best men and women in every country in the world, the best brains, the greatest workers, the noblest hearts, gave their all to communism. It has been the most unselfish, pure-hearted, political movement in the history of man. Tell him that, Ray.

RAY: Everything you've said about communism is perfectly true. But ... [*Pause*] ... it's dead.

[HUGO *stares at* RAY *for a long time. Silence.* HUGO *shifts.*]

HUGO: What do you mean, it's dead?

RAY: I mean, it was a great dream. It was tried and it's dead. [*Holding his hands up*] Manos arriba. End of story.

HUGO: Are you alright? Are you sure you know what you're saying? [RAY *nods firmly*] Ray. This is the Alzheimer's talking. You're not a bit well.

RAY: There isn't a thing wrong with me.

HUGO: But, Ray. Things are beginning to turn around again. It's on the upsurge in Poland, there's signs in Russia, Cuba's remained firm. Ray, we have to hold on.

RAY: Hugo, the Cup Final's over. We were trounced. We lost.

HUGO: That's what you think, what you really think?

RAY: It's how it is.

HUGO: I pushed your wheelchair on to a platform a year ago for you to receive a long-service award from the general secretary of the party.

RAY: And like the coward that I've been, I let you do it.

HUGO: You made a fool out of me.

RAY: I made a fool out of myself.

LEN: The world's changing, Hugo. We all have to change with it. That's what Gorbachev recognised.

HUGO: No. It's the other way round. As Marx said, the point is we have to change the world.

RAY: Every time I saw Gorbachev on the TV, he brought me joy. He brought sheer joy into this battered old heart.

HUGO: He betrayed his own party.

RAY: He had to betray his party to be true to the growth and freedom of his people.

HUGO [*standing up*]: I've heard enough. You might have thrown the towel in, Ray, but I haven't. Nobody can ever tell me this world still isn't made up of the haves and the have-nots. And I know which side I'm on. [HUGO *is preparing to leave.*]

RAY: Sit down, Hugo.

HUGO: And listen to this guff?

LEN: Surely we can agree to disagree?

RAY: C'mon, Hugo. Sit down and have another drink.

HUGO [*angrily*]: Stuff the drink.

LEN: Take it easy, Hugo.

HUGO: This is a great blow, Ray. I came here hoping to get some inspiration from you, some common sense. Just like in the old days, in Spain. You always knew exactly what to say, what to do. Like the morning you read us Eamon Downey's poem. That morning changed me. I vowed to fight for communism till the day I died. I believed in you. You used to inspire me, Ray. I always looked up to you ... now, now you're ... you're no more than a rat. A dirty, stinking, spineless rat. You're a treacherous bastard. Eamon Downey will be turning in his grave. He gave his life in Spain for what? For you to do this? Eamon Downey's arse is a better man than you! [*Exits.*]

RAY: That's why I didn't want to do it. I didn't want to lose Hugo, and all the others. I didn't want to let go.

LEN: I'll pour you a drink.

RAY: Please.

LEN: It's nearly midnight, Ray. Maybe I'd better stay here tonight. Can I sleep on your sofa?

RAY: Only if you don't snore.

[*The men chuckle. Drinks are poured.* RAY *knocks back his drink in one.*]

LEN: Don't worry, Ray. I'm sure you did the right thing.

RAY: There is no future. We're living at the end of hope. When we were young, we could dream great dreams. Now, what have the kids got? Materialism and nationalism. Bosnia. Northern Ireland. We have to sit back and watch narrow-minded men fight over lines on the map. Nationalism is scrumpy compared to the vintage bottle of wine that socialism was. All those wasted years.

LEN: Stop talking humbug, man.

RAY: I've wasted my whole life. Even my body is failing me.

LEN: Maybe it's telling you to shut up.

RAY: Even Fulham never did much. I have to ring Kate.

[*As* RAY *shuffles to stage right,* JOSEPHINA *emerges on a raised platform.*]

JOSEPHINA: I, Josephina Caricedo Martinez, as executive member of the party congress, am very proud to make this address. It is very hard to say a few words in farewell to the heroes of the International Brigades. A feeling of sorrow, an infinite grief, catches our throats. Mothers! Women of Spain! When the years pass by and the wounds of war are being staunched, then speak to your children. Tell them of the these men of the International Brigades.

YOUNG LEN [*enters*]: Kit Conway, Tipperary, Ireland.

JOSEPHINA: Tell them how they gave up everything ...

YOUNG LEN: John Cornford, Oxford.

JOSEPHINA: ... their youth, their loves, their countries, their families, and came to us ...

YOUNG HUGO [*enters*]: William Meredith, Cardiff.

JOSEPHINA: Today, they are going away. Many of them, thousands of them, are staying here with the Spanish earth for their shroud ...

YOUNG LEN: Alec McDade, Glasgow.

JOSEPHINA: Comrades of the International Brigades, you can go proudly ...

YOUNG HUGO: Charlie Donnelly, Tyrone, Northern Ireland.

JOSEPHINA: You are history. You are legend ...

YOUNG RAY [*enters*]: Wally Tapsell, London.

JOSEPHINA: We shall not forget you ...

YOUNG RAY: Ralph Cantor, Manchester.

JOSEPHINA: And when the olive tree of peace puts forth its leaves again, entwined with the laurels of the Spanish Republic's victory, come back!

YOUNG LEN: William Tumilson, Belfast.

JOSEPHINA: Long live the heroes of the International Brigades!

YOUNG HUGO: Willie Keegan, Glasgow.

YOUNG LEN: Johnny Stevens, Leeds.

YOUNG HUGO: Eamon McGrotty, Derry.

YOUNG RAY: Tommy Patton, Achill Island. Eamon Downey, Belfast.

[KATE *enters the flat with suitcase and Ray's coat. We hear Caribbean music.*]

KATE: I see the community festival is still going strong. Do you want me to shut the window?

RAY: No, they're alright. Thanks for coming back. [*Pause*] Manos arriba.

KATE: You pushed me to the wire.

RAY: I know. I almost added you to my list of casualties.

KATE: I forgive you.

RAY: You've been right about most things.

KATE: Hurry up and put your coat on. Oh, I found this in your wardrobe. [*She holds up his Spanish Civil War hat*] Do you want to take it with you?

RAY: I'll do better than that. I'll bloody well wear it. [*He puts the hat on*] It's been one hell of game.

KATE: There's still a lot to play for.

RAY: Yes. And, if I close my eyes, I can still paint a few pictures.
KATE: You look good. They'll love you.
RAY: I feel good. In the humble words of the poet, 'I feel like the green shoot, waiting for the flower'.

[*Black-out*]